"WHAT THE
HELL
IS JUSTICE?"

"WHAT THE HELL IS JUSTICE?"

•

The Life and Trials of a
Criminal Lawyer

by PAUL HOFFMAN

ꝗ♥P
A Playboy Press Book

To my colleagues of the pressroom . . . who keep the system honest.

Published simultaneously in the United States and Canada by Playboy Press, Chicago, Illinois. Printed in the United States of America. Library of Congress Catalog Card Number: 74–82480. ISBN 87223–409–6. First edition.

PLAYBOY and Rabbit Head design are trademarks of Playboy, 919 North Michigan Avenue, Chicago, Illinois 60611 (U.S.A.), Reg. U.S. Pat. Off., marca registrada, marque déposée.

Contents

	Preface	vii
1	A Week in the Life	1
2	The Making of a Mouthpiece	22
3	A Crazy Business	35
4	Around the Rim and Out	45
5	"They Are Framing Me"	61
6	A Cop Cops a Plea	76
7	Men of Respect	93
8	Appealing Propositions	111
9	A Killing in Camelot	123
10	Ring Around the Collar	136
11	The Cloud	146
12	A Year in the Arena	153
13	Black and Blue	195
	Postscript	244
	Notes	245

Preface

This is a look at the life and trials of a criminal lawyer. It is *not* an authorized, "as-told-to" account of some courtroom superstar like "How I Won My Greatest Cases." It is a candid glimpse of a "mouthpiece," the lawyer who is in the courts every day, handling everything from misdemeanors to murder, who has represented both the scum of the streets and the over-lords of the underworld, who has tried both grisly homicides and "clean" white-collar crimes, who has defended both cop-killers and killer cops.

Unlike Perry Mason, his clients are not all innocent and he doesn't win every case. Many times his clients *are* guilty and many times a jury so decides, though perhaps not as often as the prosecutors would like. More often, his only option is to admit his clients' guilt and ask the judge to "temper . . . justice with mercy." His chief skill is not the casebook law he learned at school or jury-swinging histrionics, but "street-smarts," a knowledge of how the system operates and of the men who make it function.

For a variety of reasons, I have chosen to tell the story through the vehicle of Jack Evseroff of the bar of Brooklyn,

New York. But with a change of names and dates and places a similar story could be written about a lawyer in Manhattan or Minneapolis, Boston or Dallas, Chicago or Los Angeles, or any American city where there are those who commit crimes, courts to judge them and lawyers to defend them. Even among the individualistic breed that is the criminal bar, Jack Evseroff is too colorful a character to be called "typical." But perhaps he is representative.

PAUL HOFFMAN

1 A Week in the Life

Wednesday, September 5

With an air of authority, he strode *around* the metal detector on the third floor of the Queens County Criminal Courts Building. He spotted his client in a glass-enclosed attorneys' conference room, surrounded by a bodyguard of plainclothes policemen. Except for his suit and tie, the client was indistinguishable from the casually clad cops . . . because he *was* a cop. In what had become a *cause célèbre* throughout New York's "bedroom borough," Patrolman Thomas Shea, early one spring Saturday, had shot and killed a ten-year-old black boy. Although Shea insisted that he'd mistaken the lad for a fleeing robbery suspect, the district attorney's office had charged him with first-degree murder. Jack Evseroff had been retained by the Patrolmen's Benevolent Association to defend him.

Evseroff led Shea into Part II, the courtroom of Supreme Court Justice Peter Farrell.* The attorney was tall, six-foot-

---

*A note on judicial nomenclature: The Supreme Court of New York State is a trial court, equivalent to other states' circuit or superior courts. In New York City, it is the trial court for felonies. Preliminary hearings (and trials for lesser crimes) are held in one, and lean. At 48, his black curly hair was thinning on top and silvering at the temples. He wore a bright blue Pierre Cardin suit. An ornate gold ring with the head of Moses graced his pinky, a gold ID bracelet inscribed "Jack" circled his wrist. He exuded confidence.

Once in the courtroom, Evseroff learned that the Shea case had been transferred down the hall to Part VI, the special homicide part. He left Justice Farrell's courtroom with a twinge of regret, since his "opposite number" there (the assistant district attorney assigned to the part) was an attractive blonde in a miniskirt. "I've often said what I'd like to do to prosecutors," he quipped to the cops as they marched down the corridor, "but that's the first one I've seen that I'd like to do it with."

In Part VI, Evseroff took a seat in the front row reserved for attorneys, while Shea filed into a bench two rows behind with his bodyguard, supplied by the police because anti-Shea sentiment in the black community was still at fever pitch. When the case was called, Evseroff rose and, with a wave of his hand, beckoned his client into the well of the court. While Evseroff spelled his name for the court stenographer, Shea stood beside him, hands clasped behind his back, as nonchalantly as if he were waiting to testify as the complaining officer on a traffic ticket.

The assistant D.A. in charge of the case was absent. "Second call," snapped Justice George Balbach and the clerk called the next case.

While Shea and his bodyguard waited in the part's conference room, Evseroff, lighting a Camel with a gold lighter, went downstairs for another calendar call. He found his client outside Part I on the first floor.

---

the New York City Criminal Court. Outside the city, felonies are tried in the county courts and preliminary hearings are held in the district courts. In all instances, appeals from felony convictions are taken first to the Appellate Division of Supreme Court (to the First Department, which comprises Manhattan and the Bronx, or the second, which includes Brooklyn, Queens and the Long Island and Westchester suburbs), then to the state's highest court, the Court of Appeals.

John Donnelly was a baby-faced man in his thirties. He had originally been arrested for murder, but the charge had been dropped for lack of evidence. However, he'd been tried and convicted for illegal possession of a gun and sentenced to five years in prison. That conviction had been reversed on appeal and he was back in court for rearraignment on the gun charge.

Evseroff took a seat in the front row of the larger arraignment part, beckoned the court officer and asked him to call the Donnelly case so he could get back upstairs.

"That's the biggest problem—to get them to call your case."

When the case was called, Evseroff explained the legal situation to Justice Moses Weinstein, who set September 10 for assignment to a trial part. Then Evseroff raised the question of bail. Donnelly had been freed on $60,000 bond pending appeal, but—this Evseroff didn't tell the judge—the friends who had pledged their homes as collateral were demanding release of their property. Evseroff said that the preconviction bond had been $2500 and suggested that it be reinstated.

"I'll take your word for it," Justice Weinstein said. "You have a reputation for your word to be taken."

For Evseroff it was a minor victory, but Donnelly seemed disappointed.

"I thought you were going to ask for release on my own recognizance [that is, without cash bail]," he told Evseroff in the corridor.

"I wouldn't do that."

To the veteran attorney, it was axiomatic that a man with Donnelly's record had to post some security.

Before heading back upstairs, Evseroff paused to chat with a local lawyer.

"I keep on good terms with all the lawyers. It's a good idea. I don't look on them as competitors. I look on them as sources of new business."

He joined Shea in the Part VI conference room and barely had time to take a sip of the coffee Shea had ordered for him before a court officer summoned them back into the courtroom.

Standing once again before Justice Balbach, Evseroff submitted a motion to inspect the grand jury minutes. This is a routine ploy in most New York felony cases: The defense asks the judge to review the minutes to determine if there was sufficient evidence to indict. The move results in a dismissal only once in a thousand cases.

The assistant district attorney asked for time until Monday to submit a reply.

"We have no objection to that," Evseroff said.

The judge gave him until Tuesday.

"There's another motion which we have been contemplating," Evseroff continued. "I wonder if we could have another couple of weeks."

"I certainly have enough trials to keep me busy for two weeks," the judge replied. "You can have two weeks to make your motions."

The next court appearance was set for September 19. "We'll set a date for trial then," the judge added.

In the corridor, Evseroff told Shea to come to his office the following afternoon so he could prepare the motion papers. Then he left the courthouse and crossed Queens Boulevard to a basement garage.

"I like to keep going. I don't even stop for coffee. I like to get everything out of the way. Then I can relax."

While the attendant fetched his car, Evseroff dropped a dime in a pay phone and called his office.

"It's always a good idea to check with the office. You might have a new arrest in the county you're in."

"Hello, Marie—Jack," he said to his secretary. "O.K., I'm just leaving Queens. What's doing? . . . What! You mean in Nassau? I'm not there, I'm in Queens. . . . They're in district court, right? . . . I thought it was on the sixth."

He noted the details on the back of a calling card (unlike most lawyers he rarely carries a briefcase), then climbed behind the wheel of his Cadillac El Dorado for the drive to Mineola, seat of suburban Nassau County. The air-conditioned car was a welcome relief in the 95–degree heat.

"I really have to have a comfortable car in my work. It's worth it to arrive in court in halfway decent shape so you can get to work not all sweated up or tired out."

The drive took 20 minutes. Actually, Evseroff was not going out of his way since he had a guilty plea in a grand larceny case in Mineola. He parked in a gas station on Old Country Road and crossed the street to the Nassau County Court House, a limestone structure that looks like a WPA post office.

He crossed the lobby to the first-floor courtroom of Judge Harold Spitzer and found that there had been another scheduling mix-up. His client, Carole Bucario, was absent. Somehow the message that her case was on the calendar had never reached her. Judge Spitzer suggested adjourning the case until 2 P.M., or until Thursday or Friday. Evseroff suggested next week, preferably Tuesday or Wednesday. The judge was reluctant.

"Is there going to be a disposition of this case?" he asked.

"Absolutely," Evseroff replied. "She went up and made a statement to the district attorney."

The judge agreed to Tuesday.

Before Evseroff left, he slipped into a back room and gave a court clerk a $100 check for two tickets to a fund-raising reception for a Republican judicial candidate. He had no intention of attending the gathering, nor did he expect a *quid pro quo* in court for his contribution.

"These are little things you do in this business. Whoever asks, I give."

He left the courthouse and crossed the tree-shaded mall to the low-lying District Court Building. Since he rarely handles cases in the lower courts, especially suburban ones, he was a stranger to the building. He climbed the stairs to the second floor, glanced at the notation he'd made on the calling card and looked around.

"Where's Part 7B?" he asked a passing court officer.

"1B?"

1B it was and the officer steered Evseroff to the end of the corridor. The attorney found his client sitting in the back of the tiny police court with her parents. She was a 20-year-old girl from Staten Island who'd been arrested while smoking marijuana in a parked car on a Saturday night date.

Evseroff apologized for being late. "I thought it was the sixth," he said, showing them the notation in his diary.

He filled out the appearance form and handed it to the clerk, asking him to expedite the case. He didn't have long to wait; the cases of private counsel usually receive priority over those of Legal Aid lawyers.

Evseroff offered to waive a preliminary hearing and let the case go directly to the grand jury. Judge Charles Heine summoned him to the bench.

"You might as well get two bites of the apple," he whispered to Evseroff. "These felony hearings are really conferences. You might dispose of it there."

Evseroff agreed and September 11 was set for the return appearance.

"You don't know the ropes. You go into another county and they tell you how to try your case."

Evseroff's court appearances were over for the day, but he had one more matter in Mineola. He walked across the mall to the Supreme Court Building, a modern structure of glass and marble, to confer in chambers with one of the judges. The air-conditioning system had broken down and Evseroff sat sweating in his shirt-sleeves while the judge explained why he'd sent for him.

The judge was quite concerned because the son of his former law partner had been arrested in Manhattan for selling hashish. The judge, who'd once presided over a case that Evseroff had tried and won, had suggested him as defense attorney. Evseroff agreed to take the case.

From a corridor phone booth, he called his office again: "Hello, Marie—Jack. Took care of everybody out here. What's new?"

Nothing was, so Evseroff walked to The Caucus, gathering spot for Nassau's courthouse crowd, for a leisurely lunch. Then he drove back to his office in Brooklyn to catch up on his correspondence and phone calls.

Thursday, September 6

Evseroff parked in a rundown parking lot and climbed the hill to the Richmond County Court House. Although Richmond, Staten Island, is part of New York City, it's another world, a small town in the midst of a metropolis. In Manhattan and Brooklyn, the calendars in each of 20 criminal parts were clogged with dozens of cases; the docket sheet for the lone criminal part of Staten Island's Supreme Court listed only eight.

He met his client, Edward Lino, in the sticky courthouse corridor. Lino was a dark-complexioned man in his thirties. He had a sculpted haircut, wore a modish cream-colored suit and looked like a fashion photographer. One would never guess that he'd once been, as he put it, "mixed up in a homicide." His codefendant, Salvatore Scala, was a stocky man in casual clothes.

The pair faced a variety of weapons and assault charges. Lino had come home drunk early one morning, gotten into an argument with the building superintendent and pulled a gun on him. Someone had called the police and in their subsequent search they'd found two guns in Scala's apartment, where Lino had gone after the argument.

Evseroff led his client into the antique courtroom. When the case was called, Supreme Court Justice Vito Titone set it down for a "conference" (the courthouse euphemism for a plea-bargaining session). Lino and Scala waited in the corridor while Evseroff and Scala's counsel, Albert Aronne, a solo practitioner who rents space in Evseroff's office, mounted the stairs and followed the black-robed judge to his chambers.

The assistant district attorney, Philip Minardo, opened by asking: "How can we get rid of this thing?"

"This is a bullshit case," Evseroff shot back, ticking off the legal objections.

After fencing for several minutes, Minardo offered to reduce the charges against Lino to a single misdemeanor, carrying a maximum sentence of one year, rather than the seven-year sentence Lino faced on the felony charges. Justice Titone added that he wouldn't impose a sentence of more than six months. Evseroff held out for three.

"What are you worried about?" the judge asked. "You'll have him back again."

"Not if you send him away for too long," Evseroff replied.

Minardo agreed to a three-month sentence for Lino. Then a complication arose: The prosecutor wouldn't accept Lino's plea without a plea by Scala, and Aronne, on behalf of his client, was not about to plead guilty. After more fencing, it was finally agreed that Scala would also plead guilty to a reduced charge and be let off with a $250 fine.

"I'm not a good negotiator. A trial man is not a good negotiator."

The session broke up and the attorneys returned to explain the arrangement to their clients. A second complication arose: Lino balked. He said he expected to be indicted in another case and didn't want to be in jail when it was handed up.

"I don't understand you," Evseroff said. "I really don't."

Scala and a companion finally persuaded Lino that it was best to "cop a plea." The parties returned to court for the formalities, including the legal fiction that there had been "no promises as to what the sentence will be."

Evseroff stood with his hands in his pockets while Justice Titone questioned Lino:

"Mr. Lino, would you please tell me what happened?"

Lino and Evseroff conferred in whispers. Then Lino faced the judge again: "We had a fight in an elevator."

"With whom?"

Lino didn't answer.

"If I tell you his name, will you remember? Frank Salzillo?"

"Yes."

"Who hit whom first?"

"I hit him first."

"In the course of this fight, did you display a gun?"

"Yes."

Justice Titone accepted the guilty plea. When court adjourned, the defendants walked away smiling to the probation office.

Evseroff was pleased with his morning's work. Instead of the prospect of seven years behind bars, his client would serve only three months—actually two with time off for good behavior.

"And it's good for them [the D.A.'s office] too. They're getting their pound of flesh."

After lunch, Evseroff drove across the Verrazano Bridge to Brooklyn. He parked in a basement garage on Livingston Street near Borough Hall and walked around the corner to an office building at 186 Joralemon Street. On the tenth floor a bronze plaque proclaimed the office of Evseroff, Newman & Sonenshine. Evseroff breezed through the open door.

"I got a good disposition in the Lino case today," he announced to his partners. "I got a plea to a misdemeanor."

"What did you get?" asked Gustave Newman, a distinguished-looking man with a professorial salt-and-pepper beard.

"One year?" guessed William Sonenshine, a wiry man with a cast in one eye.

"Ninety days," Evseroff said proudly.

After some shop talk, the three attorneys gathered around the receptionist's desk to divide the next day's calendar calls. A mimeographed sheet was ruled into boxes, each labeled with a different court; the defendants and the parts were written in the appropriate places. Friday's calendar listed cases in Manhattan's Supreme Court and the federal courts for the southern and eastern districts in Manhattan and Brooklyn.

"You take Manhattan tomorrow—O.K., Jack?" Sonenshine suggested.

"O.K."

Evseroff then retired to his office for the afternoon's appointments. It was a spartan room, bare and functional—a desk, two chairs and a vinyl-covered couch. There were no bookshelves, no law books. The only decorations on the plywood-paneled walls were Evseroff's diplomas and legal certificates; the only flash of color, Kodachrome portraits of his twin sons beside the desk. The sooty window looked out on the slums of Red Hook and the Brooklyn docks, but, if one stood in the far corner and leaned over the radiator, he could catch a glimpse of the Statue of Liberty.

His first callers were the suburban lawyer and his 26-year-old son accused of selling five pounds of hashish to an undercover agent. Evseroff elicited the son's background: At 19, he'd been arrested in Arizona for smoking hash. He'd been treated as a youthful offender and the conviction had been officially expunged. He'd served as a helicopter pilot in Vietnam and, like many Viet vets, had experimented with drugs during his off-duty hours. After his discharge, he'd drifted back into drugs and drug dealing.

"I never thought I was doing anything wrong," he said.

"Would you permit me to express an opinion?" Evseroff replied. "You're full of shit!"

When they left, Evseroff called Frank Rogers, New York's special narcotics prosecutor, to discuss the case. He learned that the father had already visited Rogers to plead for leniency, but he'd neglected to mention his son's Arizona arrest. It was a gaffe no criminal counsel would make. Rogers had learned of the arrest through a routine check of the son's record. He felt that he'd been deliberately misled and was definitely disinclined to make a deal for a softer sentence. Evseroff decided to let Rogers's Irish temper cool for a while.

Patrolman Shea arrived next. While his bodyguard was lodged in an anteroom, Evseroff led Shea into his office and explained what he had in mind. Shea insisted on his innocence. Would he be willing to take a lie-detector test to prove it? Shea said he was.

Normally, the results of lie-detector tests cannot be admitted into evidence, but Evseroff felt that there was an outside chance in this case. First, though, he wanted to administer his own test. If Shea failed, no one ever need hear of it. If he passed, Evseroff would move for a court-administered test. Even if the motion lost, there would be benefits. The PBA could call a press conference and announce the results—for Evseroff to do it would be unethical—and thus "precondition" potential jurors. Evseroff asked Shea to return the next day to meet with a polygraph expert.

As Evseroff was packing up for the day, a court clerk called to announce that a Brooklyn judge had ordered a general calendar call the following morning. Evseroff speculated aloud that the administrative judge was riding herd on him to clear his calendar and reduce his caseload. The partners had to rejuggle their schedules. Evseroff agreed to field the "crash call" in Brooklyn Supreme Court, while their secretary got on the phone to alert the clients to come to court.

That evening, Evseroff relaxed at a Manhattan movie and over a few drinks at a jazz club. He got home around midnight and went to bed.

At 1:30 A.M., he was awakened by a phone call from an old client with a new case, a friend's narcotics arrest. Evseroff told her to let Legal Aid handle the arraignment in the morning and, after they had posted bail, to come to his office. He'd decide *then* whether or not he'd take the case. He hung up and went back to sleep.

Friday, September 7

Brooklyn's Supreme Court Building, a concrete structure of "Mussolini modern" design, was only a short walk from the office. Evseroff arrived a few minutes after 10 A.M. and spent nearly a half-hour milling around in the corridor, conversing with his clients and other attorneys. As far as he was concerned, the "crash call" was a waste of time.

Court sessions are scheduled to start at 10, but the courtroom doors weren't unlocked until 10:30. "In God we trust" is inscribed on the walls of most New York courtrooms, but each courtroom in Brooklyn Supreme has its own individual edifying quotation. This courtroom's read: "Let justice be done though the heavens fall—Watson." The heavens might fall, but justice couldn't be done until there was a Supreme Court justice on the bench.

"Where's the judge?" one defendant asked loudly.

"The judge takes his time," a companion replied. "We're only trash."

The judge mounted the bench at 10:38. After a few minutes, Evseroff's first case was called.

His client, Eugene Lagana, was a thin, mustached man in a worn gray suit. He looked like a file clerk, but he'd reputedly been a member of the notorious Joey Gallo gang and had a long criminal record.

One night in 1970, Lagana allegedly had gotten into a barroom brawl. After being cut with a bottle, he'd left—only to return with a gun and pump four bullets into his attacker. He'd been arrested in flight and the police had found a machine gun in the trunk of his car. He'd been tried for murder and, even though the key eyewitness mysteriously disappeared, never to be seen again, convicted of manslaughter.

"The only murder trial I ever lost."

Lagana was back in court on the machine-gun charge. Evseroff explained that the district attorney's office had agreed to put off the case pending appeal of the manslaughter conviction.

"The case is marked off," the judge said reluctantly.

Evseroff asked the court to call his other cases. The clerk called the case of Samuel Pichkur, Alexander Vitkur and Nicholas Esposito, two detectives and a civilian friend accused of taking a $900 bribe.

None of the defendants was in court. Evseroff explained that he'd been unable to reach them on such short notice. He asked that the case be adjourned for several weeks.

"I want to get these cases disposed of," the judge insisted.

"These are cases that are going to be tried," Evseroff replied. "I am going to start a case with Mr. Sobel [an assistant district attorney] Monday which is going to take three or four weeks —a commercial fraud case."

"What about your capable associates?"

"They don't know the case," Evseroff explained. "Besides, Mr. Sobel is going to try the case."

"Let them get another assistant."

The judge finally agreed, again reluctantly, to an adjournment until October 15. For Evseroff, the delay was welcome.

The general rule is that time is on the side of the defendant. Why? Because 1) passions cool; 2) memories fade; 3) witnesses become unavailable because they move, they die or they change their minds. So it's to the defendant's advantage to delay a trial —that's presupposing he's made bail and is on the street. A man who's incarcerated generally wants a speedy trial.

Evseroff's next case involved five men accused of hijacking a truck. He asked for several weeks to prepare motions.

"You're giving me the same line on each one," the judge complained.

"The line is a little different in each," Evseroff insisted.

"Your office has quite a few cases," the judge continued. "You can't tie up these calendars. You have to get help."

From the spectator seats, an attorney volunteered: "I need a job, Jack."

Another adjournment was granted until October 9.

In the corridor, Evseroff consulted his calendar and told his clients to come to his office the following Tuesday so he could prepare the motion papers.

The motions were a tactical diversion. Evseroff was really "judge-shopping." Judges rotate parts each month, but the cases normally remain in one part. By the time the motions would be filed, another judge would be sitting on the case.

I don't want to try the case in front of this judge. He's a nice guy, but he's a lightweight. There are some touchy legal issues in this case. I want to get them before a knowledgeable judge.

He left the courthouse, picked up a container of coffee at the Zum Zum restaurant on Court Street and returned to his office. After taking care of a few housekeeping chores, he left the unfinished coffee on his desk and drove off to Mineola for a "hand-holding" session with the judge who'd recommended him in the hashish case and to stop at the father's law office to pick up a copy of the Arizona arrest record. Then a quick lunch at a greasy spoon and back to Brooklyn.

Most of the afternoon was spent in conference with Patrolman Shea and Victor Kaufman, a retired police lieutenant in charge of polygraph operations for the Sentor Security Group. The conference was interrupted by a call from the distraught wife of one of the office's clients, Seymour Goldes, an accountant who'd pleaded guilty to embezzling $1.2 million from *Candid Camera*'s Allen Funt. Goldes was due for sentencing the following Monday and seemed certain to draw a prison term.

Joan Goldes told Evseroff that her husband had not returned home the night before.

"If you're really concerned about him," Evseroff told her, "don't call me—call the police."

As a rule, criminal counsel can't concern themselves with the problems posed by errant spouses.

Evseroff hung up and returned to the matter at hand. He arranged for Shea to visit Kaufman's office the following week, first to work up the lie-detector questions, then to take the test.

Normally, Evseroff doesn't socialize with clients. Considering the clientele of criminal practice, his reluctance is understandable. But this night was an exception. He'd scheduled a dinner meeting with clients in two separate cases at his favorite restaurant, the Steak Casino in Greenwich Village.

One client was William Landsman, a travel agent facing a federal charge of trying to extort payment of a gambling debt. He apprised Landsman of the progress of the case, noting that he'd hired a private detective to track down a missing witness.

"In about half the cases that go to trial, we use private detec-

tives. They go and find witnesses, they interview witnesses, they take pictures of locations. They're invariably retired New York City detectives."

The other client was Anthony Granata, a 36-year-old reputed *mafioso* who'd been cited by the State Commission of Investigations as "the largest smuggler of bootleg cigarettes in New York." Evseroff was representing him on a charge of smuggling a truckload of 11,000 untaxed cartons.

For Evseroff, the meeting with Granata was mainly hand-holding; there was no real business to discuss. *"But that's very important in this business."* Most of the hand-holding consisted of digging into a hearty meal.

Saturday & Sunday, September 8 & 9

Evseroff relaxed over the weekend. On Saturday, he attended the *bar mitzvah* of Sonenshine's son. Thirty hours later, Sonenshine called with sadder tidings: Seymour Goldes had been found dead in a room at the Biltmore Hotel, an apparent suicide from an overdose of sleeping pills.

"It's a tragedy," Evseroff said. "The whole fucking thing is a tragedy."

Monday, September 10

Like a boxer before a big bout, Evseroff was keyed up, his adrenaline flowing in anticipation of an impending trial. For once he was carrying a briefcase, filled with the documents he'd need in the complex commercial fraud case.

His first stop was the special narcotics part on the ninth floor of Brooklyn's Supreme Court Building. The courtroom was crowded—Monday's calendars are always the heaviest of the week. He took a seat in the first row and showed off his new digital watch to the other lawyers. As far as he was concerned, each flash of the electronic dial signaled another wasted minute of a wasted stop.

Evseroff represented Ernest Solomon, one of the firm's few black clients.

"Most black defendants can't afford private counsel. And those that can prefer to hire black lawyers."

Solomon was also one of the firm's few clients who wasn't free on bail. He'd originally been charged with conspiracy to sell narcotics. While out on bail, he'd been arrested again, for the murder of the woman who'd referred him to Evseroff's office. To the district attorney, the murder case, handled by another attorney, obviously took priority. The narcotics case would only be adjourned again.

Tired of waiting while the court plodded through the lengthy calendar, Evseroff arranged for another lawyer to appear for Solomon and to relay the adjourn date to his office.

He went downstairs to the fifth floor and found another client waiting in the corridor. Frank Maloney was a jaunty man in his late thirties with the bantam bounce of a young James Cagney. Evseroff slapped him on the shoulder. "I was thinking of you this morning. I'm running out of shaving cream."

Maloney was a druggist. He and three codefendants were accused of passing off 75,000 bottles of an inferior preparation as Wella Balsam hair shampoo.

The four defendants, Evseroff and his co-counsel filed into Part XX, the courtroom of Justice Franklin Morton, where a jury trial was under way. At the first recess, the judge summoned them into the well of the court and explained that the trial wouldn't be concluded for another day. Their case was put off until Wednesday.

While the others filed out, Evseroff and the assistant D.A. remained before the bar.

"Your Honor," Evseroff said, "I wonder if you could accommodate Mr. Sobel and myself. We have another case on the calendar."

So the assault case of Rudolph Farone was called.

"October eighth," said Justice Morton.

"That's Columbus Day, judge," a clerk advised.

"October fifteenth."

Evseroff marked the date in his diary and slipped next door to Part XIX, where Justice Aaron Koota was presiding at a hearing. Seeing Evseroff file into the front row, he interrupted the questioning.

"You have something on?" he asked Evseroff.

"Yes, Your Honor."

Evseroff beckoned his client forward from the spectator seats. Anthony Lisi was a short, white-haired man of about 60, a soft-spoken, conservatively dressed "Godfather" type. He faced a contempt charge for refusing to answer questions at a grand jury's organized-crime inquiry.

"Your Honor was the district attorney at the time of this case," Evseroff said.

"What's the name of the case?"

"Lisi—Anthony Lisi."

The name made no impression on Justice Koota, but he readily agreed to an adjournment. It would be a blatant conflict of interest for him to sit in judgment on a case he'd initially prosecuted. Lisi's case was adjourned until October 15. Everyone knew it wouldn't be tried then either, because an appeal in a companion case was wending its way through the courts.

"This case has whiskers already," Lisi quipped as he walked with Evseroff to the elevator. "If you had a dollar for each day you came here, you'd be retired."

Evseroff cracked a smile, but it had been a disappointing day. *"I came here all full of piss and vinegar. I was all set to try a case."*

Tuesday, September 11

Mineola again. Evseroff drove along the Long Island Expressway, stalled in the traffic of what's been called "the world's longest parking lot." He had two cases on the calendar, but he was more concerned about his amateur photography. Only five frames on the film he'd picked up at the camera store in the morning had come out.

Thirty-five minutes late, he arrived at the Nassau County Court House and found his client in the lobby. Carole Bucario was a fat woman in a bright floral-print dress. She was accused of helping plot the theft of a truckload of dresses from a plush suburban store.

Despite her girth, she was a small fry in the eyes of the authorities. They were willing to be lenient to secure her cooperation against a codefendant, Pasquale Fuca. Fuca had been a supporting character in one of the most celebrated crimes of modern times. He'd owned the candy store that had served as the distribution center for the 112 pounds of "French Connection" heroin. He'd pleaded guilty to his part in the plot and had been sentenced to ten years in prison. He'd been released two years before and the authorities were anxious to return him behind bars.

Evseroff led Mrs. Bucario into the courtroom where her guilty plea to a reduced charge was quickly taken. Judge Spitzer suggested October 18 for sentencing.

"Is that all right with you?" he asked Evseroff.

"That sounds as good as any other date."

Evseroff left the courthouse and crossed the mall to the District Court Building. The hot spell had broken and his client, the Staten Island girl on the marijuana charge, and her father were waiting outside. Evseroff led them upstairs and left them in the courtroom while he slipped off to confer with the assistant district attorney. He returned a few minutes later, led them into the corridor and told them the good news.

"I told them that you had no previous record, that you come from a good family. You live at home, you work in a bank and you're going to college. He said they'd have to check it out and, if everything's O.K., the charge will be a.c.d.'d."

He explained that meant "adjourned in contemplation of

dismissal." There wouldn't even be a conviction on her record. She wouldn't have to go back to court today, but she'd have to return on October 18. He'd scheduled the adjournment for the same day as Mrs. Bucario's sentence, obviating a second trip to the suburbs.

"How's that?" he asked.

The girl broke into a broad grin. "That's great."

"I just hope that you won't get into any trouble between now and October eighteenth."

She beamed again and breathed a sigh of relief. "I won't."

Evseroff instructed the father to send another check to his office. The father agreed; he appeared eager to pay.

Before they left, Evseroff double-checked with his client: "You did start college?"

"Yesterday."

"Wagner?"

"Staten Island Community College."

Father and daughter departed. Evseroff dashed back to the courtroom to tell the assistant D.A. that it was Staten Island Community College, not Wagner College.

"You know, that judge was right. This was better than letting it go to the grand jury."

Killing three birds with one visit, Evseroff utilized his trip to Mineola to do more hand-holding on the hashish case—another visit with the judge and then a leisurely lunch with the father.

"It's a great honor to be recommended by a judge, so you do a little more."

Wednesday, September 12

Briefcase in hand, Evseroff arrived at Brooklyn's Supreme Court as the clock in the adjoining Borough Hall tower struck ten. Dapper as ever, he wore a black silk suit with a red rose design sewn on the lapel.

"Clothes are very important in my business. Your appearance

counts a lot with clients and with the court. You've got to look up-to-date—but not too much."

The first item on his agenda was a sentencing, but his client was nowhere to be seen. While the attorney waited in the corridor outside Part XI, Frank Maloney, Evseroff's druggist client, arrived with word that the Wella Balsam case had been put off until 2 P.M. He added that the defendants and the defense lawyers planned to meet in a few minutes to plot trial strategy, across the mall in the office of attorney Michael Gillen.

"I'll be there," Evseroff said.

He entered Part XI to discuss the problem posed by his missing client, conferring at the bench with the judge.

"Go do what you have to do and come back later," the judge advised him.

"What about the defendant?"

"Fuck him! Let him sit here."

Evseroff attended the conference, then returned to court shortly before noon to find that his missing client had arrived. It turned out that Evseroff's secretary had misread the Arabic numeral "II" and had directed him to Part II.

The client was an addict who'd been arrested nearly two years before on a gun charge. Since then, his record was clean. He'd gotten a job and had enrolled in a methadone maintenance program. The judge was inclined to place him on probation, in the custody of the clinic.

But there was a legal complication. As a certified addict, the defendant was not eligible for probation. Under the law, he had to be committed to the custody of the state's Narcotics Addiction Control Commission for up to three years. The commission, one of Governor Rockefeller's vaunted projects in the election year of 1966, had proved to be a billion-dollar failure. It offered little in the way of rehabilitation and its recidivism rate was astronomical. Its custody was the equivalent of a prison sentence.

During a whispered conference at the bench, the judge suggested an alternative, another legal fiction. The judge would hold a hearing at which Evseroff would contest the finding of addiction; the judge would rule that the defendant was *not* an addict, then commit him to the methadone maintenance program! He scheduled the session for the following afternoon.

Evseroff was back in court at 2 P.M. Along with the four defendants and two other attorneys in the Wella Balsam case, he stood before Justice Morton in the tiny courtroom of Part XX.

"The defendants are ready to proceed, Your Honor," Gillen announced.

"The people are ready," responded the hippie-haired assistant D.A., Henry Sobel. "The people now move the case of *The People* versus *Donovan, Donovan, Vitri and Maloney,* case number 1793 of 1972."

"The motion is granted," Justice Morton ruled. "The case is now on trial."

And so was Jack Evseroff. . . .

2 The Making of a Mouthpiece

Jack Evseroff is a member of a rare breed—the criminal defense bar.

Of the approximately 360,000 lawyers in the United States, only a relative handful have ever defended a criminal case and even fewer practice regularly in the criminal courts. In smaller communities, the lawyer still may be a jack-of-all-trades, fielding whatever legal business is thrown his way, a divorce one day, a will or a real-estate closing the next, perhaps a criminal case the day after. But in the big cities, where the bulk of legal business and, therefore, of lawyers is concentrated, the bar is segmented into specialities. Among the 22,000 lawyers in New York City, the criminal bar numbers only a few hundred. Few of the other attorneys would deign to defend so much as a traffic ticket, much less a murder case.

Reasons for this reluctance are not hard to find. Most lawyers consider criminal practice "grubby." Other branches of law offer more money, more regular hours and surely a more congenial clientele. Far better to be ensconced in a skyscraper office pushing papers across a desk than to confer with clients through the bars of a jail cell. Far better to practice in a civil court among men of substance than in a criminal courtroom crowded with the dregs of society. Far better to have a corporation on a regular retainer than to have to badger clients for fees. And U.S. Steel never issues a midnight summons, calling its counsel to some police precinct house.

So the criminal bar has become a netherworld of the legal profession. The WASPs who attended Harvard and Yale law schools graduate to the Wall Street and Park Avenue "law factories"; the Jews, Irish and Italians who went to Brooklyn and St. John's hang out their shingles on streetcorners. The lawyers who represent giant corporations get their names in the *Social Register;* those who defend Mafia chieftains get subpoenas from the grand jury.

Beyond this social stigma, there's the unique chemistry of the criminal lawyer. He has to have more than legal lore; he has to be a bit of the ham and a lot of the gambler. He has to thrive on the tensions of the courtroom; to think on his feet, hurling questions at a witness and objections at a judge; to stake his reputation on the all-or-nothing of a jury's verdict of guilty or not guilty. Small wonder then that so few are "called" to the criminal bar.

If there were a scientific scale for rating criminal counsel, Jack Evseroff would fall somewhere in the second rank. He's not a superstar like Edward Bennett Williams, F. Lee Bailey or Percy Foreman. He'd be the first to admit that he's a journeyman. His is a trade as well as a profession.

In law school, he took only one one-semester course in criminal law and applies "just about none of it" in his daily practice. "I would have to say," he explains, "that about seventy-five percent of the practice of criminal law is attributable to experience in the practice of criminal law. Only twenty-five percent is attributable to cold hard research with respect to legal concepts. You learn by doing. You learn how to try a case by trying a case."

In Evseroff's case, the making of a mouthpiece took 36 years.

Jacob Robert Evseroff was born in Brooklyn on April 7, 1925. His father, an emigrant from Russia, was in the "rag trade," owner of a small sweater-manufacturing shop in Manhattan's garment center. An only child, Evseroff grew up in Brooklyn and attended public schools. He entered Brooklyn College in 1942 as an engineering student, although, he says, "I was eminently poor in mathematics and physics and all the requisite subjects to be an engineer."

Before he could complete his sophomore year, he was drafted. After basic training at Fort Benning, Georgia, he was shipped out for further engineering studies to Clemson College in South Carolina. Within five months, the program was canceled and he was returned to a line unit as a combat infantryman. He was soon shipped off to the European theater.

He landed on Omaha Beach shortly after D-Day and was fed as a replacement into the front lines, as a member of C Company, 379th Infantry Regiment, 95th Division, Third Army, under the command of General George S. Patton, Jr. "I never met him, but I saw him," Evseroff says. Unlike most Third Army dogfaces, he saw a hero, not a hate object. "I thought he was God. I worshipped him. I thought he personified everything that an American leader should be."

Evseroff fought his way across France. After the summer campaign, what had been a rifle company of 190 men was reduced to about 20. There were only two men left in Evseroff's platoon, "of which I was one."

He soon became a casualty himself. With the American advance bogged down in the winter snows near Metz, Evseroff came down with trenchfoot and was invalided home shortly before the Battle of the Bulge. He was discharged on August 29, 1945, four days before the war officially ended.

He returned to Brooklyn College, this time majoring in political science and economics. In the army, he'd decided to forsake engineering for law. "I'd read a lot about the law," he explains.

"Then when I came home, the government told me, pursuant to Public Law 16 [the precursor of the GI Bill of Rights], that I had to have a career objective. I told them that I wanted to be a lawyer."

In his freshman year, Evseroff had been on the Brooklyn College wrestling team. When he returned, he played intercollegiate football, as a 195-pound tackle. "I wasn't a very good player," he admits.

He met his future wife, Helaine Rifkin, on the Brooklyn campus. "It was a college romance. She was a beautiful coed. I was a returned veteran. There weren't too many men around at the time."

After his junior year, Evseroff entered St. John's University Law School in Brooklyn. By going to classes year round, he completed three years' work in two. He graduated in February 1949 and passed the bar examination a month later. He got married and got a job, of sorts, assisting a solo practitioner on Wall Street, Harold Halperin, who specialized in airline negligence cases.

"He was a very nice guy," Evseroff recalls, "but he didn't believe in paying any munificent salaries. At the time, they had what was known as 'the 52–20 club.' You could get twenty dollars a week for fifty-two weeks from the government as unemployment which was a benefit they accorded to returning veterans. He [Halperin] said, 'I'm not hiring, I'm not paying anything. But if you want the experience, you can hang around here.'"

So Evseroff hung around for a year, collecting his $20 a week from the government and learning a little about legal practice. Then he went uptown to work, at $20 a week, for a lawyer named Arnold Katz, who handled collections. Among his clients was Bergdorf Goodman, the plush Fifth Avenue store. "I learned a little about civil work," he says, "and I didn't like it at all. I didn't like all the paperwork."

At that time, one of Evseroff's old college professors, Louis Warsoff, was running for Democratic district leader in Brook-

lyn. Along with a number of Warsoff's former students, Evseroff was enlisted in the campaign. Warsoff won, and as a
reward for his efforts, Evseroff received a piece of political
patronage, appointment as a criminal-law investigator in the
Kings County district attorney's office.

Under Miles McDonald and his successor, Edward Silver,
the Brooklyn D.A.'s office, as it had for years, served not only
as a prosecutor of miscreants and felons, but as an employment
agency for the Brooklyn Democratic organization. Across the
river in Manhattan, the late Frank Hogan, then a third of the
way through a 32-year career as district attorney, was building
a professional prosecutor's office that would become the model
for the nation, with assistants recruited on merit from the leading law schools.

But in Brooklyn, the old order prevailed. The assistants owed
allegiance not to the district attorney, but to the district leaders
who were their political "rabbis." Few were interested in prosecution as such or were necessarily adept at it. To most assistants, the job was a way station on the political path that led
to a seat in the state legislature or city council and ultimately
(they hoped) to a sinecure on the bench.

Also, unlike Manhattan where assistant D.A.s were full-time
prosecutors, those in Brooklyn were permitted to maintain outside civil-law practices. By mid-afternoon, the criminal courtrooms would be deserted, as assistants forsook public prosecu-
tions for private profits. Since most assistants had outside
incomes, salaries could be kept low. When Evseroff started in
1951, he was paid $3000 a year.

"As a criminal-law investigator," he says, "my duties were
exactly the same as an assistant district attorney's, except I
didn't have the title or get the money. I used to go out with a
stenographer and investigate major occurrences and crimes.
Those were the days where there was no *Miranda* warning or
anything like that. The district attorneys probably won the
greater part of their cases based on the statements we took."

Evseroff moved up the bureaucratic ladder to become first a

junior assistant D.A. (at $3500 a year); then, in 1954, a full-fledged assistant. His first assignment was to the old Court of Special Sessions, prosecuting misdemeanors before a three-judge panel.*

"I must have tried several thousand cases," he recalls. "My best estimate would be three or four thousand cases. We used to try five or six cases a day. This really was the workshop of a trial lawyer. This was where you learned to think on your feet."

In the argot of the courthouse, Special Sessions cases were "tried on a matchbook"—an expression derived from the attorneys' habit of jotting salient points on small scraps of paper during hurried pretrial conferences with witnesses in the courthouse corridors. "There was no preparation," Evseroff continues. "If you had an opportunity to speak to your complaining witness or your policeman before the trial, it was a big thing. In most cases, you would just put the witness on the stand, pick up the papers, not even knowing what the case was all about, who the defendant was, what the charge was, and say to the policeman, 'Officer, on such-and-such a day, at such-and-such a time, were you at such-and-such a place?'

"And he would say, 'Yes.'

"And you would say, 'What happened?'

"The biggest problem that we had was disposing of our calendars, which, at the time, seemed monumental. They seem minuscule by comparison with today's."

Needless to say, most of these thousands of Special Sessions cases tend to blur together in Evseroff's memory. But a few stand out.

"My daughter Leslie was born on October 17, 1958, which was a Friday," he recalls. "The following Monday, I went to court. Here I was, a new father. I had cigars for everybody. I

---

*In 1962, Special Sessions and the Magistrates' Court, which tried offenses and held preliminary hearings on more serious crimes, were merged into the new Criminal Court. At the same time, the county courts in New York City (called the Court of General Sessions in Manhattan) became a part of the state Supreme Court.

was trying a case where a man was charged with impairing the morals of a minor, his daughter. The defendant was represented by the Legal Aid Society, by a very lovely and capable woman named Caroline Davidson.

"At lunchtime we went out together—Caroline Davidson, myself and two of the three judges—which was not unusual. We never discussed our cases or did anything improper, and everybody paid his own check. I was giving out cigars. I remember I gave her a cigar for her husband, and told them all about my beautiful little girl.

"We had a nice lunch and went back to finish trying the case. The defendant took the stand. He testified on direct examination that, yes, it was his daughter, and, yes, she was in bed with him, but he didn't do anything improper, all he did was play with her.

"I started cross-examining him with my best prosecutorial venom. I said to him, 'You mean she was in bed with you?'

"And he said, 'Yes.'

" 'You mean you were *playing* with her?'

"And he said, 'Yes.'

" 'And that's all you were doing was just *playing* with her?'

"And he said, 'Yes.'

" 'What do you mean by *playing* with her?'

"At that, the presiding judge, who had not been out to lunch with us, got pretty mad. He thought I was harassing the defendant, which I suppose I was. He said to me, 'Mr. Evseroff, do you have any children?'

"I had to stop and think. 'Yes.'

" 'Do you have a daughter?'

" 'Yes.'

"At this point, the other two judges and Caroline began to snicker a little because they could see what was coming.

"He said to me, getting madder and madder when he saw them smiling, 'Did you ever play with your daughter?'

"I said, 'No.'

"He said, *'Never?'*

"I said, 'Never.'

" 'How come?'

" 'She's only three days old.' "

Evseroff also recalls a case in which *he* asked the wrong question. Again, it involved a morals charge.

"The defendant denied his guilt and put on character witnesses. One of them was a Catholic priest. He testified on direct examination that he knew the man, that he had occasion to discuss the man's reputation for truth and honesty and morality, that he knew that reputation to be excellent. That was the sum of his direct examination.

"And me—Mr. Smartass District Attorney—on cross-examination got up and asked him the following question: 'Father, you testified that you had occasion to inquire into this man's reputation for truth and honesty and morality. What was that occasion?'

"You ask a question and you get an answer. He said to me: 'This man had applied for membership in the Holy Name Society in my parish. Before I'd approve his application, I felt it incumbent upon me to go to other parishioners'—and he rattled off the names of ten or twelve—'and I spoke to them concerning his reputation for truth and honesty and morality, and they all in unison agreed that his reputation was excellent.'

"I was then called up to the bench by the presiding judge, who was Catholic. He said, 'Jack, you just blew it.' And he was right, they acquitted him."

From Special Sessions, Evseroff was rotated to grand jury duty. After the heady atmosphere of trial combat, he didn't relish the *ex parte* proceedings of the grand jury. But he found other compensations.

"I presented every conceivable case to the grand jury, from murders to bigamy," he recalls. "I think that that's the place where you learn the substantive law."

The next rotation shifted him to County Court and the trial of felony cases before a jury. He was assigned to the courtroom of Judge Hyman Barshay. His partner was an assistant named

Joseph Hoey, who later became U.S. attorney for New York's eastern district.

"I stayed about a week," Evseroff recalls. "I tried one case. Then I asked to be transferred to Judge Liebowitz's part. They thought I was crazy; no assistant wanted to work in that part."

In the two decades between World Wars, Samuel S. Liebowitz was a legendary figure in the law, the greatest defense lawyer of his time, the successor to Clarence Darrow, Earl Rogers and Max Steuer. He had represented, among others, Al Capone, Bugsy Siegel and the Scottsboro Boys. To many, he was the miracle mouthpiece who could "spring" any guilty defendant.

In 1940, Liebowitz chucked practice before the bar to preside behind the bench. His perspectives also took a 180-degree turn. From the last hope of the guilty, he became the scourge of the accused, guilty and innocent alike. Those who were convicted in his courtroom, and few defendants escaped, got the book thrown at them on sentence. He was a terror at plea-bargaining sessions, so much so that, in later years, the mere fact of having pleaded guilty before Judge Liebowitz was practically *prima facie* evidence for reversal.

In the flesh, Liebowitz was a beefy, bald man with the scowl of a bulldog and the pugnacity of a barroom brawler. Whatever his personal or philosophical differences with him, no one depreciated Liebowitz's ability or his dedication to duty. Although he was then nearing 70, "Sam Liebowitz," as Evseroff notes, "was the toughest taskmaster and the hardest worker, the epitome of a martinet.

"I wanted to work in his part," he continues, "because I thought that I could get more experience and learn more about the trial of a case there than any other conceivable place. And that sure was true.

"I went into his part and introduced myself and told him that I was an assistant and I had asked to work in his part and I knew very little about trying a case before a jury. Surprisingly, he was very nice to me. He liked me. He was tremendously helpful to me. He would have me in his chambers incessantly and he would discuss with me the manner in which the case should be tried, what I should do, how I should handle this, how I should elicit the testimony. I learned more about the tactics of trying a case from him than I did from any other single human being.

"I've never met a man who had as great an insight into the manner in which jurors react. He could look at a juror and he could ask him one or two questions and he could predict with a great degree of certainty how that person would vote. I've never met anybody else who possessed that ability.

"I've never seen him try a case, but I have no doubt that of all the lawyers I've met in my lifetime he must have been the most brilliant. I've never met anybody who inspired the awe in me that this man did. I think the man was head and shoulders over any other lawyer I've ever seen."

In five months, Evseroff prosecuted 26 cases before Judge Liebowitz, and in 25 of them the jury brought back verdicts of guilty. "In those days," he says, "I was imbued with the idea that it was my prowess as a trial lawyer that resulted in the conviction of all those people in that part. I have since learned better. It had very little, if anything, to do with my innate ability and certainly not with my experience.

"It was very, very difficult to escape Judge Liebowitz if you were a defendant in his part. The statistics ran about one or two acquittals in a year, out of perhaps one-hundred-odd trials. Statistically speaking, there was something going for the prosecution which was impossible for me to see when I was a prosecutor."

According to the scuttlebutt of the courthouse corridors, Liebowitz was a master at conveying to the jury by facial gesture or vocal intonation, which, of course, wouldn't show on the record when reviewed by a higher court, what he thought the verdict should be. And the verdict in almost every case, as far as he was concerned, invariably should have been, and usually was, "Guilty."

"Any trial in front of Liebowitz," Evseroff continues, "was characterized by the fact that the judge himself would become a participant in the trial. He would not sit there just with a view to keeping order and making rulings on objections. He could not resist the temptation to jump into the case and become an advocate himself.

"This, I believe, he did perhaps without trying—he had been an advocate for so long that it just came naturally to him. He used to tell me in chambers that he was disgusted with watching incompetent counsel and, of course, he was right. He used to tell me that he would like to get off the bench once a year to prosecute one case and to defend one case."

Evseroff remembers the one case he lost in Judge Liebowitz's courtroom. The defendant was a young black accused of mugging a Puerto Rican pimp. "The defense was an alibi, that he was at work at the time," Evseroff recalls. "They put the defendant on and three alibi witnesses. I remember very well: They were his three bosses. One was Jewish, one was Irish and one was Italian."

In a city where the ethnically balanced ticket is a political necessity and the "Three I League" refers to Ireland, Italy and Israel, it was an unbeatable combination.

"It was my feeling at the time that he was guilty," Evseroff continues, "because my feelings as a prosecutor were that *everybody* who was charged with a crime was guilty. To use the vernacular that we D.A.s used to use, 'If he wasn't guilty, who told him to get locked up?' "

Evseroff also remembers a case he won—but for different reasons. To him, it will always be "the quadruplet murder case." The defendant was Woodrow Miller, a 30-year-old black who'd shot and killed a liquor-store owner during an abortive stickup in 1957. He'd been convicted of felony murder and sentenced to death in the electric chair. But the Court of Appeals reversed, because, among other things, the prosecutor had brought out that the victim had been the father of seven children, four of them quadruplets. This was ruled "inflammatory."

Evseroff caught the case on retrial. As he recalls: "The case consisted entirely of his admission, which was a 25-page stenographic report of his reenactment of the crime. We had a guilty verdict in less than two hours.

"I remember the sentencing day. I watched the defendant. He was impassive, but as the judge imposed the death sentence on him, I saw his legs shaking.

"I'd forgotten all about the case. Sometime later I was having lunch and somebody said to me, 'Hey, look at the *Post!* Didn't you try that case?' I looked, and there was an account of the electrocution as only the *New York Post* could do it":

Weeping and praying . . . he could mutter no last words. The condemned man spent his last day huddled in his cell, at times trembling and repeatedly muttering to himself. "I don't know what got into me," he said once.

"I didn't feel very good about it," Evseroff continues. "It was at that particular moment, I think, that I decided that I didn't believe in capital punishment. I had been one of two assistant D.A.s at the trial. I had performed my job and the man had been properly convicted and executed pursuant to law. But at that point, I began to have very, very gnawing doubts about the moral propriety of taking another life."

After five months of prosecuting cases before Judge Liebowitz, Evseroff was rotated back to grand jury duty. He wasn't happy about it because he wanted to keep trying cases. In addition, he was making only $6500 a year after ten years in the office. Liebowitz advised him to quit if he couldn't try cases.

"I heeded his advice. I left."

Like other assistant D.A.s, Evseroff had maintained an outside civil practice, originally in partnership with a college classmate named Bernard Jeffrey.

"We did very little work," he says. "We had a couple of commercial clients, some personal injury, some real-estate closings and occasionally a nonlitigated matrimonial. If I made

$100 a week on the side, I was doing great."

One day a lawyer named Gustave Newman, who had once worked alongside Jeffrey selling pants in Gimbels' basement, came to the office with a case. The client remained to become a partner in the renamed law firm of Evseroff, Jeffrey & Newman.

Their office in downtown Brooklyn had more rooms than they could use, so they rented space to other lawyers. One tenant was Evseroff's colleague in the D.A.'s office, William Sonenshine, an assistant in the rackets bureau, who needed a place for his private practice.

In August 1961, when Evseroff left the D.A.'s office, the other lawyers who shared the suite were also making career decisions. Jeffrey decided to move his practice to the Long Island suburbs. Evseroff and Sonenshine decided to team in criminal practice. Their inconsequential civil business was shelved and they persuaded Newman, who had never tried a criminal case, to make the shift from civil law.

So the firm of Evseroff, Newman & Sonenshine was born. From the start, it was an equal partnership, with the profits to be split evenly, three ways.

That autumn, the new partners rented a nine-room suite on the tenth floor of an office building at 186 Joralemon Street, a half-block from Brooklyn's Borough Hall, hung out their shingle and sat back to wait for their first criminal clients.

3   A Crazy Business

Early in his career, Evseroff was trying an assault case. During a family squabble, Jack Buscarella had allegedly fired a shot at his father-in-law, Raymond Corbett, president of the New York State AFL-CIO. Evseroff had launched the defense with a series of character witnesses.

"I suddenly became aware that the jurors weren't looking at me or listening to the witness," he recalls, "but looking right past me to the defendant. I looked around and saw that he had taken off his shoes and socks and was chewing his socks in the courtroom. He was hallucinating that there were bugs on the floor and he was trying to stamp them out with his bare feet."

The judge declared a mistrial and sent Buscarella for psychiatric observation. He was found legally sane, retried with another lawyer representing him, and acquitted. But it remains a case Evseroff can't forget.

"All kinds of things happen in this business," he notes. "You're dealing with people who are *in extremis,* both legally and emotionally. It's a crazy business. It's not a staid, logical or reasonable exploration of the substantive law, as is a commercial practice. It's a business that's replete with emotion and requires a humanistic approach to people. It's a face-to-face relationship with clients, which is one of the most startling things I discovered when I left the D.A.'s office.

"When I was in the D.A.'s office, I had no contact with defendants at all. To me, a defendant was a name on a folder, who I would see when he came to court to be tried, who I would have no contact with, never speak to. I had no idea of his background, except perhaps what I was told by my investigators or by the police.

"Here you have a face-to-face rapport with the client, and learn that they are human beings. Just because somebody has a legal problem which happens to be criminal doesn't mean that he's an animal or some type of subhuman. Quite the contrary. Most people, in my judgment at least, who are involved in criminal trouble are unfortunates. They're not hardened criminals; they're not professional criminals. Sure, there are some, but by and large they're not."

Despite this humanistic approach, Evseroff does not consider himself a bleeding heart. Far from it.

"I think I have a very clinical, very surgical approach to the practice," he explains. "If you don't, if you allow yourself to become emotionally involved in the righteousness of your client's cause, I don't think that, professionally speaking, you can do the job for him that you have been paid to do. You have to have a clinical approach to be able to properly assess the case in terms of the law and in terms of the facts and the evidence, and to apply your professional skill and experience to try to reach a result which is going to be satisfactory to your client.

"The role of the defense lawyer is to protect the rights of the individual irrespective of his particular proclivities, irrespective of the popularity of his cause, irrespective of whether they happen to be *mafiosi,* politicians, left-wing hippies, black activists, fascists, communists or what have you. Under our judicial system, everybody is entitled to be defended." Even if they're guilty!

In fact, most criminal counsel prefer to defend clients they know (or believe) are guilty. It enables them to sleep nights. If they win, they have the exhilaration of having proved their prowess as trial lawyers. If they lose, they have the satisfaction that justice has been done. Either way, it's a better feeling than going home after an "innocent" man has been packed off to prison.

"If somebody comes in and tells me that they did it," Evseroff says, "I then ask them what they want to do with respect to the case. Even if somebody claims that they're guilty, if they feel that they want a trial of the issues, they're entitled to have a trial of the issues. I certainly would not advocate to somebody like that that he take the stand and commit perjury in his own behalf, because I'm not about to suborn perjury, not for any client. It's a crime, I won't do it. But their right to a trial is inviolate.

"I don't press people—I never have—on the question 'Are they, in fact, guilty?' I don't care. Your job is to defend, not to judge. You have to take people with their problems and you have to evaluate their problems legally and factually and make a determination how the matter should be handled."

Every once in a while, Evseroff's phone will ring in the middle of the night. On the line will be an old client with an urgent message: A friend or relative has just been arrested; will Evseroff take the case?

His reply is invariably the same: Let Legal Aid handle the arraignment in the morning. Then, once he's posted bail, have him make an appointment and come to the office. Evseroff will decide *then* whether or not he'll take the case.

It's not because of a natural reluctance to stumble out of bed at an ungodly hour and go dashing to some dismal police lockup; it's insurance against getting locked into defending someone before he knows if the client can foot the fee.

The legal journals, the bar association oratory, the canons of ethics may be filled with pious pronouncements about an attorney's duty to his clients, to the law, to the concept of justice; but lawyers hang out their shingles not to chase the elusive butterflies of abstract ideals, but to make money. Criminal practice may be "a crazy business," but it's still a business. And a business needs customers. A lawyer without clients is like an actor without an audience: He can't perform. In civil practice, the solution is simple: One good client can "make" a lawyer. A bank with unpaid loans to collect, an insurance company with disputed claims against it, a real-estate operator with lots of closings, a corporation that's conglomerating—one such client and the lawyer may be set for life.

Criminal practice doesn't work that way. A criminal counsel can't have clients on a regular retainer; that would constitute foreknowledge that particular persons planned to commit crimes. He has to be summoned separately in each case. Hence, his practice is a ceaseless struggle for survival.

He can get clients in many ways. For years, private practitioners were appointed to represent indigent defendants in New York courts. Though their services were supposed to be *gratis*, many succeeded in shaking down their clients for $5, $50, whatever the traffic would bear. And many a marginal lawyer eked out an existence by hanging around the courthouse, "taking cases from the magistrate."

In recent years, however, the Legal Aid Society has been designated to represent indigent defendants throughout the five boroughs of New York City. As a result, the practices of many criminal lawyers have been confined largely to representing bookmakers and numbers runners. On the assumption that the crime syndicate can foot the fees for its minions, Legal Aid won't take gambling cases.

Some lawyers still loiter around the courthouse, buttonholing likely prospects in the corridors and whispering, "You need a good lawyer?" They practice almost exclusively in the lower courts, trying their cases before a judge without a jury, the trials seldom lasting longer than an hour. If their clients face more serious charges, they either cop a plea or refer the case to another lawyer. Not only do they lack the skills and experience to try a case before a jury, theirs is a volume business; they can't afford to be tied up for a week or longer on one trial.

Some, perhaps, would like to graduate to greater things, but they never got the break of getting a case that let them show their stuff and spread their reputation among the bar and their prospective clientele. As a result, they languish for the rest of their legal careers trying penny-ante cases.

From the outset, Evseroff aimed higher. He found no difficulty in making the psychological adjustment in switching from prosecution to defense. "I have no emotional involvement at all in what I'm doing," he explains. "I'm a mechanic. One day I'm fixing a Cadillac, the next day I'm fixing a Chrysler."

He was fortunate in that two of the "Chryslers" brought in for repairs during his first year of private practice were Imperial limousines—major cases that would establish his reputation in the criminal bar. The first was the basketball-fix trial of Jack Molinas; the second was the murder trial of Anthony Dellernia.

"In the beginning," he notes, "we had a lot of lower-court cases. But now we generally spend our time with motion practice, jury trials and appeals. It's not feasible for us to take a case in the lower courts because there's not enough money in it."

The firm gets its clients from three main sources. First, cops. After ten years in the Brooklyn district attorney's office, Evseroff knew a large percentage of the borough's policemen. When he entered private practice, it was natural for many cops in trouble, whether for something on or off duty, to come to him, or to refer the cases of their friends and relatives. In the years since, the firm has had a steady stream of police clients and policemen-referred cases, and is frequently retained by the PBA and other police unions to defend errant cops.

The second source is other lawyers, both civil and criminal. In such instances, it's customary for the lawyer who referred the client to receive a one-third "forwarding fee." "That's ethical," Evseroff says of this fee-splitting. "That's not illegal or anything. The canons of ethics provide for it."

What *is* both unethical and illegal is for a lawyer to split his fee with a nonlawyer. But it is a prohibition more honored in the breach. It's common knowledge that many criminal lawyers, especially those on the lower levels of practice, split fees with the bail bondsmen who refer clients to them. Evseroff insists that his firm does *not* split fees with bondsmen.

"I guess the theory of it is that legal fees should be confined to lawyers," he says. "They are practicing law when they see a client and interview him and in their judgment deem that he should be represented by somebody who's a specialist in a particular field. They are practicing the profession, as distinguished from a layman who's just hustling a fee."

The firm sometimes refers cases to other lawyers if the fee is too small to make it worth their while, if the case conflicts with their schedules or is geographically inconvenient, or if there's a conflict of interest. "Strictly speaking," Evseroff explains, "if we referred somebody on a conflict-of-interest basis, we wouldn't take any forwarding fee and we wouldn't actually refer. What we would do is give the client the names of three or four lawyers who we know are competent and let him make his own decision."

Conflicts of interest usually arise when one of the firm's clients cops a plea and cooperates with the authorities. "I had a situation like that a number of years ago," Evseroff says. "I had a fellow who had a federal narcotics arrest. He took a plea and he became an informer. He had informed against a lot of different people, so I found out later.

"Of course, I had nothing to do with what he tells them. I don't go there when he talks to them. I don't want to be privy to any of the information he gives the government, so that if there's a leak I can't be accused of having leaked it.

"Sometime later, maybe a year later, some guy came to us with a narcotics case. He told us that he'd been referred by this particular client. I got very suspicious when I heard that. I called up the client and had him come over. And, sure enough, I found out that he had informed against this guy. The guy didn't know it. I just told him, 'Get another lawyer. I can't handle it.' "

The third, and biggest, source of business is former clients, either back after a fresh arrest or referring friends and relatives. After all, a client who's out on the streets is a walking advertisement for his lawyer.

Under New York law, lawyers appointed to represent indigent defendants are now paid on an hourly basis—$15 for each hour in court, $10 for each hour outside. The federal courts are more liberal—$30 and $15—but fees of more than $1000 are subject to review and are usually trimmed, often drastically.

For private clients, more rudimentary rules of thumb are used. As Evseroff explains, "Fees are determined on the following basis: First, they're determined by the amount of labor that's required in a particular case. Is it a case that's going to require protracted motions and trial, or is it a case that can be disposed of by way of a plea? Second, they're determined by the ability of the client to pay. Third, they're determined by what I would call the status of the lawyer in the legal community.

"There are lawyers of some stature, who, because of their know-how and experience, are entitled to higher fees than people who don't fall into that category. The lawyers who get the very, very high fees are few and far between. I suspect that there is a great exaggeration with respect to the magnificent numbers they're supposed to get.

"I think our fees are kind of in the middle. I don't think we're low and I don't think we're high. A lot of people are under the impression that our fees are very, very high. That hurts in this business. I lose a lot of business from people who don't want to come here because they heard that we're very, very expensive."

And then some walk away once he quotes a figure. What his fees are is one of a lawyer's best-kept secrets. Evseroff is no exception. "That's my business," he insists. But how they're set may be illustrated by the following incident:

In February 1974, a woman phoned Evseroff. Her son had been arrested on a narcotics charge and a civil lawyer had recommended Evseroff. But, she said, "I hear you're very expensive."

Evseroff suggested that she come to his office the next day and they'd talk it over. As soon as she hung up, he phoned the lawyer who'd recommended him to find out more about his prospective client. He learned that the boy's father was a substantial businessman, in the $40,000-a-year range. In his mind, Evseroff fancied a fee of $2500.

The woman and her son came to the office the next day.

"It was a narcotics case in a suburban county," Evseroff notes. "A young man who's twenty-one years old, who had no record, a college student who works part-time for IRS. And he had some hashish in a pipe and he was arrested in a car.

"There's possibly a search-and-seizure question. There's a very good possibility that the court might a.c.d. it [adjourn it in contemplation of dismissal] because of his youth and his good record. It doesn't look like a trial of any kind.

"I sized them up when they came in here. They're nice middle-class people. She's divorced and she said she didn't even think she wants to tell her ex-husband about this. So she's footing the bill herself.

"I charged her a fee of fifteen hundred dollars. I think fifteen hundred dollars is a fair fee."

It may be fair, but it's still a healthy bite for a middle-income family. And fees for criminal counsel are not tax deductible. It's a problem Evseroff is well aware of:

"We need some kind of a system whereby the middle-class guy who gets in trouble is afforded some kind of adequate counsel. He's the person who's caught in the middle. If somebody is a person of means, he's O.K., he can afford competent counsel. If he's a person of no means and can't afford counsel, he's adequately represented by the Legal Aid Society or the 18(b) lawyers. [Article 35, §18(b) of the County Law provides for appointment and remuneration of private counsel to represent indigents when Legal Aid cannot.] But it's the guy who makes a little too much money for free legal help and who doesn't make enough money to afford competent counsel who's caught in the middle. This is one of the hidden problems that nobody knows about, that nobody gives a damn about.

"You can take a man who earns two hundred and fifty dollars a week. He's got a wife and he's got a couple of kids. He's getting by and he has no great accumulated savings. He's never been able to save anything, because he's spent most of what he's earned just to keep alive. And suddenly he's charged with a crime. He's charged with robbery. Let's assume that the man is innocent—a case of mistaken identity, which happens. The judge sets ten thousand dollars bail. He's got to have money for the bail-bond premium; he's got to have collateral to secure that bail bond. He's ineligible for Legal Aid, because he makes two hundred and fifty dollars a week. He's incapable of going to a private defense counsel, who'd invariably charge him at least twenty-five hundred to five thousand dollars in a case like that, maybe more.

"This man is in the middle. He's in trouble. This is one area in which we need help badly."

When Evseroff was an assistant D.A., he once announced that he was ready for trial in a case. The defense lawyer, an old-time practitioner, replied: "If Your Honor please, I respectfully request an adjournment on the ground that one of my witnesses is missing—Mr. Green."

The judge readily acceded to his request.

Afterward, Evseroff approached the lawyer and asked: "Hey, who is this Mr. Green? What's he got to do with the case?"

"Don't you know what that means?" the older lawyer asked incredulously.

"No."

So he explained the cardinal rule of criminal practice: Don't go to trial until you've been paid. After all, a client who's in the pokey isn't apt to ante up what he owes; and one who goes free is likely to abscond, as Ben Gazzara did to Jimmy Stewart in *Anatomy of a Murder.*

"As a practical matter," Evseroff observes, "most judges don't object to an adjournment on that basis, unless it's a case which the prosecutor and the judge think has to go to trial *now*. 'My missing witness, Mr. Green'—those are the secret magic words.

"I haven't used it. I don't use it because I don't think it's anybody's business to know that I haven't been paid. I think the financial operation of this practice, bad as it may be, is something that should be within the firm, not publicized."

Evseroff may not request adjournments to go searching for the elusive "Mr. Green," but he still likes payment in advance.

"It's the hoped-for eventuality, which unfortunately does not materialize in all cases," he notes. "As a matter of fact, it materializes only in a very small percentage of cases that you get your fee 'up front,' in the vernacular. Most people don't have it to give to you 'up front.' Most people who get involved in criminal trouble are not rich people."

4 *Around the Rim and Out*

Jacob L. Molinas—like his lawyer, he'd dropped the Old Testament "Jacob" in favor of the more American "Jack"—grew up in the Tremont section of the Bronx. His father was an upright, hard-working man who owned a restaurant in Coney Island. He'd tried to instill his values in his son, a boy blessed with both brains and athletic ability. Jack Molinas was an honor student at Stuyvesant, one of New York City's elite academic high schools, stood six-foot-five and was a natural on the basketball court.

But he was also cursed with what every observer, even Evseroff, has described as "amorality." It caused him to scorn the accepted routes and to look for the angle, the hustle, the quick buck. Around the Bronx, they weren't hard to find. As a high-school kid, Molinas had placed bets with Joe Hacken, the neighborhood bookie, and had played on the basketball team that Hacken sponsored. After Molinas moved on to become an All-American cager at Columbia, he'd continued his dealings with Hacken, but on a more pernicious plane.

Basketball bets are based on a "point spread." The successful bettor not only must pick the winning team, but the margin of victory. For example, Columbia is favored over CCNY by ten points. If Columbia wins, 88–75, the man who put his money on Columbia wins. But if the final score is only Columbia 83, CCNY 75, he loses.

Such a setup was an easy mark for an angle-player like Molinas. A muffed lay-up, a fumbled rebound, a deliberate foul, and a crafty player could control the point spread with no one the wiser. It's called point shaving.

Somehow, both Molinas and Hacken escaped detection in the basketball-fix scandals of the early 1950s. But Molinas was not so fortunate when he entered the professional ranks. He was an outstanding rookie with the Fort Wayne (now Detroit) Pistons in 1954, but he was caught betting on the games and was suspended for life from the National Basketball Association.

But that didn't end his career on the courts. He became player-coach (and later part owner) of the Williamsport Billies in the Eastern League. Meanwhile, he went to Brooklyn Law School at night, breezed through his courses and the bar examination and somehow slipped past the scrutiny of the character and fitness committee. In 1957, he hung out his shingle on Manhattan's Park Place, specializing in personal-injury cases. In his first year of practice, he earned $25,000, but he continued to look for the angle that would bring him even bigger money.

He filed a $3-million antitrust suit against the NBA. The league, fearful of the suit's implications on its cherished reserve clause, offered him an out-of-court settlement. Molinas turned it down. Cocky as ever, he staked everything on making the big score. His case was thrown out of court, but he was already working another angle—the old combination of college basketball, gambling and the fix.

The nation's second major basketball-fix scandal in a decade exploded into the headlines over the winter of 1960–61. It was broken by the office of Manhattan's "Mister District Attorney," Frank Hogan, and quickly spilled over into a half-dozen other states. By the time Hogan's inquiry ended, 49 players at 25 colleges had been implicated in fixing 67 games over three seasons. Among those accused of bribing the players were bookmaker Joe Hacken and gambler Aaron Wagman, a one-time Yankee Stadium souvenir vendor who had been Molinas's boyhood buddy in the Bronx.

Midway through the inquiry, in January 1962, Dennis William Reed, a Bowling Green player, was flown to New York for questioning. At Newark Airport to meet the lanky black youth was his attorney, Jack Molinas. The detective escorting Reed exploded with a mixture of incredulity and outrage: "You can't interfere here! You're the target of this investigation."

Since it was an obvious conflict of interest for a lawyer to represent a prospective witness against himself, Molinas was forced to drop Reed as a client. What he didn't know then was that Reed had already been cooperating with the authorities, that he'd been "wired" and his conversations with Molinas had been recorded.

The indictment against Molinas, handed up May 17, 1962, marked the culmination of the investigation. It contained an overall count charging Molinas with conspiring with 11 others to bribe 22 players in 12 colleges to shave points in 25 games, three counts of bribery, each involving a $1000 payment to Reed to shave points in three games of the 1959–60 season, and one count of attempted subornation of perjury for allegedly urging Reed to lie to the grand jury. Hogan called Molinas the "master-fixer."

Not even indictment daunted Molinas. Ever the optimist, he expected to be freed by some big break and he made little preparation for his defense. Like a coach juggling his lineup in midgame, he bounced from one lawyer to another. In August 1962, with the trial scheduled to start barely a month away, he finally landed in Evseroff's office.

"We put it together as quickly as we could," Evseroff recalls. "We did our preparation as we went along." He needed no crystal ball to know that the odds were against him.

In contrast to Evseroff, the prosecutor had been working on the case for more than two years. Assistant District Attorney

Peter Andreoli was one of the senior men in Hogan's rackets bureau. He may have been a plodder, a prosecutor without a flair for the dramatic, but he had a firm grasp of the law and an inside-out knowledge of the evidence.

Evseroff knew he *had* to have solid evidence. The rackets bureau had developed the reputation of not bringing an indictment until the case was airtight. Those accused by the bureau generally conceded defeat, admitted their guilt and made the best deal they could. Of the ten persons indicted in the basketball-fix scandal, only Molinas chose to stand trial.

"It was a very, very strong case," Evseroff says. "It was a blockbuster case. I was told by the district attorney's office that the case consisted of the testimony of Wagman, who was a co-conspirator, the testimony of Reed and the 'wires.'"

The "wires" were the most important. Under New York law, a defendant cannot be convicted on the testimony of co-conspirators alone. No matter how many persons testified that they'd helped Molinas bribe basketball players, no matter how many players admitted that they'd taken the bribes, unless there was independent corroboration, Molinas would have walked out of court a free man. Reed's recordings provided that corroboration—in Molinas's own words. Had Molinas not attempted to cover up, there would have been no case against him.

The choice of the trial judge was another blow to the defense. Supreme Court Justice Joseph Sarafite, a soft-spoken, white-haired man in his sixties, had spent a decade as the number-two man in Hogan's office, then served briefly as the city's commissioner of investigations before going on the bench. Of all the judges in Manhattan's criminal parts, he was considered the most pro-prosecution, and his sentences were the most severe.

"He's a very conscionable man," Evseroff says of Justice Sarafite. "But try as he may to be fair—and I've seen many instances of his trying to lean over backwards—his predilections, his inclinations and his background conditioned him to be 'a D.A.'s man.'"

Evseroff explained the difficulties to Molinas. With Andreoli he explored the possibilities of a plea: "We were offered a disposition in the case. It was indicated that he wouldn't be incarcerated for more than a year or a year and a half, something like that."

But Molinas remained cocky, confident of getting the big break that would set him free. "He didn't want it," Evseroff says of the plea offer. "He didn't want to take a plea to anything. He wanted his day in court. And he got it."

Unlike the basketball court, there's no 24-second rule in Supreme Court. Molinas found the trial slow going. Throughout the five days of jury selection, he sat at an angle, unable to fit his long legs under the counsel table, and drummed nervously on the tabletop with his fingers. After questioning each prospective juror, Evseroff returned to the table and conferred with his client. Molinas would scrutinize the man, then whisper in Evseroff's ear before the attorney announced whether he was accepted or excused.

"I don't treat him as I would an ordinary client," he explained at the time. "He's a lawyer and I consult with him and I respect his opinion. But I'm the captain of the ship. If we have a disagreement, I make the decision and we sink or swim by that decision."

If there was a pattern to the selection process, it was Evseroff's exclusion of former athletes and sports fans, particularly those with a knowledge of basketball betting. "I didn't want people who would have a predisposition to believe that everything was fixed," he explains.

But Andreoli saw it another way: "He really used the old defense technique to get everybody off that jury who had any intelligence at all."

A jury of eight men and four women was finally impaneled. On November 1, the attorneys opened. They were a study in contrasts. Andreoli led off with a two-hour, matter-of-fact description of what he said the people would prove. Evseroff's response was as flashy as his clothes. In an impassioned 15-minute statement, he called Molinas "the number-one victim in this case" and said the evidence against him would come from "crooks, chislers, thieves and corrupt college kids who would say anything to save their own skins. . . .

"We do not deny that there was any conspiracy in this case," he continued. "What we do deny, ladies and gentlemen, is that Jack Molinas . . . was a conspirator. . . . There was a conspiracy . . . a conspiracy between a number of well-known chislers and gamblers and fixers and a number of corrupt college men. . . .

"Jack Molinas is guilty—but he is not guilty of any of the crimes charged in the indictment. He is not guilty of conspiracy. He is not guilty of three counts of bribery. And he is not guilty of attempted subornation of perjury. He is guilty—and what is he guilty of? He is guilty of guilt by association."

Andreoli's lead-off witness was Aaron Wagman. Short, slight, with a pool-hall pallor, the 29-year-old gambler was a walking encyclopedia of sports statistics. Sitting with the NCAA yearbooks on his lap to trigger his memory, he rattled off a complete catalog of every player the fixers had bribed, every game they had fixed, and even a few fixes that backfired. He was also able to recall the "line" on virtually every game.

Wagman told how he, Hacken and another gambler named Joseph Green had enlisted Molinas in the scheme in the fall of 1957. After a couple of abortive efforts, they fixed their first game—the Georgia–South Carolina contest on December 29, 1957. Their mode of operation was perfected over the following seasons: Molinas would scout prospects, cultivate their friendship, give them "coffee money" and even procure prostitutes for them. Then he'd introduce them to Wagman, Hacken or Green, who'd make the point-shaving pitch.

They had little difficulty lining up prospects. Few of the star players were real students. They were really paid professionals merely carried on the academic rolls, who received athletic scholarships and various forms of under-the-counter aid. The fixers knew that "amateurs" who were paid to score points could also be paid *not* to score them. Within a few months, the fixers were reaping thousands of dollars in profits on every crooked game, though Wagman's winnings were squandered on losing bets on unfixed games.

But there was no honor among fixers. Molinas had recruited a backer, David Goldberg, a St. Louis gambler, to put up the "front" money for the players' bribes. But Wagman cheated by selling the inside information to a second backer. When Molinas found out, he was angry, but agreed to continue the arrangement, letting each backer think he had sole knowledge of the fixes, while Molinas and Wagman split half the front money they'd been advanced.

This situation gave them an anxious hour during the Alabama–Tulane game of February 14, 1959. Wagman told his backer, Frank Cardone, a Pittsburgh gambler, that he'd bribed Alabama's Lenny Kaplan to shave points so that the Crimson Tide would lose or win by less than the four-point line. Molinas passed on the same information to Goldberg. But by that time, the odds had fallen and Goldberg wasn't interested in betting against Alabama. He told Molinas to tell Kaplan to get out and win.

To satisfy both backers, Alabama had to win, but by less than four points. Kaplan managed to pull it off. In the final 15 seconds, he broke up a tie game by sinking a field goal to give Alabama a 74–72 victory.

"Kaplan was the hero of the game," Wagman said. "He won the game—and he also 'dumped' the game."

Wagman's direct examination lasted five days. Evseroff hammered at him for three more, but failed to shake his story. Occasionally, one of his questions backfired. At one point, he asked Wagman how he'd learned to fix basketball games.

"I heard about it in the neighborhood," the Bronx boy replied.

"From whom?"

"From Molinas."

Billy Reed followed Wagman to the stand. While the gambler had been self-assured and voluble, the athlete from Flushing was flustered and nervous. His mumbled words were barely audible.

He told how Molinas had approached him on Bowling Green's campus the night before the Michigan State game in 1959: "He asked me if I would like to earn a little extra spending money by controlling the points in the basketball games. . . . He said it wasn't such a difficult thing to do. It could be done by missing foul shots, throwing the ball away, or in general giving an inferior performance."

Reed said he'd been "hesitant," but finally agreed to shave points in return for $500 for the Michigan State game and $1000 each for subsequent games.

When he was subpoenaed before the grand jury, Reed continued, he'd consulted Molinas. The lawyer had urged him to lie. "Act as if they asked you if you robbed the First National Bank," he quoted Molinas as saying. By that time, he'd agreed to cooperate with the D.A.'s office and had been carrying a concealed tape recorder.

That set the stage for playing the tapes.

Evseroff pulled out all the stops in his effort to block their introduction. He forced Andreoli to parade eight witnesses to the stand to prove that the tapes had not been, and could not have been, tampered with.

An even greater legal argument erupted over the transcripts. Unlike the bugs of *The Anderson Tapes* or other mystery movies, real-life recordings rarely come off with perfect fidelity. Often they're unintelligible to the uninitiated listener. Only by playing and replaying the tapes for hours were two detectives, assisted by Reed and armed with a knowledge of the subject under discussion, able to piece together what was said and provide a transcript for the jury to follow.

Evseroff protested that the transcript was merely one man's or two men's version of what was actually on the tapes. He had his secretary, Maxene Richter (who would soon become the second Mrs. Evseroff), listen to the tapes when they were played in court, transcribe what she heard and offer her version for the jury's consideration. It was part of his effort to show that the tapes were unintelligible, but Justice Sarafite barred it.

After three days of legal wrangling, the 42-minute tape was played to a jury armed with the detectives' transcript. On the tape, Molinas could be heard telling Reed: "If they told you that I—did I ever give you six hundred dollars, the answer is 'no.' There's nobody can come up and say 'I was there' when [I gave you] the six hundred. There's nobody can do it." He could also be heard telling Reed that, if he were asked about things the D.A.'s office might be able to prove, like long-distance phone calls, he should answer, "I don't remember."

The tapes not only showed Molinas's attempt to suborn perjury, but provided proof that he'd bribed Reed. Evseroff considers them the most potent piece of prosecution evidence: "Without the tapes, they wouldn't have had a Chinaman's chance. It would have been a very rough road to sell to the jury—Reed's credibility absent the tapes."

On cross-examination, Evseroff did much to damage that credibility. He forced the player to admit that in some of the games he'd "dumped" he'd turned in his best scoring performances of the season—14 points against Michigan State as opposed to three in the unfixed game against Hillsdale.

The long day of cross-examination was nearly over when Molinas pulled a document from his pocket and handed it to Evseroff. It was a two-page affidavit Reed had signed at Molinas's behest months before. In it, Reed stated:

> . . . I never accepted any money, or any promise of any money, from Mr. Molinas, directly or indirectly, or from anyone, not to do my best in any athletic contest in which I participated.

Evseroff asked Reed if he'd signed the statement. Reed replied that he'd signed something, but hadn't read what it was and couldn't recall swearing to it or having his signature notarized. But after Evseroff presented three witnesses who testified that Reed had signed and sworn to the statement, Justice Sarafite let it be read to the jury.

The remainder of Andreoli's case consisted of further corroboration of the conspiracy charge. Lenny Kaplan, the former Alabama player, testified that Molinas had promised him $2000 to control the scores in two games, but had paid only $200. On cross-examination, Evseroff attempted to prove that the $200 was a bonus paid to Kaplan to sign with Molinas's Williamsport team. To back up his contention, *he* confronted Kaplan with the fruits of a concealed recording.

A few days before the trial started, Molinas and George Palocsik, a private detective Evseroff had hired, had visited Kaplan at the Pimlico Hotel, a plush Baltimore restaurant Kaplan's family owned. Palocsik had been wired.

Evseroff asked Kaplan if he'd told Molinas at that meeting: "It could be the truth that you gave me the money to play ball."

"That's possible," Kaplan replied.

The war of the wires escalated the following day. Gary Kaufman, a former College of the Pacific player, testified that Molinas had bribed him to dump the St. Mary's game in 1960. A year later, with the investigation in full swing, Molinas had visited the Kaufman family home in Brooklyn. Like Reed, Kaufman had been cooperating with Hogan's office, and Molinas's words had been picked up by a microphone secreted in the basement TV set.

On the tape recording, Molinas was heard warning Kaufman not to implicate him or his backers. If he did, Molinas said, they might get killed.

"I'm not kidding," Molinas said on the tape. "It's the old Capone mob from Chicago. . . . Don't ever identify them . . . regardless of what you do, don't ever do that—for your own good."

Andreoli considered that tape the final coffin nail in the prosecution's case.

A few more players testified. Then, at the opening of the

session on November 29, Andreoli surprised the court by announcing: "If Your Honor pleases, that's the people's case." In 16 trial days, he'd presented 30 witnesses—and he had more in reserve. As he noted, "I could have gone on forever."

Now it was the defense's turn.

"The only way I can win this case," Evseroff quipped during one recess as he paced the courthouse corridor, "is for the defendant to get on the stand and lie his head off."

Evseroff may have been the captain of the ship, but his one-man crew mutinied. "Jack Molinas did not want to testify in his own behalf," he recalls. "He was adamant on the subject. He did not want to take the stand."

As a result, Evseroff says, "the defense was very, very difficult to put in. I believed then and I believe now that the only successful defense in a case like this is an affirmative defense. It requires someone to get on the stand and say, 'I didn't do it.' "

He led off by parading more than two dozen character witnesses to the stand. With the first, Molinas's Williamsport teammate Carl Green, Andreoli found an opportunity to get a previously forbidden subject into evidence.

"Have you heard, Mr. Green," he asked, "that Mr. Molinas was thrown out of the National Basketball Association for violating the code of ethics by betting on games in which he was a participant? Have you heard it, sir?"

Evseroff leaped to his feet. "I respectfully object to the question and I respectfully move for . . . the declaration of a mistrial on the ground that this statement by the district attorney was so prejudicial as to preclude any possibility of the defendant receiving a fair trial in this court."

"This man testified to an opinion," Justice Sarafite ruled, "and on cross-examination, in my opinion, this is a proper question. Your objection is overruled. Your motion for a mistrial is denied."

"Will you answer the question, Mr. Green?" Andreoli continued.

"Yes, I've heard."

Normally, character witnesses are presented as a buttress to a defendant's own testimony. They vouch for his reputation for truth and honesty so that a jury will be more inclined to believe him. But it became apparent on the first day of the defense that Molinas would *not* testify in his own behalf.

Toward late afternoon, Evseroff ran out of witnesses. He asked for an adjournment until the following morning but the judge was loath to grant it. "I ask you again," he said to Evseroff, "have you any witness now in the courtroom that is going to take the stand in this case?"

Since witnesses had been barred from attending the trial, Molinas himself was the only potential witness in the courtroom. Evseroff was forced to say no.

He did produce a few substantive witnesses in the following days. A young couple who had joined Molinas and Billy Reed for dinner the night the player had flown in from Bowling Green testified that Reed had said he didn't know why he'd been called because he'd never taken any bribes or thrown any games.

Another witness was Joseph Panzer, a gamblers' court lawyer whom Molinas had retained at one point to represent Wagman.

"Did he [Wagman] say anything about Jack Molinas?" Evseroff asked.

"Oh, yes. Yes, he did. Yes, he did. He said that the D.A.'s office is trying to get Molinas into the picture too. And he says he don't know anything about Molinas doing anything. He said, 'He's innocent,' he says. And from what he hears and from what he's been told, that they want to get Molinas into this as a defendant.

"I said to him, 'Well, what has Molinas got to do with this?'

"He says, 'As far as I know, Molinas has got nothing to do with this.'

"I said, 'Are you sure about this?'

"He says, 'I'm positive about it.' "

Emilio Sincola testified that Molinas had been with him on December 21, 1957, the date Wagman claimed he and Molinas had met at the Hotel Lexington to plot their first fix. He remembered the day, he said, because they'd driven to Williamsport through a blizzard. In rebuttal, Andreoli produced a weather report showing no snow that day.

All in all, the defense testimony scarcely scratched the overwhelming mass of prosecution evidence. Yet Molinas took the trial with the aplomb of an ace whiling away an hour or two in a streetcorner pickup game.

"He was a very charming and personable guy, a very intelligent guy," Evseroff says. "We became pretty friendly socially and we had dinner together many times. I really liked him, liked him as a person, and I felt bad for him. I found it very hard to realize that he was involved in this type of activity."

During one dinner, Molinas mused about writing his autobiography. It would be titled "Around the Rim and Out." Molinas's unofficial biographer, Milton Gross, the late *New York Post* sports columnist, interviewed the master-fixer during midtrial, heard him talk of wandering over to Madison Square Garden to catch a few basketball games and exclaimed, "Jack, you have *chutzpah!*"

On December 3, it seemed as if Molinas's *chutzpah*—his decision to stand trial and risk everything on some big break—had finally paid off. Justice Sarafite was stricken by a kidney ailment and the trial was recessed indefinitely. If he could not continue, the trial would be over—and retrying Molinas might constitute double jeopardy.

But the bedridden judge hung on and refused to terminate the trial. He returned to the bench on January 3, 1963, and the testimony resumed. Evseroff called his final witness, private-eye Palocsik, but it turned out that Palocsik's surreptitious recording of Gary Kaplan was inaudible. On that note of anticlimax, the defense rested.

Andreoli called one witness in rebuttal, a police document expert who said that the notarization on Reed's affidavit had been added *after* the original document was typed.

That left only the summations, the judge's charge . . . and the verdict.

Since he had declined to testify in his own behalf, Evseroff says, "I suggested to Molinas, who was a nice-looking, very articulate, very personable guy, an alternative which I considered a viable alternative—I suggested that I would prepare the summation in the case and he would deliver it to the jury. I thought it would be very, very effective for him to speak in his own behalf and advance the arguments I had prepared without the district attorney having the opportunity to cross-examine him.

"History is replete with cases where lawyers have summed up in their own behalf. Colonel Kleinman [the late William Kleinman, a prominent criminal lawyer] in Brooklyn when he was indicted. And recently Roy Cohn. I think Darrow did it when he was indicted.

"But Molinas didn't want to do it. I think he was afraid to do it. I think he was so emotionally involved because it was his own case that he couldn't handle it."

So Evseroff summed up, taking two hours. Andreoli took six. The jury took eight, returning on January 8 to find Molinas guilty on all five counts.

On February 11, Justice Sarafite threw the book at him. Calling Molinas "a completely amoral person," he imposed a 10-to-15-year prison sentence on the master-fixer.

Evseroff's partner, Bill Sonenshine, took over on the appeal. His first task was to secure Molinas's release on bail. If his sentence was severe, Justice Sarafite was equally stern in insisting that it start immediately. It took Sonenshine two months to secure a certificate of reasonable doubt—that is, a reasonable doubt that the conviction would be sustained on appeal—from Supreme Court Justice Samuel Hofstadter, freeing Molinas on $35,000 bond.

Sonenshine wrote the brief, arguing primarily that the trial should have been terminated rather than allowed to lapse during the judge's illness. He was prepared to argue the case before the Appellate Division.

Then, Gus Newman recalls, "Molinas got the idea that somebody else, particularly O. John Rogge, should argue the appeal. He felt that Rogge [an elderly attorney who had defended a variety of left-wing causes] had prestige and was widely accepted. I said that rather than add prestige to it, it would have the opposite effect: They would think he's bringing in somebody to talk down to them, or somebody to influence the court outside the brief."

The Appellate Division handed Molinas a severe setback, unanimously upholding his conviction. It ruled that the five-week lapse, in itself, was not grounds for reversal. Molinas would have had to prove that the jurors had been prejudiced by it. Molinas could find consolation only in the court's finding that the sentence was "unnecessarily excessive." But the court did not reduce his prison term. For it to do so, it ruled, would saddle the other fixers with disproportionately heavy sentences. (Hacken had drawn seven and one-half to eight years; Green, six to seven; Wagman, three to five suspended, since he was already serving a five-year sentence in Florida.)

"The next step," Newman continues, "was to get leave to go to the Court of Appeals."

Molinas's method was a textbook example of how *not* to "judge-shop."

At the time, leave to appeal to the state's highest court could be granted by any one of the seven judges. Those most favored by criminal lawyers, because they tended to be the most liberal, were Chief Judge Charles Desmond and Judge Stanley Fuld, who would succeed Desmond as chief.

"There was an unwritten rule," Newman notes, "that the judge who grants leave can't write the majority opinion. Molinas was so concerned with the ultimate, so preoccupied with who was going to write the majority opinion reversing his conviction, that he didn't want to go to somebody like Fuld or Desmond, because that would preclude them from writing the majority opinion. Instead, he picked Burke, figuring that leave would be *pro forma* and that would leave Fuld and Desmond available."

Judge Adrian Burke was one of the court's more conservative members.

"Molinas took Burke and the rest is history," Newman observes. "He didn't get leave."

His appeal denied, on July 10, 1964, Molinas went off to prison. That fall, in accordance with the Appellate Division's recommendation, Justice Sarafite trimmed his 10-to-15-year sentence to 7 to 12 1/2 years. Molinas made two unsuccessful appeals to the U.S. Supreme Court to get his conviction reversed.

But he was already working another "angle" for his early release, this time through the more accepted route of cooperation with the authorities. After bouncing through several other attorneys since he'd shelved Sonenshine for Rogge, he retained Evseroff to represent him in the Brooklyn district attorney's successful investigation of a $1-million check-forging scheme and an abortive probe of harness-race fixing. As a result of his cooperation, Molinas was paroled after serving only four years behind bars.

For the nation, the Molinas case was a revelation that almost destroyed college basketball as a big-money game. For the defense lawyer, it was a long stride forward in his career.

"That was my first big case," Evseroff says. "It was important because of the attendant publicity. Even though I lost, it got known in the trade that I could try a case."

It also had a personal effect on the lawyer. "The case was replete with all kinds of innuendos and information concerning corruption in sports. As a result, my interest in and my attendance at basketball games, both college and professional, diminished markedly. I developed a suspicion of all kinds of sporting events which I still harbor today."

5 "They Are Framing Me"

On the afternoon of Friday, May 18, 1962, detectives Luke Fallon and John Finnegan were on patrol in the Borough Park section of Brooklyn, posing as the driver and passenger of a taxicab. It was near the end of their week-long tour of duty. Finnegan decided to stop at the Boro Park Tobacco Company, a tobacco and candy wholesaler, to buy a box of candy for his wife. After he made the purchase, the two detectives headed for their cab. They had gone about 100 yards when they heard a shot in the store. Guns drawn, they dashed back.

Fallon, 56 and the senior of the pair, entered first. He was hit immediately with a point-blank shot in the heart. Finnegan, 28, managed to fire five shots before he was felled by three bullets. Both detectives were killed. It was 3:45 P.M.

Police quickly pieced together what had happened: As soon as the two detectives had left, two other customers had pulled guns and announced a stickup. The owner had handed over some money, but it wasn't enough.

"If I don't get some more dough, somebody's going to get hurt," one robber had warned.

To punctuate his point, he'd fired a bullet into the ceiling which brought the detectives running to their fatal ambush. The gunmen had fled with about $3000.

It was a shocking crime, the first double slaying of New York City policemen in 35 years, and the force was outraged. Three hundred men were assigned to the investigation and hundreds of off-duty cops volunteered their services. Within 24 hours, as the result of what Police Inspector Raymond Martin called "intensive routine work," alarms were issued for three suspects: Anthony (Baldy) Portelli, 26, identified as the man who'd fired the fatal shots; his companion, Jerome Rosenberg, 24; and Anthony Dellernia, 34, who'd allegedly driven the getaway car. All were ex-convicts who were regarded by the authorities as professional criminals.

Three days after the double slaying, Portelli was arrested in a Chicago motel room. The following day, Dellernia, who'd been hiding in the woods since the night of the murders, surrendered to police in Norwich, Connecticut, where he'd been serving out his parole. He was brought back to Brooklyn for arraignment before Magistrate Benjamin Schor (soon to become an Evseroff client himself) and held without bail.

There is a famous photograph of Dellernia in custody. Police Captain Albert Seedman (later chief of detectives) is shown pulling Dellernia's head back by the hair so the cameras could catch his face. Newspaper editorials decried the action, civil-rights groups filed protests and the police commissioner was forced to issue a formal rebuke.

The incident illustrates the old adage "One picture is worth more than ten thousand words." The public hair-pulling was trivial by comparison with the back-room tortures of the "intensive routine work." At a corollary hearing to Dellernia's, two men who had helped Portelli flee to Chicago were arraigned—Frank Lino (a cousin of Edward Lino, Evseroff's Staten Island client) and Anthony Acerino. Lino's left arm was in a cast, broken during the intensive interrogation to learn Portelli's whereabouts. It was the first hint of police brutality in the case, but there were no photos and nothing was said about it.

On May 23, the massive manhunt ended when Rosenberg turned himself in to the *Daily News.*

Dellernia was Evseroff's second major case. Like Molinas, the client initially came to him through the firm's tenant, Al Aronne.

"I didn't want to take the case," he recalls. "I had known Finnegan and Fallon, particularly Fallon, very well during their lifetimes. It was only after I did some looking into the case —and I mean looking into it—that I became convinced that Dellernia was not guilty.

"Anthony Dellernia was a man of thirty-four. He was married. He came from a family with a number of brothers and sisters. He was a man of no great intellectual stature, no great degree of education, no great degree of articulation. He was what I would characterize as a 'Bath Beach boy.' He at all times protested his innocence.

"In the preparation of the case, I became aware of the extreme brutality practiced on a number of people by the police. I had a man who came to this office—they had wanted him as a witness concerning a meeting prior to the stickup which he was supposed to have overheard or seen. He was the subject of physical torture. They took him, they burned him with cigarettes, they tied ropes around his testicles, they beat him, they whipped him, they did everything with him. They put him before a grand jury and he testified to things which he told me were not true, because it had been extracted from him.

"I hid him in this office for three days until I got the district attorney's office to agree to protect him. The district attorney then put him back before the grand jury, after calming him down and assuring him that he wasn't going to be beaten to death, and allowed him to retract his testimony. Ultimately, he was never used as a witness at the trial."

The trial opened on January 14, 1963, less than a week after the Molinas jury returned its verdict. The prosecutor was Thomas D. Selzer, one of the top trial assistants in the Brooklyn D.A.'s office.

As indigents, Portelli and Rosenberg had assigned attorneys.

At the time, the state provided $2000 counsel fees for indigent defendants in a capital case. It was a small patronage pork-barrel for criminal judges. In Brooklyn, it was the custom for the judge to assign three or four lawyers for each such defendant—one a veteran who would do the work, plus two or three personal or political cronies who would collect $500 or more for doing nothing except initialing the documents.

Needless to say, the defense table was crowded—eight attorneys (three each for Portelli and Rosenberg, Evseroff and Aronne for Dellernia), the three defendants and the three court officers guarding them. Security was tight. Evseroff protested in vain to the judge that he was not even permitted to sit next to his own client.

The judge was Evseroff's old mentor, Sam Liebowitz. "No matter how much I admired him as an assistant," Evseroff says, "no matter how much I owed him, all vestiges of friendship and admiration and all the natural humanistic traits that we all think we possess disappeared in one fell swoop as soon as I started at the other counsel table."

As a defense attorney, Evseroff had already tried two cases before Liebowitz. In the first, he had represented a policeman who had participated in a stickup. Fearful of the verdict and the severity of the sentence, he'd copped a plea to a lesser charge while the jury was deliberating. In the second, he had represented a burglar named Anthony Messina, who had been tried along with two others and convicted as a second-felony offender. The Appellate Division had reversed the conviction because Justice Liebowitz had permitted the prosecutor to prejudice the jury: He'd cited the prior convictions of two of the defendants and had "castigated Grande for consorting with ex-convicts [i.e., Orr and Messina] and quoted the old adage about 'birds of a feather.' "

Before the Dellernia trial opened, Evseroff approached Justice Liebowitz in the robing room and asked him to disqualify himself. He pointed out that in 1946 the judge had taken Dellernia's guilty plea to robbery. At the time, he had told Dellernia and a companion: "You are only kids now, but you are potential holdup killers."

Justice Liebowitz didn't agree that he was prejudiced: "There is no question in my mind that I can give this defendant a fair trial. What happened in that case, or the expression of the court in that case, sixteen years ago has not the slightest bearing on whether this defendant will get a fair trial. The motion is denied."

So the parties moved into the courtroom to start picking a jury. Evseroff's fears of Justice Liebowitz's pro-prosecution proclivities quickly proved justified. The prosecutor and the three defendants were allowed 20 peremptory challenges each: They could excuse 20 prospective jurors without citing any reason. They were allowed unlimited challenges for cause, if the prospect showed prejudice.

As Evseroff recalls: "We continually objected and there was extensive argument over the fact that the judge was assisting the district attorney in the exercise of his peremptory challenges. We felt that he was systematically excluding blacks, Italians and Jews by taking over the questioning and excusing for cause, so the district attorney would not have to use his peremptory challenges."

After three days of heated argument, a panel of 11 men and one woman was sworn and sequestered and the trial got under way. Under Justice Liebowitz, the sessions sometimes lasted as late as 11 P.M. and never broke before six.

"The trial was as rough as you can imagine," Evseroff says. "It was replete with argument, replete with skirmishes between the court and counsel, so many instances I can't even remember. It was a rough, rough trial."

Before the opening arguments, while the jury was excused as technical exhibits were marked in evidence, Dellernia shouted out: "Why don't you tell them to stop? They are framing me."

Justice Liebowitz admonished Evseroff to keep his client in order. The jury was then brought in and Selzer opened, for two hours outlining the evidence he'd present. The attorneys for

Portelli and Rosenberg waived opening, but Evseroff rose. His remarks to the jury lasted little more than a minute:

"Mr. Foreman, lady and gentlemen of the jury: In the course of this trial, you will have presented to you evidence on behalf of my client, Anthony Dellernia, which evidence will show you that Anthony Dellernia never intended any agreement with anyone to commit any robbery; he never furnished any guns to anybody in furtherance of the robbery; and most particularly, he never went to the scene of the robbery for the purpose of picking up anybody or delivering them, or having anything whatsoever to do with the alleged robbery. Lady and gentlemen: This will be presented to you on behalf of Anthony Dellernia by good, honest, competent and credible witnesses. Thank you."

On January 17, Selzer started presenting his case, a total of 38 witnesses in six days. He had eyewitnesses who identified Portelli and Rosenberg as the robbers and Portelli as the killer, ballistics experts who identified the murder gun and fingerprint experts who identified Portelli's print on it. On the third day of testimony, he called a small-time crook named Richard Melville to the stand. Melville told how he'd provided asylum for Portelli, how Portelli had admitted the murders ("I panicked") and how he'd helped Portelli disguise himself and flee to Chicago.

Portelli's counsel, Lawrence Wild, cross-examined, asking Melville about his initial interrogation by the police. He responded with a tale of torture more appropriate to the Spanish Inquisition than to the supposed scientific methods of "New York's Finest." Melville said he'd been taken to the basement of the stationhouse and slapped and slugged by the cops. When he'd persisted in denying that he knew Portelli or anything about the crime, they'd stripped him naked and beaten him with wooden sticks and a rubber hose. He'd been whipped on the testicles and lighted cigarettes had been ground into his back. After more than two hours of this torture, he'd finally admitted his dealings with Portelli.

"How long—" Wild started at one point.

Justice Liebowitz interrupted him: "What did you say to them when they struck you and kept on giving you the beating?"

"I said, 'No.' "

"As to whether you knew Anthony Portelli?"

"I said, 'No.' "

"Was that true or untrue?"

"Untrue."

"I cannot hear you."

"Untrue," he said louder.

Because Melville insisted that his testimony in court was the truth, Justice Liebowitz let it stand, regardless of the means by which it had been extracted.

Later that day, Justice Liebowitz excused the jury and convened a hearing on threats John Dellernia, the defendant's brother, had allegedly made to Melville's wife during the trial. While Liebowitz was questioning Detective Edwin Lambert, Dellernia jumped up.

"They are trying to frame me," he shouted. "He is the guy trying to frame me. He told me I was innocent. He knew it. Now you are trying to frame my brother."

"Keep quiet, mister!" Justice Liebowitz shouted back.

"You liar!" Dellernia yelled at the detective. "He told me I was innocent. He swore that I was innocent. He wanted me to testify and if I won't, he says, 'I will frame you'—him and Seedman. Bastard! I have a wife and kids."

"Quiet!" the judge shouted.

"He is framing me, judge. I swear. Give me a lie-detector test. Give me anything. He is lying. You lying bastard!"

"Don't use that language!"

"He wants to frame my family," Dellernia insisted. "Isn't it enough with me?"

The judge finally succeeded in restoring order.

"It was fraught with some of the greatest drama I've ever seen in the courtroom," Evseroff remembers. "My impression is that Liebowitz was really impressed by it."

Throughout the first three days of testimony, Evseroff had little to do. None of the evidence affected his client; Dellernia's name was hardly mentioned.

The first evidence against Dellernia came from Louis Ferrara, a 16-year-old dropout known as "Louis the Gee" (as in "geezer") who'd helped out in John Dellernia's candy store. He said that, a few days before the murder, when he'd gone on a drive with Dellernia, a man had given Dellernia a gun. Dellernia had put it under the floorboard mat. Later, he'd overheard Portelli, Rosenberg and Dellernia discussing a "score."

Finally, he said that at 2:25 on the afternoon of the murders, he'd heard Dellernia ask his brother for the car: "Give me the keys. I have to pick up Jerry Rosenberg."

Evseroff's difficulties with Justice Liebowitz can be illustrated by this colloquy from his cross-examination of Ferrara:

"At any time, Louis, did you ever see anyone remove that gun from under the mat?"

"No."

"At any time, did you ever see that gun in the Dellernia candy store?"

"No."

"At any time that day, did you see Anthony Dellernia remove that gun from underneath that mat?"

"No."

"Did you see Anthony Dellernia—"

"He said he didn't see," Justice Liebowitz interrupted.

"I'm asking another question," Evseroff explained.

"He said he didn't see the gun removed by anybody," the judge continued. "Anybody means anybody, including Dellernia."

"Thank you."

"So that settles that as far as the testimony is concerned."

Three more witnesses linked Dellernia peripherally to the crime—Robert Briggs, owner of a gun shop in Aberdeen, Maryland, his wife and their son-in-law, a military policeman at the Aberdeen Proving Ground. They identified Dellernia as the man who had bought the murder weapon from them, using an alias, on February 10, 1962. Mrs. Briggs recalled that he was "dressed like *The Untouchables.*"

When Briggs identified Dellernia, the defendant let loose again: "I never saw the guy before in my life."

This set the stage for Linda Manzione.

"The whole case against Dellernia consisted of the testimony of Linda Manzione," Evseroff says. "She was a beautiful, beautiful girl. She looked like a madonna. She had the face of an angel, but she was not what she looked like. She did not possess the morality or the good character or reputation consistent with her appearance. She was, in the vernacular, a 'knock-around broad.' And she knocked around pretty good from what we came upon."

Linda Manzione testified that on the afternoon of the murders, she'd seen Rosenberg take a gun from a shelf in John Dellernia's candy store. Later, she'd gone for a drive with Dellernia when he'd picked up Portelli and Rosenberg and dropped them off near the Boro Park tobacco wholesalers. She quoted Dellernia as telling them: "I will leave you off here because I don't want to get mixed up in anything."

They had returned to the candy store, but a few minutes later Dellernia drove back to the Boro Park shop, taking her with him. He'd parked nearby and waited. Then they'd heard shots.

"He pulled away very fast," she said. "He said, 'He never learns, he never learns.' And I said, 'Who?' And he said, 'Jerry.' . . . And then he said, 'I hope nothing happened.' "

On cross-examination, Evseroff hammered not so much at her story as at her morals. Miss Manzione admitted that she'd been Rosenberg's girl-friend, but denied that she'd been intimate with him. She denied that she'd told girl-friends that she'd feared she'd become pregnant by him. She even denied petting with him.

With each answer, Evseroff's voice took on an increasing tone of incredulity. Justice Liebowitz finally excused the jury and admonished him.

"The record does not show your demeanor and attitude when

you passed that remark. The jury is not here. I will caution you not to try that again or I will hold you in contempt of the court."

"Will Your Honor hear me?" Evseroff asked.

"No. Just behave yourself."

"I want the record to show that Your Honor is screaming at me."

"I am not screaming," the judge screamed. "And I want you to remember that you are in a courtroom and not in a barroom. Don't try that again."

The defense, such as it was, opened on January 24. Portelli's attorneys produced three witnesses, two of them inconsequential, the third a fingerprint expert whose testimony backfired completely. He said that the latent print *was* Portelli's. Rosenberg rested without calling a witness.

"I was the only one that put in a defense," Evseroff says. "I had some twelve witnesses that I was putting on for the defense. It was a very, very well prepared defense because I believed then, and I believe now, that Dellernia wasn't guilty. That feeling is one that a defense lawyer doesn't have too often."

A cocktail waitress told how she was being driven to work by a Joseph Lombardi when a tire blew out. Lombardi went to call someone for help and Dellernia arrived to complete the lift. He'd been accompanied by two girls named "Linda and Phyllis." That was at about 2:30 P.M.

Another Dellernia brother, Ignazio, told how Dellernia had received a call at the candy store and had borrowed his car to pick up "Joe L." Dellernia had been accompanied by Linda Manzione and another girl named Phyllis Russo.

Marie Spano, an 18-year-old in-law of Dellernia, said she'd seen the defendant "at a little after three" at her sister's home in Bath Beach after he'd just come out of the shower. Selzer protested that she was an alibi witness.

Contrary to popular usage, "alibi" has a strict legal definition: "in another place," the defendant was elsewhere when the crime was committed. Under New York law, the defense, on demand, must announce if it intends to call alibi witnesses and disclose their names. Selzer had served notice and Evseroff had produced no names.

Justice Liebowitz called counsel to the bench.

"Do you still claim that she is not an alibi witness?" he whispered to Evseroff.

"Yes, sir."

"This is fantastic!" the judge exclaimed.

Strictly speaking, she wasn't an alibi witness since the murder occurred at about 3:45. But the inference was clear: Dellernia couldn't have come out of the shower in Bath Beach at "a little after three" and made it halfway across Brooklyn to Borough Park in a half-hour or so.

Mary Ann Dellernia, the defendant's 18-year-old niece, testified that Linda Manzione had told her: "I haven't menstruated for a while now and I am afraid I am pregnant. . . . It's all Jerry's fault."

"What did you say to her when she said that?" Evseroff asked.

"I was dumbfounded. I didn't know what to say to her. I didn't know she was like that."

Evseroff's most important witness turned out to be one who testified on a minor matter. Savino Tamborra, Dellernia's brother-in-law and an attorney in Norwich, Connecticut, said that Dellernia had been at a birthday party in Norwich on February 10, the day he'd allegedly bought the gun in Aberdeen, Maryland.

Tamborra had also arranged Dellernia's surrender to the Connecticut State Police. On cross-examination Selzer zeroed in on that and asked Tamborra if he'd discussed the matter with anyone in Hartford, the state capital.

"No," the witness replied. Then he corrected himself. "Wait a minute. By telephone, I have spoken with, I believe it was his parole officer."

Evseroff leaped to his feet. "I object to that, if Your Honor pleases."

It's a cardinal principle of law that a defendant's criminal record cannot be disclosed to the jury unless he takes the stand or his character is put in issue.

"Overruled," Justice Liebowitz said. "He was not asked that. He volunteered it."

"I will ask Your Honor to instruct the jury to disregard it," Evseroff continued.

"No, I shall not."

The defense attorney pressed the point. "At this time, I respectfully move for . . . the declaration of a mistrial."

"Your motion is denied."

As Evseroff recalls: "That was on a Friday. When we came in Monday morning, Liebowitz called me into chambers. I understand, from what I heard through the grapevine, he had spent the weekend going over the entire record of the trial. He called me into chambers and he said to me, 'If you renew that motion for a mistrial, I will grant it.' "

The stenographer was called in and Evseroff repeated the motion, arguing that Tamborra's "statement . . . is so prejudicial to my [client] as to, perhaps, preclude the possibility of his receiving a fair consideration from the jury, based on the statement made by that witness, and if Your Honor—"

Justice Liebowitz cut him short. "You don't intend to put your client on the stand?"

"No, Your Honor."

Given Dellernia's record, it was inconceivable that he'd testify, no matter how profuse his protestations of innocence.

"Because," the judge continued, "if you put him on the stand, his criminal record would be disclosed and, therefore, that information given by the witness would merely be cumulative."

"I do not intend to put him on the stand."

"I am going to grant the motion and declare a mistrial."

For virtually the first time in the trial, it was Selzer's turn to object. And for once Justice Liebowitz had to admonish the prosecutor:

"A judge must have courage regardless what his opinion is as to whether the man is guilty or not, and a judge who does not have courage does not belong on the bench. I am not a patsy for the district attorney's office."

Dellernia was severed from the case. Two days later, after Justice Liebowitz delivered a typical Liebowitz charge, the jurors retired, deliberated for an hour, then found both Portelli and Rosenberg guilty of first-degree murder with no recommendation for mercy. On February 18, Justice Liebowitz sentenced them to death in the electric chair.

Portelli and Rosenberg appealed their convictions. Faced with the prospect of the "hot seat," they shucked their court-appointed attorneys and scrounged up the money for private counsel. Portelli hired Evseroff's partners, Bill Sonenshine and Gus Newman, while Rosenberg retained the veteran criminal lawyer Maurice Edelbaum. The main thrust of their appeal was the torture of Melville.

On March 11, 1965, the Court of Appeals handed down its ruling. The court stated that the evidence against Portelli and Rosenberg was "more than sufficient." As for the torture, the court noted:

Testimony given from the witness stand by a witness who was, some eight months earlier, compelled by police brutality to give a statement implicating a defendant stands on a footing very different from an out-of-court confession coerced from a defendant and sought to be used against him at the trial. While the latter will be excluded as a matter of law, the testimony of a witness who, although previously forced to make a pretrial statement, asserts that his testimony at the trial is truthful is for the consideration and appraisal of the jury.

An appeal to the U.S. Supreme Court was unsuccessful. Before the death sentences could be carried out, the legislature abolished capital punishment in New York, except for the murder of policemen and prison guards. Although the statute was not retroactive, Governor Rockefeller commuted *all* pending death sentences to life imprisonment. Portelli and Rosenberg remain behind bars.

They left society the court's curious ruling, now public policy in New York State, that while confessions extracted by torture from defendants, guilty or innocent, are barred, no such judicial restraints apply to evidence extracted by torturing innocent (or not-so-innocent) witnesses!

Three months after he was severed from the case, Dellernia went on trial again, this time before Justice Julius Helfand.

"An interesting thing developed between the first trial and the second trial which was crucial to our defense," Evseroff notes. "Linda Manzione went to a lawyer and told the lawyer that her testimony at the first trial was untrue and that she would sign an affidavit to that effect, saying that her testimony had been extracted from her by the police and by threats from the district attorney.

"Before the second trial, they got ahold of her again and brought her up to the D.A.'s office and, in the vernacular, 'they straightened her out.' But, of course, the statement she made to the lawyer and his testimony was used in the second trial by me. It really was devastating.

"The judge didn't interfere with the trial, the judge performed with a great amount of judicial demeanor and temperament, so much so that after he charged the jury and the jury went out, Dellernia jumped up and thanked the judge for giving him a fair trial—*prior* to the time that the verdict came in."

The all-male jury retired on June 5. Confronted by the self-contradictions of the prosecution's star witness, it returned in ten hours with a not-guilty verdict.

If the Molinas case marked a long stride forward in his

career, the Dellernia trial established Evseroff in private practice. After all, two co-defendants were sentenced to death in the electric chair, but Evseroff's client was acquitted. But the verdict was not welcomed everywhere.

"I incurred the enmity of many, many members of the police department and it lasted a lot of years," Evseroff notes. "I'd always had a good relationship with the police, being a former assistant district attorney, and I'd represented policemen for little or nothing when they themselves got into trouble. But they didn't consider it right or proper that I should get involved in this case. I didn't win any popularity contests as a result of it."

Nor did he get much credit from his client. After the acquittal, Dellernia was not set free. He was immediately rearrested for violating his parole and returned to prison to serve out the remainder of his robbery sentence.

"And do you know," Evseroff observes ten years later, "I never heard from him again. I have no idea what happened to him."

6   A Cop Cops a Plea

The real-life criminal lawyer does not live the life of Perry Mason.

First of all, he doesn't have the luxury of handling one case at a time, a murder a week, wrapped up, tied with a red ribbon and disposed of in time for the next client to walk through the door. At any given time, he has dozens of cases at various stages of the legal process. Except when he's actually on trial, he can seldom devote more than an hour or two a day to any one client. Even when he's on trial, he must answer calendar calls on other cases and must arrange his schedule with the skill of a juggler keeping a half-dozen balls aloft at once.

Second, his clients are not all white, wealthy and well connected. Society matrons rarely commit murder and bank presidents don't stick up gas stations. Except for an occasional college student caught with a stash of pot or an accountant nabbed with his hand in the till, his clients come from the strata of society most likely to commit crimes—the lower classes.

Third, and most important, his clients are not all innocent, waiting to be sprung by some fantastic feat of legal legerdemain in time for the 11 o'clock news. Although mistakes do occur occasionally, the authorities are not in the habit of arresting and indicting innocent men. Most of a real-life criminal lawyer's clients have done *something*—not necessarily the full extent of the crimes charged in their indictments—that merits consideration by a judge or jury. Even the best criminal lawyers don't win every case, often not even a majority of them.

The statistics tell the story: In fiscal 1971–72, 27,870 persons were indicted in New York City.

Charges against 2063 were dismissed before trial. A total of 17,755 pleaded guilty.

Only 1124 defendants went to trial; of these, 643 were convicted, 340 acquitted, charges against 51 were dismissed, while 56 cases ended in hung juries or other mistrials. (Because indictments are not necessarily tried during the same year they're returned, the figures for dispositions do not correspond with the number of indictments.)

Thus, in 88 percent of the cases adjudicated, the defendant either pleaded or was found guilty. If Perry Mason had compiled such a record, he couldn't have lasted long in private practice—or on television!

But then the criminal lawyer's job is *not* to play the part of Perry Mason. In all but a handful of cases, his task is not to prove his client's innocence and secure his acquittal, but to admit his guilt and make the best deal he can. This comes about by the process known as "plea-bargaining."

The results of plea-bargaining are simple and evident: The defendant "cops a plea," admits his guilt to a lesser charge and receives a correspondingly lesser sentence. But the process is complex and conducted behind the scenes, often requiring long hours of negotiation between the prosecutor and the defense attorney and sometimes the judge.

"Plea-bargaining is a very necessary expedient," Everoff says. "The connotation in the public mind is that there's something dirty, ugly and corrupt about it, when that's not the case at all. It is a practical, legitimate, much maligned and misunderstood expedient in the administration of justice. It's an absolute necessity. If we didn't do it, everybody would go to trial. If that happened, we'd need ten times the number of judges, prosecutors, court personnel and courtrooms to handle the load."

For all parties, plea-bargaining is a process for hedge-bettors. It offers a sure thing against the risks of a larger loss: for the defendant, a short sentence against the risk of a stiff one; for the prosecutor, a sure conviction against the risk of an acquittal; for the judge, a case cleared from the calendar without a lengthy trial, which often is the most important consideration of all.

The most famous example of plea-bargaining in recent years came in the case of Vice President Spiro Agnew. The Nixon administration's preacher against permissiveness faced the prospect of an almost certain conviction of extortion. ("I have never seen a stronger extortion case," said James Thompson, the U.S. attorney in Chicago, who reviewed the evidence. "If it had gone to trial, a conviction would have resulted.") So Agnew's attorneys entered into extensive negotiations with the Justice Department. Eventually, the bargain was struck: Agnew resigned as vice president, pleaded *nolo contendere* (no contest) to one count of income-tax evasion, received a three-year suspended sentence and a $10,000 fine, while the entire evidence of his corrupt dealings was spread on the record.

The deal was roundly criticized. After all, how many defendants walk out of court scot-free after stealing a half-million dollars? Any defense lawyer would have been proud to make a similar disposition, but few of them could have done it. The ordinary defendant doesn't have Agnew's leverage of precipitating a constitutional crisis by choosing to stand trial.

Ordinary plea-bargaining sessions are more cut-and-dried, as routine as a tourist's haggling with a street peddler. One side says "ten," the other says "one," and eventually they compromise at five, or four, or six, depending on their skills and the leverage they wield.

Spiro Agnew said it about slums, Jack Evseroff says it about plea-bargaining: "When you've seen one, you've seen 'em all."

One example is as good as another. Take the case of Anthony Ferreri. . . .

Anthony Ferreri, a beefy man in his thirties with a beer belly, a shaggy haircut and a bit of a swagger, was a member of New York's Finest—"the finest police force that money can buy."

And Ferreri had been bought. He was on the pad of a Staten Island gambler named Nicholas Massaro. It was his chore to collect the monthly protection payoffs from Massaro and split the take with his buddies on the force.

Then Ferreri was transferred to another assignment and was replaced by Patrolman Frederick Dorner. Dorner was no more honest than Ferreri, but he had the good fortune to get caught first. Instead of prosecuting him, the police brass employed him as a "turn-around cop," using him to get the goods on other dishonest policemen. Among those he trapped was Ferreri, who was arrested in the spring of 1973 and hit with two indictments for bribery and official misconduct.

Since his client faced the prospect of seven years in prison on each indictment, Evseroff sounded out the prosecutor about the possibility of a plea. They discussed it on three occasions and got nowhere. Evseroff held out for a misdemeanor plea and probation; Assistant District Attorney Norman Morse insisted on a felony and three years in prison.

On October 23, with Ferreri's trial scheduled to start the next day, Morse handed Evseroff the transcripts of Dorner's wired conversations with Ferreri. One transcript read:

> DORNER: I got two questions I gotta ask you.
> FERRERI: All right. Hurry up, 'cause I got one for you.
> DORNER: All right. When—when you had the nut goin', how much was yours a month, about?
> FERRERI: I don't know. About a thousand a man.
> DORNER: About a thousand a man?
> FERRERI: For you the [unintelligible] was fifteen hundred.

DORNER: Mine woulda been fifteen. Okay, now can you get me or can you write me down a list—or I'll write it down—of the guys that were on, that you can remember?

FERRERI: I can't remember. I can give you the ones I remember, but it wouldn't be half of 'em.

DORNER: Oh.

FERRERI: 'Cause some of the names on the list I never heard of before. They were guys that had never been taken.

DORNER: Oh-huh.

FERRERI: But—

DORNER: Hah?

FERRERI: You didn't see the guy?

DORNER: No, that's what I'm—

FERRERI: Fine. 'Cause see him. I was talkin' to somebody the other day, all right.

DORNER: Yeah.

FERRERI: And he thinks I'm getting somethin' out of it. Do, if anybody asks, you know, I ain't gettin' anythin' out of it. They wanna put the football tickets on and they wanna give ya fifteen hundred for the season—the one with the football games on it. Eddie Doll's one of them. He's gonna see the cat to see Jimmy. In the meantime, you tell Jimmy that you want it on.

DORNER: Yeah.

FERRERI: It's—it's no fucking trouble whatsoever and it's good. I told Eddie Doll's I'd—I'd see someone, see what I could do for him.

DORNER: Okay.

FERRERI: Right, right?

DORNER: Yeah, all right.

FERRERI: See if I can help him.

DORNER: Okay.

As soon as he saw the tapes, Evseroff knew he had no viable defense for Ferreri; he'd have to negotiate a plea. His first task was selling the idea to his client.

After the calendar call in the criminal part of Staten Island's Supreme Court the next morning, Evseroff led Ferreri into a corner of the corridor and explained the situation. Ferreri balked.

"What are the alternatives, Tony?" Evseroff asked. "I think you've got to take a plea."

He handed Ferreri the transcripts. "I read it yesterday—I got sick."

Eventually, he persuaded his client. When court recessed, he joined Morse in Justice Vito Titone's chambers for the second stage of the process.

"Judge Titone is a very good negotiator," Evseroff says. "He's a man who tries very hard to be fair. We came down to a year. We kept negotiating it, talking about it. I suggested a fine. The judge suggested six months and a five-thousand-dollar fine. So we arrived at a deal. He'd enter a plea to an E felony on one indictment and an A misdemeanor on the other.*

"The E felony was attempted bribery, the A misdemeanor was official misconduct, and the unofficial commitment by the judge, which wasn't put on the record, was that he would be incarcerated for no more than six months and fined five-thousand dollars.

"If he'd been convicted, the likelihood was between three years and four years. He could have gotten seven years. He could have gotten seven-and-seven consecutive, but that's a practical impossibility.

"Sooner or later an evaluation has to be made. Am I going to gamble a defense on the possibility of up to seven years in jail, as against six months in jail?"

Evseroff returned to sell the deal to Ferreri, then all parties went back to court for the formality of putting the plea on the record. As Ferreri stood behind the defense table, his hands clasped behind the back of his leather jacket, Evseroff asked

---

*Under New York's revised Penal Law, enacted in 1967, felonies are divided into categories from A to E according to severity of sentence. A felonies (murder, kidnapping, etc.) carry 15 years to life; E felonies, probation to four years. A misdemeanors carry a one-year maximum; B, three months. An attempt to commit a crime (used primarily for pleading purposes) reduces the charge one grade.

leave to withdraw the not-guilty plea previously entered and plead guilty to two counts of the indictment.

"Is that acceptable to the people?" Justice Titone asked.

"Yes, the people ask that you accept that," Morse replied.

Justice Titone started to read the specific counts to Ferreri. The defendant stopped him, explaining that he'd agreed to plead to another count. Morse stepped to the bench and pointed out the correct charge, which the judge then read.

"Do you join in that application?" he asked Ferreri.

"I do, Your Honor."

Unlike most defendants, who mumble their admissions, as if inaudibility obviated guilt, Ferreri boomed his answers loud and clear, the way he'd been taught to testify at the police academy.

Justice Titone continued with a series of questions, asking Ferreri if he was aware of his rights. To each, the suspended policeman answered, "Yes."

"And do you still wish to plead guilty?"

"I do, Your Honor."

"Have any promises or threats been made to you by the district attorney or any officer of the court?"

"No, sir."

The amenities satisfied, Justice Titone accepted the plea. Sentencing was set for December 4.

The process was a transparent legal fiction. Everyone knew there was a deal. Why wasn't it put on the record?

"I really don't know," Evseroff says. "It's perfectly proper, it's not illegal, it's one of the facets of plea-bargaining. The legal efficacy of such a commitment is the same whether or not it's put on the record.

"I think it has to do with committing yourself in advance of the probation report—in the event that he [the judge] can't live up to his commitment because the probation report indicates that the defendant is a worse guy than we'd anticipated. Generally they let you withdraw your plea and restore you to the status quo."

In Ferreri's case, on sentencing day, Justice Titone reduced the fine to $1000. The six-month jail term stood, but he stayed its start until January 4, so Ferreri could spend Christmas with his family.

The bargain may be signed and sealed, but the judge doesn't always deliver. It happened in the case of Edward Lino.

Lino and his co-defendant Salvatore Scala copped pleas in an assault case on September 8, 1973. The promise by Justice Titone was that Lino would receive a three-month sentence and that Scala would be let off with a $250 fine.

Scala's counsel, Al Aronne, picked up the story nearly three months later:

"We got word yesterday [November 26] by letter from the probation department that they were to be sentenced today. I immediately called the probation department and yelled that we both had extensive calendars which had been prepared a month in advance and they couldn't just give us one day's notice.

"We went and got affidavits of actual engagement to show that both Jack and myself were engaged. But because I know this judge is rough, I went out there. I allowed Lino to go up by himself before the judge and to present the judge with the affirmation that showed Jack was actually engaged in Brooklyn Supreme Court and had just received notification late yesterday afternoon that he was to appear for sentence today.

"The judge said, 'Yes, I see. And Mr. Evseroff asks that we adjourn it until December 20. That's fine. Motion granted. The case is now adjourned until December 20. Defendant remanded. Take him away.'

"And they took Mr. Lino screaming into the pen. As they started to drag him off, I jumped up and I said, 'Your Honor, I have represented this man on many occasions during the time that my colleagues from the office were not present for adjournments. I feel impelled to say something in his behalf.'

"He said, 'Yes, what is it?'

"I said, 'How can you remand the man? He has two children

who are mentally retarded at home, who have nobody to depend on, and he must get home to arrange for somebody to take care of them while he's incarcerated, if you intend to send him away.'

"He said, 'Yes, I intend to send him away.'

"I said, 'But not now, judge. The man isn't ready for this. It just happened yesterday.'

" 'You're telling me what I can do?'

"To make a long story short, he held me in contempt. He fined me two hundred and fifty dollars or thirty days, which he later came off of and suspended sentence, and which later I induced him to withdraw completely. He wiped it off the record. He indicated that he knows in my zealousness to protect a client, I sometimes ask too many questions, which I did. I kept asking him, 'Why? Why? Why? Why would you do a thing like this?'

" 'You can't ask a Supreme Court justice "Why?" You know that we have the power to do it.'

" 'Yeah, but I've been practicing for twenty years and I never saw anybody exert the power the way you do.'

"He said, 'All right, we're starting again.'

"So I came off it. In any event, he finally stuck to the remand and sent Lino in and said that, if Mr. Evseroff wants to come back before the twentieth, he can. If not, he'll leave him in there until the twentieth, at which point he'll sentence.

"This judge is tough to figure. You never know what he's going to do. The last sentence I had with him, he altered. And the one before that.

"My man had a promise of a fine of two hundred and fifty dollars. He said to me in chambers, 'Your man—I'm going to give him a five-hundred-dollar fine and thirty days in jail.'

"I said, 'You can't give him thirty days in jail.'

"He said, 'Why not?'

"I said, 'Because you promised me you'd only fine him two hundred and fifty dollars and no jail term.'

" 'Where does it say that? It's not written on my file?'

"I said, 'It's written down right here, judge,' pointing to my forehead.

"The district attorney was a man and he stood up and he said, 'Judge, I remember you said you would only fine him and I believe the fine was two hundred and fifty dollars, and the other guy, you said you would give no more than ninety days. And I wrote it down on my file.' And he had it and he showed it to him.

"The judge said, 'Well!'—and he walked out.

"He gave my man a five-hundred-dollar fine. He just doubled his promise, and Lino—he still kept in remand to await Mr. Evseroff's attention. I could have taken the sentence, except I didn't know what the hell he was going to do. Another day or two wasn't going to make any difference, if he was going to give him a lot of time."

Evseroff heard what had happened when he returned to the office that afternoon. He considered dashing over to Staten Island the next morning, but he decided to let the judge's temper cool.

In fact, he waited until sentencing day, December 20, when Justice Titone, like many judges, might be imbued with the spirit of the season and inclined to be lenient.

While Lino stood beside him, dapper as ever in a blue denim suit, Evseroff made his plea for mercy. He did not try to conceal Lino's criminal record, nor his culpability. He noted that Lino had been drinking and that no one had been hurt by his action. He reminded the judge that Lino's two children were retarded, one with serious brain damage, and that his wife had been diagnosed as "schizophrenic–catatonic type" and was unable to care for them.

"Justice would best be served if he were sent home," Evseroff said, "not for his sake, but for the sake of these children."

Justice Titone turned to the defendant. "How did you like it?" he asked Lino about his month behind bars.

"Horrible."

"If I placed you on probation, do you think you could do it?"

"Yes."

So he imposed three years' probation with an 11 o'clock curfew weekdays, midnight on weekends, "and do not associate with any person with any criminal record whatsoever" and "do not enter any premises which serve alcohol." He also imposed a $1000 fine.

Evseroff asked if Lino could have time to pay the fine.

"How long do you want?"

Evseroff asked for two weeks. The judge gave him until February 4. Evseroff wished the judge "Merry Christmas" and Lino walked out of court.

Evseroff estimates that a majority of his cases never go to trial. He either wins them on pretrial motions (as in the Wella Balsam case) or disposes of them by plea-bargaining.

Yet he insists: "I'm not a good negotiator. Good negotiators invariably are lawyers who know they will not go to trial—they don't have the experience, they don't have the time, or the know-how or what have you. When I negotiate, in the back of my mind I know that I'll go to trial if I can't make a deal which is satisfactory to me and my client.

"It strengthens my hand with respect to the negotiations *per se,* because the people who negotiate with me know I'll go to trial if I have to. But it weakens my position because I don't have the stick-to-itiveness that is really required to wear somebody down in order to get what you want. I'll only talk to a point. I think it makes me a weaker negotiator, I really don't have that much experience negotiating.

"I want at least an even-money chance in the case that I'm trying. Sometimes that doesn't happen. Sometimes a client will not recognize the realities of the situation. Against my advice, he'll insist on going to trial in the face of what seems to be complete adversity—he can't win.

"I've had it happen—and I've been wrong. It happened to me in the Droner case." Evseroff will always remember it as "the case of the dancing dolls."

Peter Droner was a retired police sergeant. In 21 years on the force, he'd won four citations for bravery. Once he'd shot it out with a cop killer and although he'd been wounded in the action, he'd gotten his man. "A real cop," Evseroff says of him. After he'd started collecting his police pension, Droner worked as an investigator for a bus company and continued to carry his .38-caliber police special.

On the evening of September 16, 1964, Droner was walking through Times Square when he came across a peddler hawking dancing dolls. The paper dolls appear to be self-propelled but actually they're moved by an accomplice jerking an almost-invisible string. During his years on the force, Droner had had some run-ins with the peddler, a Negro named Clarence Ritchie, and there was bad blood between them.

As a curious crowd gathered around, Droner denounced the dolls as a fraud and a fake. Ritchie replied by calling Droner an obscene name. The argument quickly escalated. Droner kicked the string that controlled the dolls. Ritchie slugged Droner. Droner staggered back into the crowd. When he got up, he whipped out his gun and fired three shots into Ritchie's chest. The peddler died instantly. Droner was arrested and charged with first-degree murder.

Evseroff was brought into the case by a Patrolmen's Benevolent Association delegate. He reviewed the evidence and saw no hope in going to trial. He thought it best to plead to manslaughter.

"It was the only case I remember," he says, "where in the negotiating for a plea, the judge [Supreme Court Justice Irwin Davidson] took the defendant and the district attorney and myself—all of us—into chambers and spoke to the man in an effort to show him that he should take a plea. We were all in unison begging him to take a plea. His family was begging him. Notwithstanding that, the guy just wouldn't take a plea."

So, against his better judgment, Evseroff prepared for trial. "I never thought I'd win it."

His opposite number was Vincent Dermody, the ace homicide prosecutor in District Attorney Hogan's office. "I was told that he'd lost only two murder cases in thirty years," Evseroff notes.

"The jury that I selected was anything but what a defendant would normally select. There were people who had previously sat on murder cases, people who had been grand jurors, people who had been on blue-ribbon juries. They were the type of people who ordinarily you'd never want, from the defendant's standpoint, on a jury. Dermody must have thought I had never been in a courtroom and had never tried a case before. But these were just the kind of people who saw it the way that my defendant saw it.

"I brought one of his sons to court, who was a policeman. He sat in the first row in his uniform. His other son, who was a United States Marine—I got him a furlough, and he sat in the first row in his uniform. And his two daughters, his wife. It was really an exemplary family.

"He [Droner] took the stand. He testified that he recognized the man [Ritchie] as a man with a record, and that he was asserting himself as a policeman, even though he was no longer a policeman. He was punched and he didn't recall anything after that. 'If I shot him, I shot him because I reacted to my twenty-one years of police training.'

"This was bolstered by some seventeen or twenty character witnesses who testified to his exemplary character, including the fact that he had once jumped into the East River to rescue somebody."

The jury deliberated only four and one-half hours before rendering its verdict on the ex-cop who wouldn't cop a plea.

"I guess he was right," Evseroff says. "He was acquitted."

Plea-bargaining has been widely criticized for permitting the guilty to escape with minimal punishment. A lesser-known corollary is that the process sometimes induces the innocent, or at least those who profess their innocence, to plead guilty to crimes they didn't commit. And the courts have recognized such pleas as valid!

The most notable example in recent years came in the case of the "Harlem Six," a *cause célèbre* involving the arrest of six black teen-agers in 1964 for the holdup-murder of a storeowner's wife. They were tried and convicted, but the conviction was set aside on appeal. They were retried twice, but both trials ended in hung juries. (Along the way, one of the six pleaded guilty to manslaughter and was sentenced to 15 to 35 years; another was tried separately, convicted of murder and sentenced to 40 years to life.) On April 4, 1973, the remaining four came to court for their fourth trial. In what they termed a "pragmatic decision," they pleaded guilty to manslaughter and were sentenced to time served.

Despite the plea, they continued to protest their innocence. "We've said all along that we are not guilty, and what we feel the world should understand now is that we are still not guilty," said defendant William Craig. One of their attorneys, the radical lawyer William Kunstler, noted: "The fact that they had to plead guilty to crimes they didn't commit is a tragic reminder that justice is truly blind."

Evseroff has had similar, if less celebrated, cases.

Albert Fea was a short, squarely built man of 60. He looked like a bookkeeper, which he was in a way. The books he kept were the records of the bets placed with him. He was a bookie. In 1971, he was arrested, not for bookmaking, but for criminal usury. He'd allegedly lent a furrier $5000 at $1000 interest—the loansharks' classic "six for five." He retained Evseroff to defend him.

"He claims he didn't loan the money to the guy," Evseroff said. "What he did was, he invested money with the guy in a joint venture. He's very adamant about it: 'I'm not guilty, I'm innocent. I may have been a bookmaker, but *that* I didn't do.' He's got a number of witnesses who claim that they were present at the time conversations were held between them and that this was the nature of the transaction.

"However, this man has got a very, very serious heart condition. My position is, 'I don't care if you're innocent or not in this case. You're a very sick man. You have other misdemeanor convictions for bookmaking. One more isn't going to hurt you. But trial and jail could kill you.' "

So Evseroff plea-bargained, arranging for Fea to plead guilty to a misdemeanor and escape with a fine. But he had a tough time convincing his client.

"I had to sit down with him, with his cousins, with his relatives and convince them that it's the expedient thing to do —that he's likely to die if he has to stand trial."

On December 5, 1973, Fea stood in Manhattan's Supreme Court before Justice Burton Roberts, the former Bronx district attorney, a ferocious prosecutor turned compassionate judge. Evseroff offered to plead guilty to the reduced charged of attempted usury.

The assistant district attorney recommended acceptance of the plea. He noted that Fea had a coronary condition. Justice Roberts said he'd accept the plea on the understanding that if the probation report indicated that Fea was able to withstand a jail sentence, he'd allow its withdrawal.

"Is that understood by everyone," he asked.

Evseroff stooped over to whisper to Fea: "Do you understand that?"

Fea indicated that he did.

"What was the loan and what did he charge?" Justice Roberts asked the prosecutor.

The assistant D.A. needed several minutes to find the details of the charge and read them.

"Mr. Fea," Justice Roberts then continued, "did you hear the facts as stated by the district attorney?"

"Yeah," Fea mumbled.

"Are those facts true?"

"Yeah. . . ."

"Are you pleading guilty of your own free will?"

"Yeah."

"Are you pleading guilty because you are guilty?"

This time the answer had to be prodded out of him: "Yeah."

Justice Roberts accepted the plea and set sentencing for February 6 in order to give the doctors time to examine Fea and prepare their reports. (The doctors' examinations sustained the pleadings; Justice Roberts gave Fea a severe tongue-lashing and sentenced him to three years' probation and fined him $1000. Less than two months later, on March 31, on a street in Yonkers where he'd stopped to change a flat tire, Fea fell dead from a heart seizure.)

Evseroff had no regret about pleading an "innocent" man guilty. "I do think that that comes under the heading of trying to do the right thing for a client," he says.

A few days later, while he was Christmas shopping, Evseroff ran into a client whom he'd represented in a murder case a few years before.

"His case," he notes, "is a classic example of how you can help a client without the necessity of trying a case."

Louis Bolino was a 30-year-old auto salesman who eked out a marginal living. He needed a diamond ring to give his fiancée and he decided to steal it. On August 7, 1968, he went to an apartment in the Jackson Heights section of Queens and accosted Adele Berkoff on the stairway. She screamed and her husband, Joseph, a 34-year-old lawyer, came dashing out of their apartment. Bolino fled with Berkoff on his tail. As he ran down the street, Bolino turned and fired a shot at Berkoff. The bullet struck him in the abdomen. He died en route to the hospital.

"Bolino told his girl-friend about it, who promptly went and told the police about it," Evseroff recalls. "He was apprehended. He made statements which were inculpatory. He took the police to the gun. There was nothing to try.

"He knew without a doubt that she had implicated him. Nevertheless, notwithstanding that fact, he married her, which of course proves that love is a very strong and potent force in our society, or so it is alleged.

"He was indicted for murder. They didn't want to give him

any kind of a deal. They wanted him to take a plea to murder, which is punishable by 35 to life. The only thing I could do was bluff it out. I made a lot of noises with the D.A.'s office that I was going to try it and I had information and I had evidence and the statement was coerced from him and all kinds of improprieties were practiced by the Queens district attorney's office.

"So discretion being the better part of valor, they gave me a plea to manslaughter. We submitted a lot of letters and memoranda about what a prior good character he had. And he did. He came from a nice family. He did not come from a racket family. His father was in the postal service. Justice Farrell in his discretion sentenced him to an indiscriminate sentence of up to twenty years—'zip-twenty.'

"He served thirty-six months and he was released a few months ago. He was very pleased and very happy to see me. He said he was meaning to call me. That's a good example of how proper handling of the case can do a lot of good for the client, because to do thirty-six months in jail on a very bad murder when other people do twenty-five years to life for the same thing —I don't think that's bad.

"Incidentally, while he was in jail, his loving bride divorced him. Merry Christmas."

7 *Men of Respect*

In street jargon, they're "men of respect." In police files or newspaper accounts, they're the dons of the Mafia or *cosa nostra,* syndicate or mob, call it what you will. Whatever the name, they can be the backbone of a criminal lawyer's practice.

Jack Evseroff has had his share of such clients, but their patronage has not illuminated the inner workings of the underworld for him. The *mafioso's* code of *omerta* extends even to the attorney entrusted with his life or liberty.

"I never really understood what the mob is," Evseroff says. "I never really asked anybody. I've had a lot of clients of Italian extraction and I've heard or read that they are mob-connected, but I never inquired of them with respect to any of their affiliations. I never inquired into anything that was not relevant to the issue. Whatever my client's friendships are or his affinity with any individuals or any group, if he chooses to tell me about it, O.K. If he doesn't, that's his business."

Without exception, the men of respect have chosen to keep it their business. And one gathers that, for safety's sake, Evseroff hasn't pressed them too hard.

"Nobody has ever, ever volunteered to me any conversation

concerning organized crime or a Mafia or a *cosa nostra,*" he continues. "On many occasions, they've suggested to me, 'We have some mutual friends,' or, 'You've represented some friends of mine in the past,' and some names might be mentioned.

"I must say that I have felt on occasion, speaking to some of these people, that implicit in what was said was the fact that a particular client has some affinity with others, the nature of which and the extent of which and the operation of which I really don't know. But I have felt that there is an affinity, the kind of thing where nobody talks about it, they talk *around* it."

The men of respect are cool customers. They regard arrest and indictment as routine costs of doing business, the way a storeowner regards license fees and insurance premiums. "He has more experience in being involved in criminal trouble than the average layman," Evseroff observes. "As such, he has a tendency to accept the situation he's in. Emotionally, he's less upset. He's better able to cope with the circumstances that confront him. The average layman who's never been in any trouble and gets arrested or indicted—it begins to work on him."

Yet he recalls one case that was a glaring exception to the rule.

"Years ago, I had a fellow who's dead now—he died of cancer—named Joe Yancone. He was reputedly a member of the Gallo gang. He'd been involved in seven or eight major stickup cases. He was a real tough guy.

"Then he got arrested in a case in which he was charged with indecently exposing himself in a movie theater. He was adamant about his innocence. I really believed he was innocent. I never heard that man claim he was innocent in any other situation.

"I never heard anybody protest like him. A woman police officer had arrested him. He a) wanted to kill her, b) wanted to have her arrested, c) wanted to invoke in his behalf all the artifices of law that any citizen might invoke when falsely accused, particularly for a crime involving morals.

"Those who you call mob people react in exactly the same way as the average layman in a given situation. If they're falsely accused or they feel they're being framed, they vocally manifest it."

The morals charge against Yancone eventually was dropped.

To the men of respect, the lawyer is a hired hand, no more privy to the underworld's inner workings than the auto mechanic who fixes their cars or the waiter who serves their food. Yet, surprisingly for those so experienced in the criminal process, the members of the mob harbor some naïve notions as to what constitutes expertise in a criminal counsel.

The smart *mafiosi* have learned the lesson; like Frank Costello, they retain an Edward Bennett Williams. But all too often, the lesser lights of the underworld are represented by a tub-thumper with more lung power than legal lore. In short, they want a mouthpiece with a big mouth.

"These people like somebody who is very vocal in their behalf," Evseroff says. "As they put it, somebody who will 'fight for them.' Their idea of what fighting means may not necessarily be ours. It's great to scream and holler at a propitious time, in a summation perhaps, or to express your righteous indignation before a jury. But when arguing motions with respect to a grand jury proceeding, it ill behooves you to holler at a judge. It's not going to do anything except antagonize him."

Such a conflict came to a head when Evseroff represented Joseph Colombo, the head of one of the five Mafia families in the New York area. Brooklyn District Attorney Aaron Koota had been conducting one of his periodic fishing expeditions into the mob's activities. Colombo was called before the grand jury and given immunity from prosecution. When he balked at answering Koota's questions, he was cited for contempt.

"I handled him initially and then my partner Bill Sonenshine handled him," Evseroff says. "We were attacking it [the contempt citation] on a legal basis. I think that Colombo was dissatisfied because he felt we didn't holler enough. He got himself another lawyer."

Evseroff also represented Colombo's reputed successor, Vincent Aloi.

The case had its roots in the so-called Gallo-Profaci War. In the annals of organized crime, there have been few battles so bloody or so protracted. The war started in 1961 when several members of the Joseph Profaci family demanded a bigger slice of the underworld pie. The rebels were led by the colorful Joseph "Crazy Joey" Gallo. Jimmy Breslin dubbed them "The Gang That Couldn't Shoot Straight," but enough of them shot straight enough to leave a dozen dead in three years of mob rivalry.

An uneasy ceasefire settled on the scene in 1962 after Profaci died of cancer and Gallo was convicted of extortion and packed off to serve a 7-to-14-year prison sentence. Profaci's mantle passed first to Joseph Magliocco, who died of natural causes, then to Colombo.

Colombo soon startled everyone by organizing the Italian-American Civil Rights League and publicly protesting efforts to link Italians with organized crime. He picketed FBI offices, forced Paramount Pictures to delete the word Mafia from *The Godfather* and even induced the Justice Department to ban official use of Mafia and *cosa nostra*. His massive Italian-American Unity Day rally, held at Columbus Circle in 1970, drew 50,000 followers, including politicians of every party. He had created a sort of mob chic.

But there were clouds on Colombo's horizon. According to some accounts, Carlo Gambino, the underworld's new boss-of-bosses, disliked the heat generated by Colombo's antics. Perhaps more ominous, in March 1971, Gallo was released from prison and quickly reassumed leadership of what was left of his old faction.

The second Unity Day rally was held on June 28, 1971. This time Gambino's followers refused to cooperate. But Colombo was still walking proud, the peacock of the podium. As the

48-year-old crime boss posed for pictures, a black drifter posing as a photographer stepped up and fired three shots into his head. Miraculously, Colombo survived, but as a living vegetable. Vincent Aloi took over as the family's acting boss.

Who ordered the shooting—Gallo, Gambino or others—is not known, since the black assailant was killed immediately. But the Gallo-Profaci War (or Gallo-Colombo War, as it was retitled) broke out again in full force. It culminated on April 7, 1972, when Gallo was gunned down in front of his new bride while eating an early-morning snack at Umberto's Clam House on Mulberry Street.

During the investigation into Gallo's murder, Aloi was haled before a Manhattan grand jury and given immunity from prosecution. Assistant District Attorney Robert Tannenbaum fired the first question:

"Now, Mr. Aloi, do you know Carmine DeBiase?"

"May I speak to my attorney, please?"

After several minutes of argument, Aloi was allowed to step outside and confer with Gus Newman.

When he returned to the grand-jury room, Tannenbaum repeated the question: "Do you know Carmine DeBiase?"

"Yes, sir."

"How long do you know him for?"

"I don't know. From the neighborhood. I don't know."

"What neighborhood are you referring to?"

"New York."

"When you say 'New York,' exactly where do you mean?"

"Downtown New York."

"And for how long a period of time when you say you know him?"

"I don't know."

"Approximately?"

"I can't give you beginning, end, Mr. Tannenbaum. From the neighborhood."

"Approximately how old were you when you first met Mr. DeBiase?"

"I know him about ten, twelve years or so."

"And when you say you know him for ten, twelve years, in what capacity do you know him?"

"Hello and good-bye. And that's the acquaintance from the area. . . ."

"Now, when is the last time you saw Carmine DeBiase, also known as 'Sonny Pinto'?"

"To the best of my recollection, I say a year or so ago."

"Where did you see him?"

"Where did I see him?"

"Yes."

"In the neighborhood."

"Well, what neighborhood are you referring to?"

"The Lower East Side."

"Did you talk to him when you saw him?"

"Hello, good-bye."

"Did you discuss the murder of Joseph Gallo with anybody?"

"Now may I consult my attorney?"

"Did you understand the question?"

"Yes."

"What is it that you don't understand, that you [would] like to talk with your attorney?"

"I want to confer with my—"

Tannenbaum interrupted him: "The question is very important to our investigation. . . . Be kind enough to answer the question. It is: Did you discuss the murder of Joseph Gallo with anybody?"

"It was probably the topic of conversation in the neighborhood."

So it went throughout the session. Tannenbaum found it difficult to pin Aloi to any answer. Aloi said he owned a trucking company in the garment center and made $40,000 or $50,-000 a year, but he was unable to explain what he did for the money or even when he'd last visited the office.

Finally, Tannenbaum turned to Aloi's relationship with another mobster named Joseph Yacovelli.

"Did you ever see Yacovelli outside of New York City?"

"Outside of New York City?"

"Yes."

"I can't recall. . . ."

"Did you ever visit 101 Gedney Street in Nyack, New York, in your life?"

"Not to my recollection. . . ."

"Isn't it a fact, Mr. Aloi, that after the murder of Joseph Gallo on April 7, 1972, you visited Joseph Yacovelli inside apartment LK at 101 Gedney Street in Nyack?"

Aloi answered "no" and for that answer he was indicted for perjury.

"Gus [Newman] was supposed to try the case," Evseroff recalls, "but he was going on a vacation with his wife to France. Judge Murtagh was breathing very hard on Gus and he didn't want to give him any kind of adjournment because he was going on vacation. So I was prevailed upon to go up to see Judge Murtagh. He gave me an adjournment for a week or two weeks, something like that, to let *me* try the case."

So Evseroff prepared for trial. He found Aloi "a very pleasant, somewhat naïve man of forty, who, if you got to know him, absolutely belies the fact that he is a mob leader, as he is alleged in the press. You'd find it inconceivable to believe that a man like that is a big-time gangster. He's quiet, he's mild mannered, he's unassuming, he's a perfect gentleman."

Aloi, Evseroff notes, "maintained unequivocally that he had never been in the apartment."

"In discussing the case with Aloi," he continues, "it became necessary to talk to him concerning the individuals who were in that apartment. I discussed it with him to the extent of asking, 'Do you know these people?' 'How long do you know them?' 'How did you come to know them?' After all, he had already testified to this before a grand jury. But what of any other relationship businesswise or mobwise, I didn't go into it. It's not my business. It's not relevant, it's not germane, it's not necessary."

Aloi's trial opened on June 18, 1973, before Supreme Court Justice John Murtagh. The choice of judges did not bode well for the defense. As one attorney has observed: "In *causes célèbres,* where the district attorney's office desperately wants a conviction, Murtagh is apt to be assigned to the case—not only because he is conviction-prone but also because he is one of the better judges and there would be a smaller chance of reversal for technical errors." As if in confirmation, Murtagh was later named to hear all the cases brought by Maurice Nadjari, the special prosecutor appointed to investigate corruption in the administration of justice in New York City.

However, Evseroff says, "Judge Murtagh has always been very courteous to me, notwithstanding the fact that he enjoys the reputation of being a very tough judge." Murtagh granted him an adjournment midway through the Aloi trial so he could attend his daughter's graduation from junior high school. But he granted the defense nothing in his rulings.

"In my judgment," Evseroff says, "we did not try a perjury case, we were in fact trying the Joey Gallo murder case and Aloi's participation in the Joey Gallo murder."

This became apparent in Tannenbaum's opening remarks to the jury. He traced the history of the Gallo-Colombo rivalry and said that the Colombo family had let an "open-hit" contract on Gallo.

"It means simply," he explained, "whenever the opportunity would arise, Joseph Gallo would be murdered."

The prosecutor identified Aloi as "the acting head of the Colombo crime faction" and said he'd visited Yacovelli's apartment in Nyack after Gallo's death.

"You will learn," Tannenbaum continued, "that on many occasions Mr. Yacovelli and the defendant, Mr. Vincent Aloi, discussed in a very businesslike, very matter-of-fact manner how they would kill Joseph Gallo."

Evseroff objected, but, he notes, "under the guise of materiality, the district attorney was permitted to introduce all of this into evidence." Evseroff tried to keep the case in narrow focus.

"The issue in this case very simply, ladies and gentlemen," he said in his opening, "once you strip this case bare of all its bizarre surroundings, once you do not allow yourselves to be suckered into any question of the Gallo murder and all the surrounding circumstances, the issue in this case is really very simple. The issue is whether or not the people can establish beyond a reasonable doubt that Mr. Aloi [lied] when he went into that grand jury and testified under oath that he was never in that apartment—that particular apartment in Nyack as he is alleged to have been and that the indictment charges him with. And that is all the indictment charges him with. . . . Please try to keep your eye on the ball."

The key witnesses against Aloi were two FBI agents, James Kallstrom and Benjamin Purser, Jr. They gave identical accounts: Joseph Luparelli, in fear for his life, had broken with the Colombo mob, fled to California and turned informer. He told the FBI that Gallo's murder had been plotted in the Colombo family's hideout, an apartment in Nyack. He didn't know the address, but it was on the ground floor, overlooked the Hudson River and had a business name on the door.

Kallstrom and Purser set out to find the flat on April 18, 1972. They located it at apartment LK, 101 Gedney Street, ironically in the same complex where the two agents lived. Both said they'd seen Aloi arrive and say something to the doorman, who'd directed him down the hall.

The doorman identified Yacovelli's photo: "That's the fellow [who] lived in apartment LK." But he did *not* identify Aloi, nor was he asked to—by either side.

Then Luparelli took the stand, his face hidden behind sunglasses. Tannenbaum explained that Luparelli "has the sunglasses on because he's in fear of having himself seen in open court"—as if the mobsters he'd consorted with didn't know what he looked like.

Evseroff protested: " . . . one of the things a jury has a right to see, in passing upon a man's credibility and believability, is what he looks like—I mean his entire face."

But Justice Murtagh ruled otherwise, and Luparelli, his eyes still shaded, gave his account. He identified Yacovelli as the *consigliere* (counselor) of the Colombo family and Aloi as the acting boss. He said he himself had served as Yacovelli's driver and bodyguard.

He told how the Colombo family had let the open-hit contract on Gallo. He said that Aloi had visited the Nyack apartment many times and had discussed killing Gallo. On one occasion, he said, "Joseph Yacovelli and Vinny Aloi were discussing that if he [Gallo] should come in that they would take his head off."

Luparelli himself had spotted Gallo entering Umberto's and had relayed the information to Yacovelli. The family decided to stake out the Mulberry Street restaurant to await Gallo's next appearance. Aloi arrived at the apartment the next day with $500 for Yacovelli to deliver to DeBiase, whom he named as one of the actual killers.

On cross-examination, Evseroff hammered at Luparelli's record. The witness admitted to being a burglar, a loan shark and a fence for stolen goods. In addition to the Gallo slaying, he confessed that he'd been mixed up in the "Joe Wagon Wheels murder" and "just one other."

That testimony and Aloi's grand-jury testimony were the prosecution's case. Evseroff moved for dismissal, citing, among other things, another judge's ruling in another case that Luparelli was "completely unworthy of belief." Justice Murtagh denied the motion and the defense rested without calling a witness.

"Aloi should have taken the stand," Evseroff maintains. "I suggested it, but he didn't want to."

So all that was left were the summations. Evseroff scored Luparelli as "a man who comes into this court and gets on the witness stand with his dark glasses, with his sinister appearance, and he tells you very clearly and very succinctly and very plainly that he is a criminal, that he is a hood, that he has been involved in one way or another in at least three murder cases, that he hasn't done a decent day's work in over fifteen years, that he is a man who earns his livelihood in various echelons of criminal behavior. . . . Luparelli comes here and he gives you a story, a tale. He weaves a bizarre tale of a conspiracy to commit murder."

Once again, he tried to keep the case in narrow focus. "There is only one issue in this case. The one issue in the case is: Did Aloi go to that apartment at any time? That's the issue in this case, no other issue. Don't be confused, don't be steamed up, don't be prejudiced, don't be biased by the bizarre story that you heard from that killer."

But Tannenbaum opened it up again. Over Evseroff's repeated objections, he recited Aloi's criminal connections. "You know the kind of person the defendant is," he concluded. "You know the kind of person that sits in this courtroom."

The jurors retired at 3:10 P.M. on June 26. They were back in little more than an hour with a question: Should the FBI agents be considered one witness or two?

It was a good omen for the defense. Evseroff had asked Justice Murtagh to explain in his charge to the jury the "two-witness rule," that is, in perjury cases the defendant must be contradicted by more than one witness. The question obviously indicated that the jury did not believe Luparelli.

Justice Murtagh gave the only answer he could—two people are two people, regardless of occupation. The jurors retired again.

At 8:45 P.M., they reported that they were deadlocked. Justice Murtagh sent them back to deliberate further.

At 10:35, after a rereading of the agents' testimony, they returned with a verdict of guilty.

Justice Murtagh remanded Aloi immediately and on August 7 imposed the maximum sentence of up to seven years in prison. Aloi could be paroled after two and a third years, the exact term to be determined by the parole board. But the judge expressed his hope that "the period to be served should be much closer to the maximum."

The case is on appeal. Evseroff is confident that the verdict will be reversed because of the prosecutor's inflammatory statements and the witnesses' prejudicial testimony.

"It was a suspicious case to me," he reflects. "I had a strong suspicion that Aloi might very well be innocent. Of course, that presupposes that two FBI agents would perjure themselves. It's hard to believe that two FBI agents would commit perjury, although in this day and age, nothing much surprises me after what I read about Washington.

"If Aloi had been in the building many times, as Luparelli alleged, the doorman for sure would have identified him; the two FBI agents in the lobby would have shown him a picture. According to the agents, he walked up to the doorman and spoke to the doorman, who pointed to an apartment. Clearly, if the man had been there fifteen or twenty times before, why would he have gone to a doorman and asked where the apartment was?"

Above all, there's the mystery of the prosecution's motive. If, as Luparelli alleged, Aloi had ordered Gallo's execution, he should have been the target of the grand-jury inquiry. Instead, he was called before the panel and given immunity from prosecution!

"A very peculiar case," Evseroff notes. "I have a strong suspicion that there was some very substantial perjury committed there—and not by Aloi before the grand jury."

In most Mafia trials, it's not one man's word against another's, but one man's word against a defense lawyer's ability to punch holes in his story. There's never a defense of "I didn't do it," or "I did it, but . . ." It's an axiom of criminal practice that *mafiosi* don't testify. "The incidence of these kind of people ever taking the stand in their own behalf is nil," Evseroff observes. "It just doesn't happen."

This poses problems for a defense lawyer. "I believe in people taking the stand in their own defense," Evseroff continues. "Generally speaking, a jury likes to see and hear a defendant.

I think that notwithstanding a judge's admonition that 'the defendant did not take the stand although he had a right to do so and you should draw no inferences from it,' I think that juries do draw inferences from it nevertheless."

The most difficulty occurs in federal conspiracy cases, one of the government's major weapons against the mob. Unlike New York State, where independent corroboration is required to convict, in federal courts a defendant may be found guilty on the unsupported testimony of a co-conspirator. Yet Evseroff managed to win one such case against the testimony of one of the most celebrated informers of modern times—Herbert Itkin.

Itkin has been called "the ultimate con man." He was the epitome of a "shyster" lawyer, often pocketing the personal-injury settlements he won for clients. By the mid-1960s he was dabbling in Caribbean business ventures and was a registered foreign agent. At the same time, he served as a "source" for the CIA. His success as a money-mover brought him to the attention of the underworld, and he started arranging deals for the mob for a percentage of the take. By then he was an informant for the FBI, promised immunity from prosecution. He had, in effect, a license to steal.

He surfaced in the late 1960s, giving testimony that led to the jailing of James Marcus, Mayor Lindsay's water commissioner, *mafioso* "Tony Ducks" Corallo and former Tammany chieftain Carmine DeSapio. Some months later, he was the key witness in the Mid-City case.

In 1964, the Mid-City Development Company of Detroit needed a loan to buy an industrial complex in suburban Warren, Michigan. Through the intercession of a local *mafioso,* it obtained a $1-million mortage from a Teamsters' Union pension fund. But it still needed $200,000 to swing the deal and this time the mob haggled over terms.

Mid-City turned to Itkin and his business partner, John Keilly. Through James "Jimmy Doyle" Plumieri, the mob's leading garment-center loan shark, the mortgage was arranged in return for a $60,000 fee for Keilly and Itkin and a $5000 bribe to David Wenger, auditor of the Teamsters' pension fund.

The deal caused a dispute between the Detroit and New York mobsters. So a "sit-down" was arranged on neutral territory, Pittsburgh, presided over by the city's aging mob boss, Frank Amato. He ruled in favor of Detroit, with New York getting a lesser cut.

As a result of Itkin's information, Keilly, Wenger and 11 *mafiosi* from New York, Detroit and Pittsburgh were indicted for an interstate conspiracy to bribe Wenger with $5000.

The trial opened on October 26, 1970, in the federal courthouse on Foley Square before Judge Milton Pollack, who, before his appointment to the bench in 1967, had been one of New York's leading litigators. Only 11 of the 13 defendants were on hand. Three weeks before, Salvatore "Sally Burns" Garnello had been found on the Lower East Side stuffed in the trunk of a car with four bullets in his head. Plumieri was too ill to stand trial; he too would later be murdered. Evseroff's client was Edward Lanzieri of Brooklyn.

"The case hinged primarily on the testimony of Itkin," Evseroff recalls.

Like the other defense attorneys, he hammered away at Itkin's credibility on cross-examination, attempting not so much to disprove specific allegations as to cast a cloud over his character and thus his entire testimony.

"During 1964," he asked, "did you engage in any other illegal activities except this case that you have outlined to us?"

"Oh, no, sir. There were many others," Itkin answered.

"Many others in 1964?"

"Yes, sir."

"And did you engage in others in 1963?"

"Yes, sir."

"And in 1965?"

"Yes, sir."

"1966?"

"Yes, sir." . . .

"In this particular case, you got some money, I think you testified?"

"Yes, sir. I did."

"That money that you got, did you turn that money over to the government?"

"No, I did not, sir."

"Did you ever turn any money that you obtained as a result of your participation in these various enterprises over to the government?"

"No, I did not, sir."

None of the others offered a defense, but Keilly took the stand. Among other things, he denied meeting Wenger until February 1966. In rebuttal, the government called John Townsend, a Texas attorney who'd been involved in a similar deal with Itkin and Keilly. He said Keilly had introduced him to Wenger in October 1963. He added that part of his arrangement was that Wenger would split the fee he paid to Itkin and Keilly.

The jury retired on November 12 and quickly found Keilly and Wenger guilty as charged. "This had to be off Keilly's testimony," Evseroff observes. Keilly was subsequently sentenced to two years and three months in prison and fined $6000; Wenger to two years and $10,000.

All the others were acquitted. "The jury didn't buy Itkin's testimony," Evseroff explains. "Their efforts to corroborate him failed."

It was a rare victory. As he notes: "It's so awfully difficult to get anyone acquitted in a federal conspiracy trial."

The defense difficulties are compounded if the charge involves narcotics. Not only are the penalties more severe, juries are more apt to convict. All a prosecutor needs is a sample of the stuff and an informer, and dozens of people may be brought to justice—or injustice.

Among both law-enforcement agents and the underworld, many federal narcotics convictions are suspect, but none more so than that of the late Mafia boss Vito Genovese, who was found guilty of dope dealing in 1958 and sentenced to 15 years in prison. He died behind bars in 1969.

The conversations of Angelo DeCarlo, a New Jersey *capo* (captain) in Genovese's family, were bugged by the FBI for four years in the early 1960s. On these DeCarlo tapes, the mobster was overheard admitting to murder, extortion and other assorted crimes, but never to narcotics. Indeed, he advocated the death penalty for dope pushers, and he insisted that Genovese had been framed: "Vito hated narcotics all his life."

Evseroff had a similar case, but one with a happier ending for his client.

In May 1971, Michael Casale was arrested by the federal strike force, the multiagency unit sent into various jurisdictions to combat organized crime. He was indicted, along with seven others, on charges of conspiring to import and sell a $100,000 kilo of heroin.

On the FBI charts, Casale was listed as a *capo* in the family of Joseph Bonanno, better known as Joe Bananas and familar to many as the patriarch in Gay Talese's *Honor Thy Father.* Evseroff found Casale to be a 55-year-old, gray-haired man who dressed conservatively and spoke softly.

"He gives you the impression that he's been around," Evseroff says of Casale. "He's not naïve. He had a terrible record, a long, long yellow sheet [the New York police arrest record], but never anything that smacked of narcotics.

"Casale, at all times, vehemently denied the charge. He always took the position that he had nothing to do with this or any other narcotics transaction, that narcotics or anything to do with it was anathema to him. It wouldn't take you very long in speaking to him to believe completely, as I did, what he said."

The feds had the heroin and an informer who'd been in the inner councils of the conspiracy, a hood known as "Big Nose Mike" Fiore. Fiore provided the only link tying Casale to the plot; he claimed that he'd paid Casale $1000 from the proceeds.

The trial opened in July before Judge John Dooling, Jr., in Brooklyn's federal courthouse.

"We started the trial," Evseroff recalls. "Fiore came out as a witness. As he walked by the defense table, he said, 'Hello,

Mike.' I thought Casale was going to jump up and strangle him right there in the courtroom. I had to restrain him."

Fiore testified and Evseroff cross-examined. He elicited the information that, as an informer, Fiore had become a government charge and that, thus far, he'd been paid $50,000. He then turned to the question of Fiore's residence.

"Isn't it a fact," he asked, "that you now live out of New York State? Isn't it a fact that you now live in South Carolina?"

"If I told you where I lived," Fiore shot back, "I wouldn't live twenty-four hours."

Because of that inflammatory assertion, Judge Dooling declared a mistrial. He excused the jury and ordered both the prosecution and defense to be back in court the next morning to start a new trial. As Evseroff left the courtroom, he noticed Dennis Dillon, the head of the Brooklyn strike force, conversing with the prosecutor, James Drucker. He approached them.

"Jesus Christ!" he exclaimed. "I don't believe this guy's telling the truth."

Apparently the prosecutors had their doubts too, at least as to Fiore's evidence against Casale.

"What about that lie-detector test?" Dillon asked.

During one of his many protestations of innocence, Casale had demanded to take a lie-detector test.

"You want him to take a lie-detector test?" Evseroff asked incredulously.

The prosecutor assured him that he was serious.

"Sure. Fine," Evseroff said.

The agreement was quickly worked out. "We stipulated that the results of the lie-detector test would be admissible in evidence," Evseroff explains. "Judge Dooling didn't like the idea. He felt it was inadmissible, even if nobody objected to it. But he went along with it."

Casale was severed from the case and the test was administered to him at the office of Manhattan District Attorney Frank Hogan, which pioneered in the use of polygraphs. The questions had to be carefully drawn, to avoid asking Casale anything that might involve crimes outside the indictment. (Lie-detector questions, all of which take a simple "yes" or "no" answer, are made known to the subject in advance. They include several innocuous ones—"Is your name Michael Casale?"—and only one or two that go to the meat of the matter.)

"Casale passed with flying colors," Evseroff notes.

Instead of introducing the results in evidence, the government dismissed the case against Casale. Of his seven co-defendants, one was severed from the case because of illness. At the second trial, two were convicted and sentenced to five-year prison terms; two were acquitted; the jury was unable to agree as to two others. So a third trial was held; charges against one were dismissed; the other was convicted and sentenced to ten years in prison.

"I really felt very good about it," Evseroff says of Casale's case. "I think it's a great credit to the U.S. attorney's office that these people had the insight, foresight and guts to see that this man wasn't guilty."

8 *Appealing Propositions*

Each law firm develops its own *modus vivendi*. Some are casual associations, with each partner going his own way, handling his own clients, collecting his own fees. Others are assembly-line operations, with specialists handling each stage of the legal process and divvying the fees according to their status in the hierarchy. At Evseroff, Newman & Sonenshine, it was an equal division not only of fees, but of labor.

"We treat each of the cases as jointly ours," Sonenshine explained, "the exception being that a particular client may want a particular lawyer to handle his case, in which case of course we do it. But there are times when a situation requires fairly immediate action and the partner to whom the client originally came is not available; then another partner will take over. With a firm, there's always someone who can fill the breach, at least for emergencies. In fact, that was our original concept when we formed our partnership."

But one legal chore is not divided equally. Evseroff eschews the paperwork of criminal practice. The preparation of motions and appeals is handled mostly by Sonenshine. If Evseroff is the legal gladiator, fired by the head-to-head combat of the courtroom, Sonenshine is the legal scholar, equally aroused by an academic argument over a fine point of law. Where Evseroff's office is bare and functional, the walls of Sonenshine's are lined with shelves of books and his desk is cluttered with briefs, motions and copies of the latest judicial decisions.

Sonenshine was born in the Bronx and grew up in the Williamsburg section of Brooklyn. Like Evseroff, he attended the borough's public schools, then went on to Brooklyn College. After two years, he switched to night classes at Brooklyn Law School, while working days as the managing clerk of what is now the Wall Street law firm of Cleary, Gottlieb, Steen & Hamilton. He was the first night-school student to become editor-in-chief of the *Brooklyn Law Review.*

After graduating in 1951, he kicked around for a few years, working first for other lawyers, then in offices of his own in the Bronx and Brooklyn. In 1958, he joined the staff of the Brooklyn district attorney's office. In 1961, his boss, D.A. Edward Silver, was president of the National Association of Prosecuting Attorneys. He selected Sonenshine to write the association's *amicus curiae* brief in the landmark case of *Mapp* v. *Ohio,* in which the U.S. Supreme Court extended the protection of the Fourth Amendment to defendants in state criminal trials, ruling that illegally seized material could not be introduced into evidence. It was not a decision that prosecutors welcomed, and Sonenshine pleaded in vain for reconsideration.

Later that year, he joined Evseroff and Gus Newman in private practice. Sonenshine's wife, the former Mina Flax, in addition to being the mother of their four children is also a lawyer and an associate in the firm. Though her time is necessarily limited, she occasionally tries a case.

Sonenshine estimates that about one-fifth of his practice is appeals, perhaps 10 or 12 cases a year, roughly half of them cases originally tried by his office. "I enjoy them," he says of appeals, "particularly when there are really solid legal issues to deal with. I would not like to do it—and I don't do it—anywhere near exclusively. I probably spend as much or almost as much time as Jack does on trials. I wouldn't like to do that exclusively either."

The appellate process is far different from the back-room negotiations of plea-bargaining or the courtroom combat of trials.

"The first thing you've got to do with an appeal," Sonenshine explains, "is familiarize yourself with the actual case. That can be done only one way and that is to read the trial record. Of course, if you tried the case yourself, you're already familiar with it; otherwise, you have to start from scratch. The second step, if it was a case that we were not a party to originally, would be to speak to the attorney who tried it, just to get his overall impressions.

"You read the record with a view toward the legal arguments you're going to make, and these usually arise either from the rulings of the court or the charge of the court. Most laymen who've never had anything to do with an appeal think of it as a rehash of the original case, which is not true. You start out with the basic proposition that, by virtue of the conviction, all the factual issues in the case were resolved against the defendant. Except for the very rarest of situations, you cannot urge to an appellate court that a particular witness should not have been believed, or perhaps should have been believed. None of that will usually prevail. Those are what lawyers call 'issues of fact' that the appellate courts basically do not deal with.

"The basic concept of an appeal is that the defendant, in substance, is saying he didn't get a fair shake on trial because certain important rules were not complied with. Classic illustrations are where a judge permits a prosecutor to offer evidence which should not have been admitted, or conversely where a defendant wants to offer certain evidence and the trial court feels that it is irrelevant to the issue; or very often where judges in charging a jury as to what the law is charge them in a manner that is not correct."

Sometimes Sonenshine will review a record and decide that the case isn't worth appealing, that the chances of success are too slim to justify the effort. But for most clients, especially those facing protracted prison terms, any straw is worth grasping.

"The next step," Sonenshine continues, "is to make notes from your reading of those aspects of the case you think constitute a legal issue worth presenting to the appellate court. Sometimes there'll be a dozen; sometimes, just one. Normally, what I do first is formulate in my mind, based on my own knowledge without looking at any particular law books, the direction I think the argument should take. The next step is the actual legal research, which involves going to the reported decisions over the years and examining them to see whether or not any legal proposition in a prior case will support the argument that you want to make."

The materials for this research constitute a major part of the office's overhead. The firm receives the bound volumes of the *Supreme Court Reports* and the *New York Supplement* which reports the state court decisions. It also subscribes to the "advance sheets" of the Supreme Court, U.S. Court of Appeals, state Court of Appeals and the local appellate divisions, as well as the *New York Law Journal,* the daily newspaper that carries the court calendars, decisions and announcements. Even this mass of printed matter, which periodically threatens to overflow the office, may not suffice. Then Sonenshine will repair to the library, either at Brooklyn Law School or the Supreme Court Building, to search out other legal tomes.

At this point, the academic process of appeal may be diverted by a practical consideration—the convicted client already may be behind bars. If his sentence is short, he may complete it before the appeal can be heard. So Sonenshine's first task, once he has decided there is an appealable issue, may be to secure the client's release. The motion for an order fixing bail pending appeal (what used to be called a certificate of reasonable doubt) is a preview of the appeal itself.

"The next thing to do," Sonenshine continues, "is to draft what amounts to a legal argument in written form. Basically you take the prior opinions and quote from the language used there to support the argument you say is applicable in your case. Very often, cases arise where you can find precedents in either direction. Sometimes different courts take different views of the same proposition. And sometimes, very often in fact, you have to argue by analogy, because no two cases are quite alike.

"I spend a good amount of time on the actual writing of the brief. I usually do it in longhand. The writing by hand stimulates and generates other ideas as I'm doing it. In addition, I like to spend a good deal of time with the literary quality of the brief. I've had briefs that were quoted by the courts; they adopted the very language that I used. I think a well-written brief, while it's not critical, can be a very decisive factor in persuading a court.

"The final literary effort I try to do at home because there's no distraction such as phones and clients and the usual turmoil of the office. I get away from the wife and the kids by locking myself into the room I'm in, or I do it after they're asleep."

Once written, the brief is reproduced. At one time, courts required printed briefs, but most have adapted to the methods of modern technology. Briefs may be mimeographed, photo-offset or Xeroxed, at a considerable saving for the client. An even greater saving comes from elimination of the old rules requiring transcription and in some cases printing of the entire trial record. Now most courts use the appendix system, under which attorneys summarize the proceeding, reproducing the exact language only of the points at issue.

Once printed, it's served, and the prosecutor's office goes through a similar process in preparing its reply. (Occasionally, a prosecutor will appeal a successful pretrial motion to suppress evidence or to dismiss an indictment, so Sonenshine must draft the response.) Then the briefs are filed in court and the case is set down for oral argument, if requested.

"I almost invariably ask for oral argument," Sonenshine says. "I think that's a very big factor on appeal."

Appeals of misdemeanor convictions are made to the appellate term of the appropriate Supreme Court and are heard by three-judge panels. Felony appeals go to the Appellate Division of Supreme Court and are heard by five-judge panels. Federal cases are normally heard by three-judge panels of the Second Circuit Court of Appeals in the U.S. Courthouse on Manhattan's Foley Square.

The procedures vary from court to court, but the process is the same. The lawyer has 15, 20, maybe 30 minutes to state his case. Often, he barely gets a sentence out of his mouth before the judges start firing questions at him.

"I enjoy the give and take of it," Sonenshine says. "The judges are usually briefed on the case beforehand, so they have some pretty pertinent questions."

Once the case is argued, the judges take it under advisement. The decision may come anywhere from a week to months later, either in the form of a simple unsigned memorandum or a full-fledged opinion, replete with citations and accompanied by concurrences and dissents.

If he loses, the lawyer can go to a higher court. Sonenshine hits Albany about twice a year to argue before the state's highest court, the Court of Appeals. Though he's filed briefs with the U.S. Supreme Court, he's yet to argue before the tribunal. But he'd like to. In the interim, he quips that the reason he hasn't is because he's been so successful in the courts below.

Appealing can be a protracted process. Take the case of *People* v. *DeLucia.* "That's one in which I changed the law in the state of New York," Sonenshine says proudly.

The case started at 5:30 A.M. on May 14, 1962, when three detectives arrested Fred "No Nose" DeLucia and Salvator Montella in the hallway of an apartment building on Queens Boulevard.

At the trial a year later, the detectives testified that while DeLucia stood by, they saw Montella with a screwdriver trying to jimmy open a door that led from the hallway to Pep McGuire's Cabaret, a watering hole made famous in the columns of Jimmy Breslin. Montella claimed that he and DeLucia had "closed" the bar and were innocently walking along an alleyway to their car when they were accosted by the detectives and pushed through a door into the hallway. He insisted that the detectives had planted the screwdriver. DeLucia did not take the stand.

On May 2, 1963, after deliberating for 12 hours, the jury found both defendants guilty of attempted burglary and possession of burglar's tools. On June 28, Supreme Court Justice Peter Farrell sentenced DeLucia to two and a half to ten years in prison and Montella to two and a half to five years.

Sonenshine caught the case on appeal. In reviewing the record with the trial lawyer, he learned that some of the jurors had mentioned visiting the scene of the crime, which was only a block from the courthouse. He sent a private detective to ferret out further details. As a result, he secured affidavits from five of the jurors that several members of the jury had visited the scene the night before they'd deliberated.

One juror stated:

... We visited the scene because, a number of things that had been mentioned in the trial, had not been specifically clear to us, and as the result of this visit, some of the testimony now became clear. This visit, I believe helped me, clarify some puzzling aspects of the testimony given, and as a result it helped influence me when we adjourned to the jury room in coming to my decision. . . . [punctuation sic]

Another said:

... I did not go to the scene of the crime that these two men were being tried for, but I do recall that it was Mrs. Margolin who had instigated the fact that the jurors should go to the scene of the crime to get a better picture of what had actually happened and to better assure herself in the interpretation of the photos and other evidence

which had been presented by the district attorney's office.
I further recall that it was Mrs. Margolin who after visiting the scene came back to the jury room the next day and
attempted to influence others as to the guilt of the boys.
At this time she also had stated that she was convinced
that persons of this type should be removed from the
street, since her husband had been a victim of a recent
mugging. As the result of her carrying on she most certainly had influenced at least five of the other jurors, who
at the time were for voting these two young men innocent.
She, Mrs. Margolin, had stated that she had re-enacted
how these two defendants could have been apprehended.
In her discussing how she had visited this scene, I would
say that she definitely swayed the other five jurors. . . .

It was clearly improper for the jurors to have visited the
scene of the crime without permission. But Sonenshine was
confronted with what had been a principle of Anglo-Saxon
jurisprudence since Lord Mansfield rendered judgment in *Vaise*
v. *Delaval* in 1795—jurors cannot impeach their own verdict.

"The law was basically against me," he says. "My argument
was—and this was one of those situations where there was no
precedent in my favor; if anything, they were against me—that
in dealing with a criminal case, there's a constitutional right to
confrontation of the witnesses against you. And the argument
I made, without any authority at all other than the basic constitutional precept, was that the jurors, when they went to the
scene of the crime and then reported back to their fellow jurors
what had transpired without anybody knowing about it, in
effect became witnesses against the defendant."

Sonenshine's first move was a motion asking Justice Farrell
to set aside the verdict—denied on February 13, 1964. Next an
appeal to the Appellate Division—denied unanimously on June
10, 1964. Then an appeal to the state Court of Appeals—denied,
four to three, on March 18, 1965. Judges John Van Voorhis,
John Scileppi and Francis Bergan joined Marvin Dye in the
majority opinion:

. . . It has long been familiar law that jurors may not impeach their own duly rendered verdict by statements or testimony averring to their own misconduct within or without the juryroom; much less can they do so by statements presented in the form of hearsay affidavits. . . . The rule is founded on sound public policy. . . . Even though an unauthorized view of such premises is improper it is not, without more, such an impropriety as to warrant the granting of a new trial.

But Judges Stanley Fuld and Adrian Burke (now New York City's corporation counsel) agreed with Chief Judge Charles Desmond:

The catch phrase "jurors may not impeach their verdict" does not dispose of the proof that these jurors, depriving defendants of a basic protective right, went on their own to the crime scene, investigated there to check on the officers' testimony and reported back to their fellow members of the jury, all without the knowledge of court or counsel. The rule prohibiting self-impeachment by jurors is stretched too far and in the wrong direction when it is used to validate such a transgression of fundamental fair trial rules.

Finally, an appeal to the U.S. Supreme Court—*certiorari* denied on October 11, 1965. (Contrary to popular usage, denial of *certiorari* does not mean the court upheld the conviction, it simply declined to review the case. But the effect was the same —the verdict stood.)

Rebuffed on one route, Sonenshine decided to scale the ladder of the federal courts by claiming that the defendants were being held in violation of their constitutional rights. His first step was to prepare a *habeas corpus* petition. Since DeLucia and Montella were incarcerated in Dannemora prison in upstate New York, it was filed with the federal court in Albany.

On April 16, 1966, Judge James T. Foley denied the petition, but he was not as callous about it as some of the judges who

had heard the case. First, he expressed his incredulity that the
petition was "neatly prepared and well organized by a lawyer
with the unusual payment of the $5.00 filing fee." Then he
noted, "The claim here is not in the usual pattern of the standard type claims raised concerning state convictions." He went
on to rule:

> . . . No matter whether I would agree or disagree if I were
> a state judge, it is my opinion that the question is purely
> one for the state courts and the irregularity does not rise
> to the stature of being state action violative of fundamen-
> tal liberties guaranteed by the federal constitution. . . .
> Occurrences of this kind are disturbing but do occur in
> human existence. Our only consolation is that although it
> is ideal to strive for totally perfect and unblemished jus-
> tice, such is unattainable. Prejudicial and intentional un-
> fairness is not evident to me.

But Judge Foley was sufficiently disturbed that he granted
Sonenshine leave to appeal to the Second Circuit. Once again
the attorney argued that:

> . . . The prejudicial effect upon the jurors resulting from
> their clandestine investigation is amply demonstrated by
> their uncontroverted statements. The evidence received in
> court during the trial obviously left at least some of them
> unsatisfied. In their misguided zeal to find what they
> hoped would be the truth of the matter, they ran haphaz-
> ardly along a path forbidden by long established and
> wisely chosen rules of law. The end product was not a
> verdict consonant with our jurisprudence.

As before, he had difficulty pointing to a precedent. The only
case he could cite was a recent decision in which the Fifth
Circuit had ordered a post-trial hearing on a moonshine convic-
tion because a juror had conferred with a prosecution witness.
But the ruling of the Deep South court was not binding on New
York's Second Circuit.

Then, while the case was pending, the Supreme Court

handed down its decision in *Parker* v. *Gladden,* reversing an Oregon conviction because a bailiff had told the jurors that the defendant was guilty.

"Based on that decision," Sonenshine says, "I now argued for the first time with some real authority behind me."

As judges are wont to do, those of the Second Circuit sidestepped the issue. Rather than rule, on March 7, 1967, they sent the case back to the state courts for "reconsideration." But their decision contained the undisguised indication that if the state courts didn't act, the federal courts would.

So the case was reargued before the state Court of Appeals, which ruled on July 7, 1967. Again, it split four to three, this time in Sonenshine's favor. Speaking for the majority, Judge Kenneth Keating (the former senator, now ambassador to Israel) noted:

> To use the reasoning of the Supreme Court in *Parker* v. *Gladden* . . . these jurors became unsworn witnesses against the defendants in direct contravention of their right, under the Sixth Amendment, "to be confronted with the witnesses" against them. . . .
>
> In this type of case, proof of the unauthorized visit is sufficient to warrant a new trial. . . . Such a visit, in and of itself, constitutes inherent prejudice to the defendants.

Actually, no votes had been changed by the federal courts' holdings. Judges Van Voorhis, Scileppi and Bergan remained adamant in holding that, despite *Parker* v. *Gladden,* DeLucia and Montella had no right to contest the jury's verdict, and to permit them to do so would subject every future juror to potential post-trial harassment.

Only the infusion of fresh blood switched the scale. Judges Fuld (by then the chief judge) and Burke were joined by Keating (who had succeeded Dye) and Charles Breitel (who had succeeded Fuld as associate judge and who would succeed him as chief) in sending the case back to Justice Farrell for further hearings.

"We held a hearing," Sonenshine says. "I subpoenaed the

jurors. They came in and testified they had indeed gone to the scene and had told the other jurors. Justice Farrell set the conviction aside. The final outcome was that both defendants were permitted to plead guilty to misdemeanors of unlawful entry and were sentenced to the time they had already served."

As drama, the denouement was an anticlimax—but a new principle of law had been established.

For the defendants, the epilogue was less happy. Once freed, Montella was soon arrested again and charged with being the mastermind of a $130,000 burglary of a suburban department store, but he beat the rap when the key witness against him disappeared. He was convicted in federal court a year later for a bank burglary and sentenced to seven years in prison. DeLucia simply disappeared. According to the scuttlebutt of the street, he was tried by a Mafia kangaroo court, found guilty —of what is not known—and executed.

Only rarely does an appeals attorney succeed in staking out a legal landmark. Sonenshine had tried in the Portelli case and failed. But he takes some consolation because Chief Justice Earl Warren cited the case as part of the factual justification for the Supreme Court's *Miranda* decision, requiring police to advise prisoners of their right to counsel.

9   A Killing in Camelot

Jack Guarino was a compassionate cop. When he walked his beat in midtown Manhattan, he dreaded the thought that someday he might have to use his gun and possibly wound or kill someone. He became distraught when he learned that a Puerto Rican youth he'd arrested for narcotics had hanged himself in jail.

"I knew him for a number of years," Jack Evseroff says, "because I'd represented his kid brother, who was always the bad seed in the family. One day I got a call—I was trying a murder case at the time—and it was Guarino's kid brother. He said, 'Jack's been locked up for murder. He killed Cathy [Mrs. Guarino].' I couldn't believe it. Jack Guarino was always a nice quiet sort of a guy, who I assumed was happily married. I'd spoken to his wife on a number of occasions on the phone when I'd been calling to find his brother."

Evseroff agreed to undertake Guarino's defense. It was to be "the most fascinating case I ever tried."

On the morning of April 19, 1971, Guarino had gone to Mercy Hospital in suburban Rockville Centre where his estranged wife, Catherine, a nurse, was taking a refresher course.

"Is the marriage over?" he asked her.

"I feel it is," she replied, "but I don't know."

Guarino got in his car and drove off. He picked up his two-year-old adopted daughter and dropped her off at a baby-sitter's. En route, he stopped at a sporting-goods store and bought a box of 50 rounds of ammunition for his off-duty revolver. Then he drove to his sister's house, where he drank a bottle of beer and penned a suicide note:

> Bury us together. I guess we had a Camelot. It's got to end
> up as Camelot did in destruction. . . .

He returned to the hospital parking lot and hid behind a car. His wife came out shortly after 3 P.M., accompanied by her mother, Mrs. Louis Schnurr, and Mrs. Schnurr's sister, Mrs. Catherine Parsons, who was carrying a two-year-old nephew, their brother's son. Guarino accosted his wife and led her into the front seat of his car, while the older women waited outside.

"Is it over?" he asked again. "I'll get a divorce and bang you with adultery right now."

"I don't know, Jack. I'm all confused. Jack, I'm trying to work it out. Please give me some time."

Aunt Kate interrupted: "I'm getting too upset."

"I have to go," Catherine told Guarino. "I will call you when I get home."

"Leave us alone, Jack," Aunt Kate insisted. "Leave us alone."

Catherine started out of the car. Guarino pulled out his gun and shot her. Then he got out of the car and walked around it, firing through the windows until he ran out of ammunition. Catherine's body fell through the half-open door to the pavement. The two older women stood frozen, petrified with fright. Guarino reloaded his gun and fired five shots into his mother-in-law. She crumpled to the ground, moaning, "You got me too, Jack. You got me too."

Then he turned to Aunt Kate.

"Don't shoot the baby!" she screamed.

Guarino pulled the trigger. The hammer gave the metallic click of an empty weapon. He turned away, picked up his wife's body and trundled it into the back seat, then drove to his home in the nearby South Shore suburb of Massapequa. He carried Catherine's body into the house and laid it out on the bed. He pulled her skirt down to cover her exposed legs and removed her contact lenses. Then he lay down beside her, took hold of her hand and fell asleep.

He awoke about a half-hour later and made several calls to his parish priest, to his baby-sitter, to several relatives. By then, police had surrounded the house and shouted over a bull-horn for him to surrender. He walked out and gave up peaceably. He was handcuffed and placed in a squad car.

"How can I be so calm when I just killed two people?" he wondered aloud.

At the stationhouse, Detective William Rauff took charge of the investigation. He started to advise Guarino of his rights.

"Of course, I know all about it," Guarino said. "I'm on the job."

"The job?"

"I'm a policeman in New York City."

As required by law, Rauff continued his recitation of the *Miranda* warning despite Guarino's insistence, "Look, I told you I understand. I know all of these." The detective read through to the end, then asked, "Now, you understand?"

"I told you I understand."

"Do you want to talk about it?"

"Look, I did it. I shot them."

Guarino went on to dictate a five-page confession. He read through Rauff's handwritten transcription, correcting the detective's spelling of Cathy from "K" to "C," but refused to sign it.

He was held without bail on two counts of murder and two of attempted murder.

"It had all the technical aspects of a premeditated homicide," Evseroff notes. "The buying of the bullets, the taking of the gun, the hiding, the reloading of the gun. I'm not a psychiatrist—I don't profess to be—but I certainly know enough about people to wonder what would make a man go off the deep end in the manner that he did.

"I had him sent for psychiatric evaluation. I made an application and it was granted. He was evaluated and their psychiatrist said he was sane, which was not unusual. Just about everybody is declared to be sane unless they have been adjudicated incompetent before.

"I felt that I needed independent psychiatric consultation so I called in Dr. Daniel Schwartz. He's a young man but a very eminent psychiatrist, the head of forensic psychiatry at Kings County Hospital. He found Guarino fascinating. He saw him with another psychiatrist we brought in. In their opinion, he was legally insane at the time of the commission of the crime."

Evseroff had found his defense, but he knew it would be an uphill battle. There had never been an acquittal on grounds of insanity at the time of the crime in a Nassau County homicide. Even the great Sam Liebowitz had tried and failed in the 1940 trial of Alvin Dooley, a policeman who'd shot the mayor of Long Beach; the jury had found him guilty of manslaughter and the judge had given him 10 to 20 years. Jack Evseroff may have an ego as big as Brooklyn, but he knew he was no Sam Liebowitz.

"I had to sit down and evaluate how you try a case like this," he continues. "I knew that the question of insanity is a question of fact which has to be determined by the jury. I came to the conclusion that in order to try a case of this type and have the jury resolve the question of fact your way, you had to impress the jury not with the psychiatric testimony, but rather with the facts and circumstances leading up to the occurrence, so that the jury could properly be conditioned to accept the testimony of the psychiatrist as being correct. After all, what does a lay jury know of these long fancy technical terms relative to psychiatric circumstances? So I began to prepare the case. The last thing I prepared was the psychiatric testimony."

The preparation was a guided tour of Guarino's psyche. Gioaccino—his baptismal name—Guarino's home was only a suburban cottage with a white picket fence around it. But to him it was a king's castle, his Camelot.

"In all my conversations with him," Evseroff notes, "everything revolved around the image of Camelot. He always referred to himself as King Arthur and Cathy as Guinevere. His favorite record was the song 'Camelot' from the picture."

As Lerner and Loewe's Camelot was an ideal of legend, Guarino's was an idealization from his fantasies. In reality, all was not well with his wedded life. He had married in 1965 at the age of 21; his wife was older. He was a high-school dropout who pounded a beat; she was a college graduate and a registered nurse. This was enough to give him a feeling of intellectual inferiority.

His marital relations led to doubts about his manhood. The Guarinos were unable to conceive a child because Guarino's sperm count was too low, so they adopted a daughter. That might have sufficed for stability had their sex life been satisfactory, but it wasn't. Catherine was a deeply religious woman and prudish. She'd blushed crimson when Guarino had taken her to a striptease and had walked out of the movie *Joe*. A virgin when she married, her sexual acrobatics were confined to the classic missionary position. She was never able to achieve orgasm when Guarino made love to her. He finally bought a vibrator and would use it to bring her to a climax; then he'd have intercourse with her. But, "I didn't feel like a man," he admitted.

The final blow to his manhood came in December 1970. Just as Queen Guinevere had found Sir Lancelot and had run off with him, so Catherine found her ill-made knight in shining armor and left Guarino. The man she moved in with, Steve Kemplar, according to Evseroff, was "a rather effeminate, sensitive kind of a guy who didn't work regularly, a student type, an intelligentsia type she apparently found attractive." And he could turn her on without a vibrator.

Winning the policeman's wife away from him apparently wasn't enough for Kemplar. He sought further satisfaction by taunting Guarino with the intimate details of his sexual adventures with Catherine. One night, he phoned Guarino and said that Cathy was with him, that she had her arms around him and that she was begging to go to bed with him. The next day, Kemplar came with Cathy while she visited Guarino and told the cuckolded cop how he'd made love to Cathy with his mouth. All Guarino could say was, "Cathy, did you have a good time?"

On another occasion, after Kemplar told Guarino how Cathy had satisfied him orally in the shower, he went to Kemplar's house and confronted her: "Are you proud of yourself?" But he said later: "Every time I took a shower, I would think of Cathy down on her knees blowing him. . . ."

During the 112 days from the time Cathy left him until he took out his frustrations in a fusillade of bullets, Guarino sank deeper and deeper into depression and despair. He developed insomnia and loss of appetite. His weight fell from 185 pounds to 150. It was apparent to many that he was far from normal.

In January, he visited his family physician. "His hands were shaking," Dr. Anthony Mazzara recalled. "He was fidgety. His mode of speech was kind of nervous." Dr. Mazzaro prescribed a sedative, but also advised, "It is not going to cure your condition. You've got to resolve this thing one way or another, because I don't like the way you look."

He also consulted a psychiatrist, Dr. Albert Jessen, who recalled that "he was completely obsessed, one might say, with his own feelings of depression and remorse because his wife wanted to leave him." He said Guarino's responses "went well beyond the pale of what we would call a normal reaction." He'd recommended commitment.

A few days later, Guarino fired a bullet into a basement

lumber pile and told his wife that he'd attempted suicide. She called the local police, who called in the New York City cops, who took away Guarino's gun and placed him on limited duty pending psychiatric examination, "the rubber-gun squad" in police slang. Six weeks later, the police psychiatrist gave Guarino a clean bill of health. He was restored to duty and given back his gun. (As a result, Cathy's father has filed a $2-million damage suit against the city.)

It was only the first of three feigned or abortive suicide attempts. Once he tried to stab himself; the knife was wrested away from him. Later, he aimed a bullet at his head but missed. He also played Russian roulette with his service revolver.

In mid-February, while on limited duty, he visited his parish priest, Father Charles Kohli. "You're my only hope," he said. Father Kohli described Guarino as "increasingly dependent, increasingly wild." During several hours of rambling, at times incoherent, conversation, Guarino said, "I can't go on. How much can a man take?" He finally pleaded, "Commit me, father. Commit me, father." Father Kohli called the police, who took Guarino to Meadowbrook State Hospital for observation. He signed himself out the following day.

Throughout that winter of his discontent, Guarino made repeated attempts to effect a reconciliation, only to be rebuffed every time, even after Cathy had broken with Kemplar. Increasingly, he took out his frustrations by firing shots into the walls of his Camelot. Evseroff came into court with more than 100 photos of the bullet holes. On the morning of the fatal day, Guarino banged his fist through the clapboard wall of their bedroom and smashed the vibrator beneath his heel.

The trial opened on January 31, 1972, before Nassau County Court Judge Harold Spitzer, a no-nonsense jurist whose rulings left little "hook" for appeal in case the jury returned a guilty verdict. The prosecutor was Frank Dillon, the assistant D.A. in charge of the homicide bureau.

"They figured they had an airtight case, a classic case of premeditation and deliberation," Evseroff notes. He did not dispute the prosecution's evidence. "My defense was insanity," he explains. "I spent all my cross-examination on what he looked like and what he sounded like prior to and during the occurrence.

"On the defense, I put all my witnesses on to show the entire background and history. I put the priest on. I put the lawyer on [an attorney who'd represented Mrs. Guarino]. I put on his brothers and his sisters who had seen him. It wasn't a classic alibi case where you would disbelieve the relatives. They testified to specific things he did.

"I subpoenaed the boy-friend who came with a lawyer and asserted his privilege against self-incrimination. I called on the court and the district attorney to give him immunity from prosecution, which they did. They compelled him to testify. Once he started talking you couldn't stop him. He testified to everything he did with the wife. He had told all of this to the defendant so it was admissible with respect to Guarino's state of mind. He spoke about how she committed acts of sodomy in the shower, how they made love, the color of the nightgowns she wore, where they went and what they did."

At one point in his testimony, Kemplar turned and looked at Guarino and said, "Oh, Jack, I'm so sorry."

"It was perhaps the most dramatic day I've ever seen in the courtroom," Evseroff continues. "He testified on direct examination from eleven o'clock in the morning until a quarter to five. The cross-examination didn't take ten minutes. They were fascinated by this man."

And incensed. Evseroff had challenged all women off the jury. He'd wanted men who would sympathize with his cuckolded client, not women who would identify with the victim.

"This was just the kind of a witness who the jury wouldn't like," Evseroff notes, "because he was a little effeminate, just not a man's man."

The jurors weren't the only ones who came to detest Kemplar. One court officer offered the use of his gun if Guarino wanted to shoot the witness right there in the courtroom. And an assistant D.A. told Evseroff, "Why, if he'd killed this guy, I'd give him a plea to attempted double-parking."

Finally, Guarino himself took the stand, a soul more to be pitied than a menace to be eliminated. He recapitulated the events of his marriage and breakup, his futile efforts at reconciliation, his fits of frustration, anger and depression—all leading up to nothing. He had blanked out on the fatal day, he said, and couldn't remember what had happened.

Dillon cross-examined Guarino thoroughly, almost brutally, in an effort to show that if he had not acted wholly rationally, he'd at least known what he was doing.

"But it was too good an opportunity to pass up when she [Mrs. Schnurr] was there, right?" the prosecutor asked.

"Too good an opportunity to pass up?"

"Right," Dillon said. "Wasn't this a great opportunity to wipe out your mother-in-law as well as your wife?"

"No, Mr. Dillon," Guarino replied. "I never wanted to hurt either of them, Mr. Dillon. See, Mr. Dillon, you can't hurt me because I am only a shell sitting here. I have no feelings inside at this point."

"I am not trying to hurt you, sir. I am just trying to get at the truth."

"The truth is, I don't know that I killed Cathy, and I can't answer that question."

All this was prelude to the psychiatric testimony. Evseroff presented the two defense psychiatrists, Dr. Schwartz and Dr. Abraham Perlstein, who testified, as Dr. Perlstein phrased it, that "in my opinion . . . he [Guarino] lacked substantial ability —mental ability—to appreciate the consequences of his act or the wrongness of his act." It was the legal definition of insanity under the *M'Naghten* rule, propounded by the British House of Lords in 1843 and still in use in most states.

In rebuttal, Dillon called Dr. Harold Zolan, who testified that Guarino was legally sane.

"He testified on direct examination for fifteen minutes," Ev-seroff recalls. "I cross-examined him for over a day. I took him through it [his report] word by word and sentence by sentence. I cross-examined him to the point of distraction, to the point where the judge couldn't stand it anymore, to the point where no one could stand it anymore."

His thrust was not so much to discredit Dr. Zolan's opinion, which is very difficult for a lay lawyer to do with an expert witness, as to let it be lost in a welter of words. But he managed to elicit one fact that stuck in the jurors' minds. As a professional witness, Dr. Zolan was paid $500 a day for his court appearances.

When he returned to the stand for his second day of cross-examination, Evseroff greeted him with: "Good morning, doctor. Another five-hundred dollars, I presume?"

"That's right."

That the point sank in became evident after the trial when one juror wrote a letter to *Newsday,* the Long Island newspaper:

> Several weeks ago I served as a juror on a murder case in the Nassau County courthouse. One of the witnesses for the prosecution was a Long Island psychiatrist who testified for two days at $500 a day, paid him by the county of Nassau.
>
> It seems to me that in these days of high prices and high taxes, perhaps the powers that be can be a bit more concerned about spending the hard-earned money of Nassau County taxpayers.

At 11:15 A.M. on February 29, the all-male jury retired for its deliberations. It returned six hours later with a verdict of not guilty by reason of insanity. Evseroff notes: "It was really, in layman's terms, a case of temporary insanity," a plea not allowed under New York law.

But the effect was the same. Since the jury had judged Guarino insane, Judge Spitzer had no choice but to commit him to a state mental hospital. Guarino's civil lawyers immediately filed suit for his release, which the court had no choice but to grant since the state's psychiatrist had judged him sane!

A year later, on February 5, 1973, Evseroff started a trial in Brooklyn Supreme Court. He represented seven of 19 policemen accused of extorting a $20,000-a-month "pad" from gamblers in the Bedford-Stuyvesant ghetto. It was the largest group of policemen ever prosecuted in New York City, and it turned out to be one of the longest trials ever held in the Brooklyn courts.

Evseroff obtained permission from Justice Milton Mollen to take off Thursday and Friday, February 8 and 9. "My wife was nagging me to go to Florida."

She was the second Mrs. Evseroff. Ten years before, during the Molinas trial, Evseroff and his first wife had separated. After the divorce, he'd married his secretary, Maxene Richter. They eventually settled into a plush ranch-style home in Upper Brookville on Long Island with their twin sons, Paul and Kenneth.

Maxene Evseroff left on Wednesday afternoon with the twins. Evseroff followed that evening with his father and his daughter Leslie. He returned on Monday, February 12, Lincoln's Birthday, so Leslie could go back to school and he could go back to the trial. Maxene remained in Florida with the twins.

"She was going out at night 'with her friends,' " he recalls. "On Thursday [the 15th] I kept calling her. She didn't get back until two-thirty in the morning. We had a big argument on the phone.

"I spoke to her on Saturday. She said, 'Look, I'm going out with my friends again tonight. Don't call me. I don't want a repetition of what we had Thursday night. I'll be home late.'

"I told her that I'd been to see a client that night who I'd represented in three cases—in Brooklyn, tried and acquitted; a robbery in the Bronx, took a plea to a misdemeanor and got a suspended sentence; and a third case which I'd disposed of for him in Nassau with a misdemeanor and a suspended sentence.

And I'd collected five-thousand dollars in cash for a fee. She knew him because he used to come to the house to bring us ice cream. He was in the ice-cream business, among other things."

Maxene and the twins returned to Long Island on Sunday, February 18.

"She was very unhappy," Evseroff continues. "She didn't want anything to do with me."

Monday was a holiday, Washington's Birthday. Evseroff returned to court on Tuesday, the 20th.

"While I was in court, she took the five thousand dollars I had collected, she took my collection of gold coins, she took my bankbooks, she stole my checkbook stubs to show my income, she took the deed to the house and all the jewelry and the boys and left—went to Florida."

It turned out that during the week she'd remained in Florida, she'd started a liaison with a married man.

The breakup hit Evseroff hard. "I was off the wall," he recalls. "For three months I lived on martinis and Valium. I underwent the most unbelievable emotional crisis from February until June, the end of the case. I worked under the worst of conditions. I couldn't sleep. I lost weight. My waist was forty-one when the case started and thirty-five when it was over. I lost three suit sizes. I was really sick. I suffered depression. I felt I was going insane."

Evseroff moved in with his father in Brooklyn, while attorneys on both sides launched a long, costly and acrimonious divorce action. He visited his home in the suburbs occasionally to take care of the household chores and pick up items he'd need in the city.

On the night of Friday, April 27, he parked his Cadillac in the driveway and started into the house. Two men grabbed him in the breezeway and forced him into the kitchen. At gunpoint, they made him lie on the floor and took his cash and jewelry.

One of the robbers addressed him by name. "Where's the money in the house?"

"I have no money in the house," Evseroff replied. "She took it all when she left."

He noted later: "They never asked me any questions about who 'she' was or when did she leave. They apparently knew and they searched only the one room in the house where the money was kept."

The robbers asked Evseroff for the keys to his car, but they'd been lost in the scuffle. The police later found them wedged between the washer and dryer.

The men bound Evseroff's wrists with wire and stuffed him into a closet. After about 15 or 20 minutes, he managed to kick his way out. The telephone was ringing. Although his hands were bound behind his back, he managed to knock the receiver off the hook and tell the friend who was on the line to call the police. They arrived a few minutes later and untied him.

The robbery remains unsolved. Evseroff still bears a scar on one wrist from the wire. The scars on his psyche healed, however.

"And while all this was going on," he says, "I was trying my case until June 10. It wasn't until the case was over that I really came back to myself. I think the fact that I did work served as therapy. I didn't think so at the time. But it is possible to work under the worst of circumstances. I don't think my clients suffered. I think *they* may think they suffered. I think I worked as well as I've worked in any case, but it was pretty much an untenable case." Sixteen of the 19 defendants, including Evseroff's seven clients, were convicted and received sentences ranging from one to three years.

As friends do, Evseroff's rallied to offer moral support during his personal crisis. One of the first was his old client, Jack Guarino. He implored Evseroff not to do anything rash, not to do what he had done.

"What do you think I am—crazy?" Evseroff asked.

Guarino laughed.

10 Ring Around the Collar

As Mario Puzo wrote in *The Godfather*, "A lawyer with a briefcase can steal more money than a thousand men with guns." So can an accountant, banker or stockbroker. They can also afford to pay more for their defense if they're caught, which is the main reason most criminal lawyers like white-collar clients.

"A lot of lawyers," according to Evseroff, "would have you believe that there's a special significance to these kinds of cases, that they're cleaner, that you sully your hands less with them. But I don't see it that way at all. To me, a thief is a thief whether he comes from Bath Beach or Park Avenue. It's true that generally the white-collar clients have more money—they're bigger thieves."

But the defense lawyer must adopt a different bedside manner for the stockbroker from Park Avenue than for the stickup man from Bath Beach. The white-collar client usually has little experience with the criminal process or familiarity with laying his liberty on the line. It takes much more hand-holding to get him to adjust to his new situation.

He also tends to be more reticent about leveling with his

lawyer; the pertinent facts must be pried out piecemeal. Also, unlike gas-station stickups or barroom brawls, white-collar crimes usually are not one-shot situations. They take place over a protracted period and the client may have knowledge of only a small segment of the pertinent data. For the defense lawyer, such cases call for far more investigation and preparation.

The traditional white-collar crimes are embezzlement, forgery, stock fraud and tax evasion—"crimes in the suites," to use Ralph Nader's classic phrase. In recent years, the category has come to include political corruption, and the volume of such cases has swelled nationally as part of the post-Watergate syndrome and in New York City from the appointment of Maurice Nadjari as special prosecutor to investigate corruption in the courts.

Evseroff's most notable case of political corruption was the trial of Criminal Court Judge Benjamin Schor. A faithful servant of the Brooklyn Democratic organization, Schor had risen through the ladder of patronage posts to become a deputy commissioner of the State Liquor Authority under Governor Averell Harriman. In 1959, when the Republicans reassumed the reins of state government (and completely corrupted the SLA), Mayor Wagner named Schor a city magistrate. Under the court reorganization of 1962, he automatically became a criminal court judge.

"He was very, very bombastic in nature," Evseroff says. "He was tremendously outspoken. He had the worst judicial demeanor and temperament you can imagine. On occasion, he could be very, very insulting to all parties. But he was a pretty knowledgeable lawyer and he seemed to mete out substantial justice. There were many rumors around that he was dishonest, which I didn't believe."

On election eve, 1966, Schor was indicted in Queens for attempted grand larceny. He had allegedly asked $3500 for his services as a go-between to secure a liquor license for a used-car dealer who wanted to open a restaurant.

"I am innocent of the charge that has been made against

me . . ." Judge Schor insisted. "It is my intention to insist on an immediate trial at which time I shall be vindicated. This indictment cannot and will not stand impartial scrutiny by a court of law."

Schor's reading of the law was correct, but Supreme Court Justice J. Irwin Shapiro's decision was scarcely a vindication:

> We have here the sorry spectacle of one who has attained the high and exalted position of a priest of justice refusing to answer some questions, dodging and evading answers to others, and when answering, committing transparent perjury.
>
> A judge who fouls his own nest casts a shadow upon all those engaged in executing public trusts. Thus, it has been difficult to view this record with judicial objectivity. Schor's inexcusable conduct has not, however, relieved me of my judicial obligation to check my outraged feelings and to decide this case with the cold neutrality of an impartial judge, and if the crimes with which he is charged are not established by the record made before the grand jury, to unhesitatingly so declare, for "justice is truth in action" (Disraeli). . . .
>
> I hold the evidence insufficient. . . .

However, Justice Shapiro recommended that Schor be indicted for perjury before the grand jury. It took ten months to file the new indictment. In the interim, Schor, 62 and pleading ill health, had resigned from the bench. But he continued to protest his innocence: "My position today is no different [from] that [of] one year ago when the last indictment was dismissed. There is no reason to expect that there will be anything less than an exoneration of these charges."

Evseroff didn't enter the case until more than two years later. "Schor was originally represented by Bill Kleinman," he explains. "Unfortunately, he died. And his partner, Eugene Gold, had become the district attorney for Kings County. Now Benny comes to me—the case is ready for trial. I got a very, very small fee, because most of the money had been paid to Kleinman."

He had less than a week to prepare. The trial opened on January 26, 1970, before Supreme Court Justice Thomas Agresta, a new judge presiding over his first jury trial. The assistant D.A., William Leahy, presented only two substantive witnesses —the used-car dealer and a former SLA investigator, both of whom testified that Schor had set a $3500 price tag for his services as intermediary.

"Off their testimony it was a powerhouse case," Evseroff observes. "I was really worried. The perjury before the grand jury was that he had not spoken to Brodsky [the used-car dealer] about the fix. These two corroborated each other, but they weren't present at the same time. They had had two separate conversations."

Schor took the stand in his own behalf, denying that he'd discussed the fix or a $3500 fee, asserting that he'd first heard about the case when he read a newspaper account two weeks before he'd testified. But what he said was not as important as the way he said it.

"He had cancer at the time," Evseroff notes. "I managed to elicit that. I said, 'Judge, I can't hear you very clearly. Is there something wrong with your voice?' He said, 'Yes, I have cancer of the throat.' The jury managed to hear it. I don't even remember if there was an objection."

Schor was followed by what Evseroff calls "an impressive array of character witnesses," 19 in all: seven Supreme Court justices, a retired Supreme Court justice, the Kings County surrogate (probate judge), seven lawyers, two businessmen and a city councilman.

The case went to the jury at 2 P.M., January 29. After casting 11 ballots, the jurors announced that they were hopelessly deadlocked. Justice Agresta sent them back for further deliberations. At 3:29 A.M., they returned with a not-guilty verdict.

What prompted the panel to acquit in the face of what a judge had termed "transparent perjury"? Evseroff cites the character of the prosecution witnesses, the minor contradictions in their testimony and the nature of the character witnesses, but basically, "I think they were sorry for him."

For a white-collar case, the Schor trial was unusual because it did not involve reams of paper. Paper is what usually distinguishes a white-collar case from a run-of-the-mill street crime.

"I'm not happy trying paper cases," Evseroff states. "I'm at my best trying *people* cases."

Gus Newman feels quite the contrary: "I tend to be much more successful in cases that involve papers and documents, rather than the classic, 'Is this the guy that stuck you up?' " Not unnaturally, he gets most of the firm's white-collar cases.

Like Evseroff, Gustave H. Newman was Brooklyn born and bred, attended the borough's public schools and started Brooklyn College as an engineering student. After wartime service in the army, he entered New York University majoring in labor relations. "I finished half of a master's in labor law and never handled a labor case." He received his degree from NYU Law School. Unlike Evseroff and Sonenshine, his entire legal career has been in private practice, the first decade in civil law, the second in criminal.

"In dealing with a white-collar crime," Newman says, "you're dealing with paper. Take a stock-fraud case. Invariably in a stock-fraud case the prosecution will produce some of the co-conspirators, some of the people who participated in the manipulation. Although you have live witnesses, they're subject to the stigma that they've been involved. The way the prosecution tries to corroborate them is with the paper—the confirmations of the stock purchases, the checks, the correspondence, the financial statements, the offering circular.

"And the way they try to wrap it up and make it palatable for a jury is by their last witnesses, those who have lost money. If it was just a deal where a brokerage house or a bank lost money, the jury wouldn't get excited—like, 'Who cares?' But if you bring in John Q. Public who lost two thousand dollars on the representation of a broker that it would go from two to ten, that could be equated to a jury.

"From a defense point of view, you can't let the jury get hypnotized by the paper and say, 'There must be something to it, look at all the exhibits.' The defense case must make it clear that these pieces of paper do not implicate your client. They may show that there was a stock manipulation and nobody's denying that, but they don't show that your client—John Doe —was involved in it.

"I sometimes analogize it to a narcotics case. I feel that juries in a narcotics case are hypnotized by the narcotics that are introduced in evidence. All they see are the narcotics and they don't really care who's involved. They want someone to answer for those narcotics. You've got to avoid that in the white-collar case. You can't let them be hypnotized by the volume of paper. You've got to make them keep their eye on the ball: How does this establish your client's guilt beyond a reasonable doubt?

"In trying a regular criminal case, you've got witnesses and you can ask them questions: 'How far away were you?' 'What were the lighting conditions?' And you can go for direct confrontation of the witnesses and make an absolute liar out of them.

"You can't do that in a white-collar case. Let's say you have co-conspirators in a stock swindle. You can't start going into all the details because these people are usually sophisticated and they're usually very, very expert in the area they're talking about. They can just end up repeating to the jury the same story they told on direct. You *can* ask, 'How many times have you been a co-conspirator?' 'What has the government promised you?'—which may or may not be a direct confrontation of the witness.

"What you do, if you have any theory of defense, is tailor your cross-examination toward the situation. Let's say they're contending that your client should have known he was in a manipulation and your defense is that your client had no expertise, that he'd been in the laundry business. Then what you do is start setting the jury up for your defense by going at them [the co-conspirators] very subtly—how many years they had in the market, how many years it took them to understand all the transactions, how complex and involved they are. On the face of it, it doesn't seem like any kind of cross-examination. But what you're doing is getting the jury ready for your defense, so when your defense goes in, it has meaning."

As an example, he cites the case of Matthew Kelly.

Salvatore, Anthony and John Giordano were brothers who owned a used-car lot and a riding stable in Brooklyn. According to the government, they engineered an elaborate check-kiting scheme utilizing their privilege of getting immediate credit on check deposits at two separate banks, the Van Wyck branch of Bankers Trust and the Baisley Park branch of the Bank of North America.

Checks drawn on the Bankers Trust account would be deposited in the Bank of North America and new checks would be written, drawn on that deposit. Before the spurious nature of the deposit could be discovered, a check drawn on the Bank of North America would be deposited in the Bankers Trust account and the cycle would start afresh. According to the indictment, the brothers managed to float $1,213,835 in worthless checks over a 15-day period in March 1969.

The scheme came a cropper when a messenger was late delivering a batch of checks to the main branch of Bankers Trust one Friday. The following Monday, the Giordanos' account at the Bank of North America was found to be $440,000 short.

The Giordanos were indicted for conspiracy to defraud banks, along with Martin Shaughnessy, the assistant manager of the Bankers Trust branch, and Newman's client, Kelly, a vice-president of the Bank of North America and former manager of its Baisley Park branch. At the outset of the trial, which opened on April 8, 1971, before Judge John Dooling, Jr., in Brooklyn's federal court, Shaughnessy pleaded guilty and agreed to testify for the government.

"There was no way I could deny the checks," Newman says. "There was no way I could dispute that the check-kiting took place. My thrust was to show that he [Kelly] wasn't involved, that this privilege these fellows had existed long before he came in, and that the bank branch and the bank hierarchy encouraged this idea of giving immediate credit, and that it was this practice that facilitated the bank-kite, and that they really didn't need my client and so he couldn't have been criminally involved—to try to take it out of the criminal area and, at most, make it seem that all he was was negligent.

"I was able to show that he was doing all the other things a bank manager is primarily charged with doing: soliciting new business, going to social functions to make the bank's presence in the community known, increasing their loan portfolio, things like that.

"Although the prosecution put on a parade of witnesses, we ended up showing that he was a good bank manager, that the auditors came in and found no discrepancies—so how was he supposed to know?—that none of the records were falsified. If my client were involved with this, being a bank manager with expertise, he would have the wherewithal to fool around with the records to prevent anybody from discovering this.

"And most important, I tried to show that my client had no financial stake—never got a quarter—to play on the common sense of the jurors. Why would a man expose so many years of a background if he's not getting anything?

"I couldn't attack the basic things, as you might in a regular criminal trial—'Is this the guy?' and try to show that this wasn't the guy. I couldn't confront it that way. I had to deal with the fact that he was the bank manager at the time the check-kite was in operation. There was no getting away from it."

As with most white-collar cases, the trial was long, complex and boring. It went to the jury on April 26.

"It caused me greater anguish than any case I've had before, since or probably ever will have," Newman notes. "The jury was out for seventy-two hours. For three days he [Kelly] and I paced the hallways not knowing what the verdict would be.

There were forty-eight counts of the indictment, so when they finally came out, they had to read the verdict as to each of the forty-eight counts. It seemed like an eternity."

Kelly was acquitted on all 48 counts. The jury was unable to agree on the guilt or innocence of the Giordano brothers.

"Then I learned that they had reached an acquittal for him [Kelly] within the first two hours," Newman continues, "but they didn't know they could report back a separate acquittal for him when they hadn't reached a verdict on the other defendants."

The Giordano brothers were retried two years later. As the result of his performance in Kelly's case, the Giordano brothers retained Newman to represent them in the second trial. It was a more difficult assignment. Anthony and John were acquitted, but Salvatore, the eldest brother, was found guilty and sentenced to a year and a day in prison.

Most white-collar crimes are tried in the federal courts. In contrast with the skilled staffs of the SEC, IRS and other federal agencies, none of the local police or prosecutors' offices, with the exception of Manhattan's frauds bureau, has the expertise to handle such complex cases, nor the manpower to expend on such time-consuming investigations and trials. In addition, many of the crimes such as securities violations and income-tax evasion are covered only by federal statutes. Because of the concentration of financial institutions in downtown Manhattan, an unusually high percentage of such cases are filed in the southern district courts on Foley Square, which poses problems for a law firm in Brooklyn.

"We don't get the really big white-collar cases," Evseroff says. "You get such cases invariably because they're referred by other lawyers—civil lawyers—and that type of case has a tendency to gravitate to midtown Manhattan. I really don't understand it. We know our business, we're good, we're recognized as such. My feeling is that if you're well known and do the job right, people are going to come to you even if you're in a phone booth."

But not if the booth is in Brooklyn. Few clients choose to cross the East River to consult counsel, although Borough Hall is a shorter subway ride from Wall Street than Park Avenue.

"A lot of white-collar people don't seem to think you're a good lawyer unless you charge really, really big fees and put on a real big front," Evseroff continues. "They don't consider you a good man otherwise. That's part of the psychology of clients."

During the summer of 1973, the partners of Evseroff, Newman & Sonenshine contemplated moving to midtown Manhattan, primarily in hopes of attracting more high-paying white-collar clients. They even picked a tentative new office at 58th Street and Park Avenue. But they decided to defer final action until Evseroff's marital litigation was resolved and his finances were unencumbered.

Gus Newman was unwilling to wait. In October, he struck off on his own, breaking up a 12-year partnership. The firm was renamed Evseroff & Sonenshine. Its secretary-receptionist, Marie Miller, complained that the only name she could pronounce had left. For the two partners, Newman's departure did not signal a loss of business, only more work, since the caseload was now divided two ways. To ease the burden, they hired a new associate, Jeffrey Rabin, a former assistant D.A. in Brooklyn.

Newman rented space in the suite of attorney James LaRossa on Fifth Avenue. It's quite a contrast from his old quarters. Instead of a view of the Red Hook docks, his window looks out on the towers of midtown Manhattan. There are thick pile carpets on the floor and the decor is stark and modern, glass and chrome. And, he hopes, the clientele will be a different—and better-paying—breed.

"I thought it would be a different image in Manhattan. I'll know in six months whether I was right or wrong."

11   The Cloud

Early in his career as a defense lawyer, Evseroff represented a
Black Muslim named Mustapha Abdullah.

"He stood about six-foot-six," Evseroff recalls. "He wore a
flowing gown and a black cap. He looked like an Arab."

Mustapha Abdullah was charged with possession of narcotics. The case came before J. Irwin Shapiro, a Queens judge on
temporary assignment to the Brooklyn courts.

"He took a plea," Evseroff continues. "He was given a misdemeanor with a promise of no jail. On the day of the sentencing, Judge Shapiro said to him, 'Do you have anything to say
before sentence is imposed on you?'

"He said, 'Yes, I do. I went to my lawyer's office. I wired a
conversation I had with him.'

"I nearly fainted when I heard this, and so did nearly everybody else in court. Shapiro looked at him and in his judicial
wisdom said to him, 'Well, what did your lawyer say to you?'

"Abdullah said, 'My lawyer said to me, "Judge Shapiro's
sitting here and he's pretty liberal. Next month you're liable to
wind up with Judge Liebowitz and you're liable to wind up with
a lot more time."'

"With that, Shapiro had a big smile on his face. He said, 'What else did he say?'

" 'That's all.'

" 'I think your lawyer gave you good advice. Now the probation report indicates that you should get probation, but any man who goes up to his lawyer's office and wires his conversation with his lawyer when his lawyer is trying to help him is not entitled to probation.'

"And he gave him an indefinite term of up to three years in jail."

The incident illustrates what is practically an occupational handicap for criminal lawyers. Just as bullfighters get gored, coal miners get silicosis and butchers cut off their thumbs, so criminal lawyers are fair game for charges of corruption by disgruntled clients and defeated prosecutors. It's not just the street-corner shyster who gets hit; some of the biggest names in the business have been brought before the bar as defendants: Clarence Darrow, Samuel Liebowitz, F. Lee Bailey.

"When you're a criminal lawyer," Evseroff explains, "you're forever the subject of a possible attack from any and all sources. It's a natural concomitant of the profession."

Evseroff hasn't been indicted. That's an honor he doesn't seek. But he and his partners are under a cloud created by a former client, Gerald Martin Zelmanowitz.

Like Jack Molinas and Herbert Itkin, Zelmanowitz was brilliant but warped, the type who would never do anything straight when he could take a crooked shortcut. Thirty years old in 1967, he was a paper millionaire, wheeling and dealing in the netherworlds of high finance. His speciality was arbitrage, the simultaneous buying and selling of securities in the U.S. and foreign markets, profiting on the fractional differences in price. Such enterprises required vast investments of capital. Zelmanowitz got it from organized crime. His rapport with the mob also involved him in numerous shady dealings of his own.

In 1967, Zelmanowitz was charged with being part of a $67,-000 check-kiting scheme. Some years before, Gus Newman had handled Zelmanowitz's divorce, and Zelmanowitz retained Ev-seroff, Newman & Sonenshine to represent him in the criminal case.

"In the course of that case," Evseroff recalls, "we brought him to the district attorney and tried to cooperate, but they didn't believe him."

In March 1969, Zelmanowitz was arrested again on two charges of interstate transportation of $250,000 worth of stolen securities. Again, Evseroff, Newman & Sonenshine represented him.

But Zelmanowitz was working another angle on his own. He became a government witness in the federal case against Angelo DeCarlo, a powerful *capo* in the Mafia family of Vito Genovese. He was placed in protective custody, hidden away at undisclosed locations and even testified before the grand jury with his face shielded and his identity disclosed only as "Mr. X."

"I always thought I had a good rapport with him," Newman says. "He kept attesting to the fact that of every lawyer he ever had, the only one he ever respected was me, that I was the most honorable one. When he decided to cooperate, he called me just to tell me this personally."

Zelmanowitz testified against DeCarlo and supplied the key evidence of extortion that resulted in conviction and a 12-year sentence. He went on to testify against his co-defendants in the stolen securities case.

In return for his cooperation, the government persuaded the judges to give Zelmanowitz suspended sentences. To shield him from the mob's vengeance, it gave him a new identity and relocated him and his family in San Francisco. Using the name "Paul Maris" and the contrived credentials of a retired military intelligence officer, he quickly impressed a local clothing manufacturer and became the treasurer of the company. Within a year, he persuaded Creative Capital Corporation, a New York investment firm, to buy control of the company, rename it Paul Maris Company and install him as president.

For a year he lived high off the hog, in a "glittering world of Rolls-Royces and $50,000 parties," according to one account. But his extravagances disturbed his financial backers and in April 1973, he was fired.

For a man who supposedly wished to stay submerged, he did a surprisingly stupid thing: He filed suit against Creative Capital for breach of contract and asked for $5 million in damages. Creative Capital hired a private detective to check his background and his real identity was discovered. Creative Capital filed a countersuit charging him with misrepresenting himself and misappropriating $200,000 in company funds.

"My whole entire cover is being destroyed and torn apart," Zelmanowitz said. "At this moment, I am traveling very far and very fast."

He high-tailed it to Washington where he surfaced a month later under the protective custody of the Senate's Permanent Subcommittee on Investigations headed by Washington Democrat Henry "Scoop" Jackson. He testified at a subcommittee hearing on July 13, 1973, under a cloak of immunity and with the press barred from sketching or photographing him. Throughout the morning, he testified about his dealings with the mob, handling stolen securities and setting up secret Swiss bank accounts. Then, shortly after noon, Kentucky Senator Walter Huddleston switched the subject:

> SENATOR HUDDLESTON: Mr. Zelmanowitz, were you ever involved directly in the fixing of a criminal case in New York City?
>
> MR. ZELMANOWITZ: I was, sir.
>
> SENATOR HUDDLESTON: Can you describe that to the committee?
>
> MR. ZELMANOWITZ: It was in Brooklyn, New York, years ago, an acquaintance of mine named William Light—
>
> SENATOR HUDDLESTON: How many years ago? . . .
>
> MR. ZELMANOWITZ: This would have taken place approximately in 1964–65. I am giving you outside dates, Senator. I would have to check my records to get exact dates for you. Somewhere in the early mid-Sixties. There

was a law firm in Brooklyn who was Evseroff, Newman
& Sonenshine. Some of the members of this firm were
ex-attorneys for the district attorney's office of Brooklyn, New York. Their office is located in downtown
Brooklyn in the same building as the investigative squad
for the district attorney.

One of the investigators at that time, the chief investigator, was a gentleman named Walter Bookbinder.
Directly attached to that office was another office which
went under the name of Armed Forces News. Its pub-
lisher and editor—a one-man office—was Mr. William
Light. Inside the office they connect with the law firm,
actually. . . .

From time to time clients were brought in seeking
legal advice and legal help from Evseroff, Newman &
Sonenshine. They would bring them into the Armed
Forces News area where Mr. Light made arrangements
with the district attorney's office to fix cases. I personally was involved in one where five thousand dollars was
given to an attorney from the district attorney's staff to
see to it that a—

SENATOR HUDDLESTON: Can you identify that individual? Not openly, but for the record?

MR. ZELMANOWITZ: I can lead you to the identity,
Senator. This individual happened to have three convictions, prior convictions, for similar crimes. This was the
importing of cigarettes where he failed to pay taxes to
New York State. A truckload of these cigarettes were
found by the investigative squad of the district attorney.
When the trial came, he just walked out of the courtroom. The case was not processed.

I don't remember whether he received a suspended
sentence or was found not guilty. This five thousand
dollars was distributed among various people in the district attorney's office.

Mr. Bookbinder, who was chief investigator, received
a brand-new Buick at one time, as I remember. Joe

Colombo owned, was in partnership, in a dealership in Brooklyn, a Buick dealership. The district attorney's office was issuing subpoenas for some type of investigation at that time. I don't remember if it was in regards to the meeting that was held in Forest Hills, but they were arrested, or if it was prior to that time. I don't recall now. There were subpoenas issued for many people and Mr. Bookbinder was asked by us not to present the subpoenas for a period of at least a week, because Mr. Colombo had certain business he was trying to transact. He did not wish to go before the committee because he felt he would be placed in prison for failure to testify.

He was given a brand-new Buick for this. There were many instances like this taking place at this time, Senator Huddleston.

"It didn't bother me," Evseroff says of Zelmanowitz's charge. "I laughed when I saw it. I didn't get excited about it because I knew it was completely untrue."

He told *The New York Times* the charge was "absolutely 100 percent untrue." Bookbinder (who had since been indicted for perjury in an unrelated case and who is represented by Evseroff) said it's "so ridiculous it's pathetic." Aaron Koota, the Brooklyn D.A. at the time, said, "I am completely satisfied with my own integrity, of course. That's beyond question."

But some gave greater credence to the charges. Maurice Nadjari, the special prosecutor, said, "We want to see what kind of intelligence they [the Jackson subcommittee] have and if it fits in with anything we have." He described it only as a "preliminary inquiry," not a full-fledged investigation. State Senator Ralph Marino, chairman of the Joint Legislative Committee on Crime, went further. He said he'd also asked for data from the subcommittee: "They have certain information that's fairly detailed, and that's what I'm looking for." He explained that the committee had already been looking into the operations of Koota's office. When asked if it was an ongoing investigation, he replied, "We're making it one now."

However, neither Nadjari's inquiry nor Marino's investigation made much headway. "We haven't gotten to him [Zelmanowitz] yet," said one crime-committee counsel at year's end. "He's apparently being kept under wraps because there are federal warrants out for him in Newark." It seems that the IRS still had tax liens against Zelmanowitz from his arbitrage operations.

Significantly, there was no public comment from Light, who had retired to Florida. He had been a public-relations man and fund-raiser for the BARO (Brooklyn Association for the Rehabilitation of Offenders) clinic, a favorite charity of D.A. Koota. He'd given dinners honoring Koota in 1964 and 1966, but he was later "relieved of his responsibility" because of "disenchantment with his background." Light himself was an offender, how rehabilitated is not known. He'd been convicted of attempted grand larceny in 1936 and of bail-jumping in 1946. He was subsequently convicted of income-tax evasion. He was also an old friend of Zelmanowitz's. In his Senate testimony, Zelmanowitz related how he and Light had traveled together to Europe to dispose of some stolen securities.

"He was such a good connection of mine," Evseroff observes, "that I evicted him for nonpayment of rent."

As to the specifics of Zelmanowitz's charges, Evseroff notes that they relate to a period several years before Zelmanowitz became a client of the firm. The firm had represented Colombo briefly in a contempt case, but was dropped for another lawyer and had entered the case *after* he'd gone before the grand jury. As for the other charge: "I don't know what they're talking about. I've had a number of cigarette cases."

"If you read the testimony carefully," Evseroff continues, "he didn't say that *we* had anything to do with these particular cases; he said that Light did. We never had anything to do with any kind of fixes in Kings County or anywhere else. Zelmanowitz's allegations and accusations are just patently untrue."

But the cloud remains.

12   A Year in the Arena

Between September 5, 1973, when Patrolman Shea's case came up for motions, and May 8, 1974, when it went to trial, Evseroff tried four cases before a judge and jury. His clients were three cops, a travel agent and a bartender; the charges ranged from murder to extortion to bribery. Unlike the Shea case, in which the press hung on virtually every word, none of the trials rated so much as a single sentence in the papers. They may not be news, but they illustrate the times, trials and techniques of a defense lawyer.

Testing in a Can of Worms

For Evseroff, 1973 had been a rough year. His marriage had broken up and he was going through an acrimonious divorce. He had been robbed. Gus Newman had left the partnership. There was the continuing cloud of Zelmanowitz's accusation and the threat of an investigation. Worse, he hadn't won a jury trial all year. He wondered if he was jinxed, if he'd lost the magic touch.

Then came the trial of Albert Slama. To the spectators, a trial is drama. To the actors, it's supposed to be "a search for truth." As drama, *People* v. *Slama* was farce. As a search for truth, it was a wild goose chase. But to Evseroff it was a test and a turning point.

The case had been kicking around the calendars for nearly three years. On October 1, 1969, Patrolman Albert Slama had made an arrest in a barroom brawl. When another patron, Gerald Haggerty, interfered, Slama arrested him. About a year later, Haggerty told the Brooklyn district attorney's office that Slama was trying to shake him down for $200 to change his testimony. At his next court appearance, Haggerty was wired and given $100 in marked money. He met Slama on the eighth floor of the Central Courts Building at 120 Schermerhorn Street in downtown Brooklyn and ducked into the men's room with him. When they emerged, Haggerty waved his handkerchief, the prearranged signal, and Slama was arrested. As the detectives grabbed him, Slama pulled the marked money from his pocket and threw it to the floor.

The trial opened on Monday, November 5, 1973, before Supreme Court Justice William Cowin. A crotchety, white-thatched man of 71, Cowin spoke a classic Brooklynese and peered through glasses with a sun-shield flipped up against the glare of the overhead lights. He was a rarity on the Brooklyn bench—a Republican. He'd been a crony of John Crews, the late Brooklyn GOP leader, and every time there'd been a judicial vacancy in the borough, Governor Rockefeller had given him the interim appointment, and every time he'd been defeated by a Democrat for election to a full term. The Democrats finally gave in and gave him a joint endorsement.

The prosecutor was Evseroff's adversary from the five-month police-corruption case, assistant D.A. Henry Sobel, the nephew of one of the borough's most respected judges. In the courthouse vernacular, Sobel was trying it "off a matchbook," meaning he'd made little preparation. In fact, he considered the case so weak he'd urged dropping the prosecution, but his superiors ruled otherwise.

Jury selection took up most of the first day. After the panel was sworn and excused for the day, the judge and the lawyers conferred on the ground rules for the trial. Justice Cowin barred Evseroff from introducing evidence about an earlier incident in Slama's career: In 1963, the patrolman had arrested three men for hijacking; one of them had offered Slama $10,000 for his freedom, and Slama promptly charged him with bribery. The inference was clear: If Slama had turned down $10,000, why would he try to shake down Haggerty for $200.

Despite the setback, Evseroff announced: "I'm going to get it in, judge."

"I'm not going to permit you to ask him about it," Justice Cowin ruled.

"I'm not going to ask him," Evseroff replied. "I'll tell you exactly how I'm going to get it in. I'm going to get it in through the character witnesses."

"You can't ask them either."

"Judge, I'll tell you exactly what questions I'm going to ask them," Evseroff said, reciting the standard litany of questions for character witnesses: "Do you know the defendant? How did you come to know him? Do you know others who know him? Have you had occasion to discuss with them his reputation for truth, honesty and veracity? What is that reputation? *What was that occasion?*"

The rest of the trial would be a cat-and-mouse game, with Evseroff trying to slip in the forbidden subject when the judge wasn't looking.

Tuesday was Election Day and the courts were closed. Sobel opened on Wednesday, announcing that he wouldn't play the tape Haggerty had recorded because it was inaudible. Evseroff replied, insisting that Slama had been set up by Haggerty. It seemed a simple question of one man's word against another's, a case that should last only a day or two. But it was a can of worms that crawled across nearly two weeks of the court calendar.

Haggerty was the first of five prosecution witnesses. He stood six-foot-three and looked like a man who could get involved in a barroom brawl. He told of his arrest and said that Slama had slugged him in the squad car and at the stationhouse. He related the shakedown demand and told how he'd been wired and given $100 in marked money. (Why the D.A.'s office gave Haggerty $100 when Slama supposedly had asked for $200 was one of several discrepancies that were never clarified.) When Slama entered the men's room, Haggerty continued, he'd inspected the stalls to make sure they were alone, then demanded the money. Haggerty asked for his promise that he'd get off and Slama gave it. Haggerty then handed him the money, Slama counted it and stuck the wad in his pants pocket. They then left the room and Slama was arrested.

On cross-examination, Evseroff brought out that Haggerty was no novice at getting arrested. He'd served one jail term for unlawful entry (reduced from burglary) and escaped another only by "psychoing" himself into Pilgrim State Hospital for nine months.

"I was laying the groundwork for argument on summation. I wanted to show that this was a man who was experienced in the ways of trying to avoid prosecution."

Haggerty was followed to the stand by his girl-friend— "paramour," Evseroff termed her—Carol McCadwin, a chunky former nurse who corroborated Haggerty's account of the shakedown demand.

Justice Cowin took a folksy approach to the conduct of the trial. He opened the third day's session by telling the jury: "You know, when I walk into court, the officer bangs the door and everybody stands up. When I walk into my home, I bang the door and my wife says, 'Take out the garbage.' "

Then he turned to the stenographer: "Don't put that in the record." He explained that in another case he'd excused himself for a few minutes because he'd had diarrhea and *that* had been entered in the record to be reviewed by the higher courts.

Indeed, the judge seemed edgy about letting any of the legal arguments be transcribed. At one point, when Evseroff insisted that a colloquy be taken down, he protested: "Every time I take a breath which is not material to the issue, you want to put it in the record."

Sobel's third witness was Edward Levine, the assistant chief investigator for the Brooklyn D.A.'s office. He was a squat man with a pot belly who showed up in court wearing a T-shirt and wash pants. He told of giving Haggerty the marked money dusted with a fluorescent powder and of getting it back after Slama's arrest. He also related how Slama, while in custody at the D.A.'s office, had played with a piece of Scotch tape in an apparent effort to remove the telltale traces of powder.

But Levine was hopelessly confused about the dates, and on cross-examination Evseroff showed that his handling of the investigation was, at best, inept. He'd made no memos and kept no records. The defense lawyer also brought out that, despite his gun and shield, Levine was not a cop; before joining the D.A.'s staff, he'd been a butcher.

"Perhaps you're wondering why I made such a monkey out of Levine. We don't deny any of his evidence. That's not our defense in this case. But it's conditioning the jury. By the time I put my man on the stand, I want the jury to hate the prosecution."

Detective Kenneth McCabe, who assisted in the arrest, testified to Slama's throwing the marked money to the floor. Then Sobel said that his final witness would not be available until the following day because he was in Buffalo.

"Buffalo!" the judge exclaimed. "What's he doing up there? Watching O. J. Thompson?"

"That's *Simpson!*" a half-dozen persons shouted.

One juror turned to another and asked, "Who's O. J. Simpson?"

Sic transit gloria Monday night football.

The jurors were excused for the day. Once they'd left, Sobel announced that he was *not* going to offer the marked money in evidence, because it had disappeared. In a city where $70 million worth of "French Connection" heroin could be stolen from the police property clerk's office, the loss of $100 was not unusual but it was a blow to the prosecution's case. First the tapes, then the money—no wonder Sobel had wanted to drop the case!

Evseroff insisted that *he* had the right to bring up the matter of the missing money for the jury, and Justice Cowin agreed. Friday's session opened with Levine back on the stand.

"Where is the money now?" Evseroff asked him.

"I have no idea."

"It disappeared?"

"Yes. . . ."

"Yes, it disappeared in your office?"

"Yes."

"I have no further questions."

Sobel's final witness was a retired crime-lab detective who had driven in, not from Buffalo but from his home in Saranac, at the opposite end of the state. He testified that he'd found traces of the fluorescent powder from the bills in the right-hand trousers pocket of Slama's uniform.

The jury was excused again, and Sobel announced that he had one more piece of evidence: After three years, they'd discovered that a portion of the tape *was* audible, "less than a minute," Sobel said. It supposedly included Haggerty saying, "Here's the money I promised you. You'll get me off?" and Slama answering, "Guaranteed."

Slama shook his head sadly and whispered to Evseroff: "I never said that."

The defense attorney protested vehemently against introduction of the tape. He said it was untimely, that he was entitled to an audibility hearing *before* trial. He claimed "surprise"—evidence not indicated in the prosecutor's opening. He insisted that the tape be submitted to the FBI or some independent laboratory for testing its authenticity, which would take weeks and which could cause a mistrial and the possibility of double jeopardy.

Justice Cowin was obviously overwhelmed by the complex legal situation. He was also anxious to get to the hospital for some minor nasal surgery he'd scheduled. He announced that he'd rule on Monday, giving him time to consult more learned authorities.

Monday's session opened with Sobel completing his double-reverse. He said he would *not* introduce the tape. He explained that Haggerty, the only person who could identify the voices, had left town after he'd testified.

Justice Cowin seemed disappointed. "Gee, I had a beautiful opinion written up."

But Evseroff was not surprised. "How would he [Sobel] look to the jury, putting in the tape after telling them that it was inaudible? Can't you hear me screaming, 'Fabrication'?"

The jury was brought in to hear Sobel rise and recite a single sentence: "Your Honor, at this juncture, the people rest."

Since Sobel had been scheduled to present more evidence, Evseroff had no witnesses available. The trial went over until Tuesday.

The defense opened with the character witnesses. First was Slama's next-door neighbor, Joseph LoVerde. Evseroff went through the standard litany, then asked the trigger question: "What occasion did you have for discussing this defendant's reputation for truth and honesty with others?"

"A few years back when he made a hijacking—" LoVerde started.

"Objection!" Sobel shouted.

"The objection is sustained," Justice Cowin ruled.

The jury was excused again for the legal arguments. Evseroff insisted on a clear-cut ruling: "Am I being forbidden to ask this witness, 'What occasion did you have for discussing with others his reputation for truth, honesty and veracity'?"

"You can ask him what that reputation was," the judge replied.

"I've asked you one question and you've answered something else," Evseroff protested.

"I'm dumb," the judge said. "I didn't understand the question."

The arguments continued. Justice Cowin finally ruled that

Evseroff could *not* ask the question. "I may be wrong," he said, "but I'm never in doubt"—which was doubtful.

Evseroff was satisfied. He was convinced that the judge's ruling was "reversible error."

The defense lawyer presented four more character witnesses who testified to Slama's good reputation, but each time he tried to slip in the forbidden evidence, Sobel objected and Justice Cowin sustained the objection.

After the mid-morning recess, Evseroff turned to his client: "Take the stand."

Slama is a casting director's dream of what a cop should look like: 38, husky, handsome, blond and blue-eyed and very ill-at-ease in the suit and tie Evseroff made him wear to court.

He testified to making the initial arrest on November 1, 1969. He said that Haggerty had threatened, "I'm going to get your fucking ass." He denied beating Haggerty, adding that in 13 years on the force, he'd made some 300 arrests without a complaint of brutality or a charge of shakedown. He said he'd never seen Miss McCadwin until she'd testified in court and had never discussed a shakedown with her or anyone else.

Evseroff attempted to introduce police records showing that Slama, rather than having set up the payoff for December 11, had asked for the day off. Sobel objected and again the judge sustained him.

The legal arguments were interrupted while Justice Cowin rummaged over his desktop. "Who stole my pen?"

Slama reached into the pile of papers on the bench and extracted the pen. "Here it is, sir."

Then he gave his version of what had happened inside the men's room. As soon as they'd gone inside, Haggerty had edged closer to him and said, "I told you I was going to get even with you."

"He pushed something into my pocket," Slama continued. "Then he pushed me aside and ran out."

Slama said he'd started after him, but was arrested almost as soon as he'd stepped out the door.

"Are you guilty of this charge in any manner, form, shape?" Evseroff shouted.

"No, sir."

"Did you do what Haggerty said?"

"No, sir."

"Or his girl-friend?"

"No, sir."

Then he turned and said softly to Sobel, "You may inquire."

Most of the cross-examination dealt with the passage of money. Sobel had Slama don his old police blouse and demonstrate with one of the court officers how Haggerty had slipped the money into his pants pocket. Sobel was trying to show that it couldn't have happened as Slama said, that the patrolman's gun would have been in the way. He tried to have Slama hitch on a holster, but the belt he provided was too small for Slama's stocky frame. He also reached into his wallet to provide bills. This time Evseroff objected successfully.

"If he has the money in question, I have no objection," he added sarcastically.

On redirect, Evseroff made one more stab at the forbidden subject: "Prior to this occasion, did anyone offer you a bribe?"

The replies came in unison: From the witness, "Yes, they did"; from the prosecutor, "Objection!"; and from the judge, "Sustained."

One of Evseroff's witnesses had not shown up, so the trial was recessed until the following morning. In the corridor, Evseroff pulled Slama aside and laid down the law to the lawman: "I want you to get her [the missing witness] and get her here in court tomorrow at ten o'clock."

Slama produced the witness, but there was another legal hassle as to whether her testimony was admissible. She was a 70-year-old restaurant owner named Gina Constanza who claimed that Miss McCadwin had attempted to shake down Slama for $4000. Sobel protested that this was a collateral attack on his witness.

Justice Cowin had difficulty comprehending the conflicting

accounts of who had demanded money from whom: "I must be dumb. I can't follow that."

So the lawyers repeated their arguments slowly. This time the judge seemed to grasp the point. "I think that in the interests of justice I'm going to allow it," he ruled.

Mrs. Constanza gave a long, rambling account in broken English of how Miss McCadwin had used her as a go-between to Slama, relaying word that for $4000 Haggerty would leave town and not testify against him. She quoted Slama as replying: "I'm not going to pay that woman twenty-five cents, because I'm innocent." To prove her point, she turned to Justice Cowin and informed him: "Judge, you can call the woman up yourself."

Needless to say, Sobel had difficulty cross-examining her. After 20 minutes, during which he ascertained little more than the fact that Italian restaurateurs do favors for each other like loaning Mozzarella cheese, he gave up.

But he produced two rebuttal witnesses: Detective John Morris, who testified that Slama had walked about 50 feet from the men's room before he'd been arrested; and McCabe again, who said that Slama had worn his gun over his right-hand pocket.

After the mid-morning recess, summations started. Evseroff said the basic issue was Haggerty's word against Slama's. "Believe Haggerty?" he shouted. "Believe a burglar? This is a cop-fighter. This is a man who above all does not want to go to jail. . . ."

But his main point involved a matter not in evidence: If Slama had stood in the men's room counting the money, as Haggerty had testified, he would have had traces of powder on *both* hands; if, as Slama claimed, he'd touched the money only when he'd pulled it from his pocket, he would have had a stain only on the right.

"Nobody took the stand to testify that he had luminescent powder on both hands," Evseroff shouted.

He launched his peroration standing in the center of the courtroom, his face flushed, his voice booming:

"If you convict this police officer, you better lock up your houses pretty good, because Haggerty will think up some other way to get out and this man—" he pointed to Sobel "—will be there to help him."

"Objection!" Sobel shouted.

"Sustained."

Evseroff paused to sip some water, in part because his throat was parched, in part to let his point penetrate. He offered a paper cup to Sobel, but the prosecutor declined.

"What do you want—some gin?" the judge asked.

Evseroff concluded, calling it "an *inversion* of justice that lets a burglar go free because he put one hundred dollars in the pocket of an honest policeman."

By contrast, Sobel was low-key, almost apologetic in his argument.

The jury was excused again while the attorneys debated the judge's charge. Justice Cowin expressed the opinion that Haggerty was an accomplice and that his testimony had to be corroborated.

"What is your evidence that there was corroboration?" he asked Sobel.

"I don't know of any evidence of corroboration," he replied.

The prosecutor argued that Haggerty was not an accomplice, but an agent of the district attorney's office.

"He's conceding entrapment," Evseroff chimed in joyfully.

He walked out of the courtroom chuckling. He knew the judge was wrong, but since the error, for once, benefited his client, he was not going out of his way to correct it.

Justice Cowin's charge, delivered the following morning, struck Evseroff as surprisingly good. The jury retired at 11:15 A.M.

Evseroff relaxed over lunch, hopeful that he'd get an early verdict of not guilty. "Three years ago, there would have been no doubt about it. Now I don't know. After Watergate, after the Knapp Commission, after everything else, people are ready to believe anything about cops."

He speculated aloud that Slama really might be *not* guilty. "Of course, he told me all along that he was innocent. But I operate on the principle that they're *all* guilty, even when they tell me they're innocent."

But as the afternoon wore on, his confidence waned. The jury continued to deliberate, sending out several requests: first, to examine Slama's uniform, which was granted; next, to visit the scene of the "alleged crime," which was denied; finally, to have portions of Haggerty's and Detective Morris's testimony reread to them. There was a key contradiction in their accounts. Haggerty had said that he'd walked out of the men's room first, followed by Slama, had made a right turn and hadn't seen what had happened behind him. Morris said that they'd walked out together, had made two right turns and had gone about 50 feet before the arrest.

Evseroff downed two Gibsons with his shrimp dinner at Gage and Tollner's, one of Brooklyn's finest restaurants, then returned to the deserted courthouse to await the verdict.

"You never get used to it. You can try cases for a hundred years and you never get used to it. You can pretend you don't care. You can say, 'I've done my job, I've done my best, there's nothing more I can do,' but you never get used to it. You grow a little older with each case you try. And any lawyer who tells you otherwise is full of shit!"

Sobel waited out the verdict in his office in the Municipal Building watching *Kung Fu* on TV. Evseroff either paced the darkened corridor with his client or lounged in the courtroom with Justice Cowin and the court attendants. But he declined to join in their speculations as to what the verdict might be.

"I've been trying cases for twenty-four years and I have no idea of what makes jurors tick," he told them. "I know how to try a case. I know how to question witnesses on direct examination and how to cross-examine them. I know how to object and how to conduct an offer of proof. But when it comes to what goes on inside jurors' heads, I know nothing."

As the night wore on, the possibility of a hung jury loomed. Justice Cowin had to attend a judicial conference on Friday, so there was no question of locking up the jury overnight. If there wasn't a verdict by midnight, he'd declare a mistrial.

That prospect was never reached. The jury sent word at 11:12 that they'd reached a verdict.

"What do you think?" Slama asked Evseroff when word came to them in the corridor.

"I don't know." He clasped a hand on Slama's shoulder. "If I knew, I'd tell you, baby."

He cautioned both Slama and his wife, Lulu, a flashy brunette, "No demonstrations—either way."

Sobel dashed over from his office and they filed into the courtroom.

"How say you as to count number one . . . ?" the clerk asked.

"We find the defendant not guilty," the foreman replied.

"How say you as to count number two . . . ?"

"We find the defendant not guilty."

Trial over, verdict rendered, Evseroff was finally permitted to tell the jurors what he'd been trying to tell them for two weeks —of the bribery arrest Slama had made ten years before.

"I had a hunch it was something like that," one juror said.

Slama rushed over to shake hands with the departing jurors, then joined his wife in congratulating Evseroff. The attorney advised Slama to contact his office the following week so they could prepare for the departmental hearing, which would determine if the suspended patrolman would be reinstated and receive three years' back pay. Then Slama ripped off his tie, undid his collar button and went off to celebrate.

One of the jurors, a man of Italian extraction, asked Evseroff for his card. The attorney gave it to him, then wandered outside into the chill November night.

"You know," Evseroff commented, "I'll bet he has relatives in one of the 'families.' I think I'll be getting some business from them."

"The Best Burglar in Brooklyn"

On November 29, the Appellate Division reversed the man-slaughter conviction of Eugene Lagana and dismissed the murder indictment against him. As a result of the ruling, Evseroff was in the enviable position of never having lost a murder trial. It was a distinction he'd keep for only 19 days.

Back in October, while he was in Suffolk County Supreme Court on his wife's motion for temporary alimony, Evseroff ran into a local lawyer he knew, Robert LaBord, then in the process of closing out his practice because he'd received an appointment as a professor at Delaware Law School. The two had lunch together.

"Jack, I have a murder case for you," LaBord said. "It's a very interesting case. I can't try it because there's a conflict of interest. I believe you should try it."

"Sure, Bob," Evseroff replied. "Come and see me."

"There's no great fee involved," LaBord continued, "but there's a conflict of interest. I believe you should try it."

Evseroff returned to Brooklyn, reimmersed himself in his practice and forgot about the case.

On Tuesday, December 4, LaBord stopped at his office.

"Jack, I'm going to have to start that case," he said. "I'll bring the people up to see you."

"O.K.," Evseroff replied. "When is it on?"

"Next week some time."

It was shorter notice than Evseroff had hoped for.

LaBord returned on Friday with the client, Walter Reagan, a six-foot-four bartender with the build of a football tackle.

"I'm picking a jury in the case," LaBord said. "Don't worry, you won't have to be there until Tuesday to try it."

"What!" Evseroff exclaimed. "What's it all about?"

LaBord proceeded to outline the case: Reagan and a co-defendant, Charles Jackson, a chunky black known as "Butch," were accused of felony murder. After hours, in the early morning of May 19, 1972, in the Flatbush saloon where Reagan worked, they'd allegedly slugged Edward Appnel with a length of iron pipe, taken a wad of bills from his pocket and dumped him in the gutter outside, where he was found dead. The murder weapon was never recovered.

The chief witness against them was the saloon's Filipino porter, Lawrence Layus. He'd been questioned by police at the scene and in subsequent days and had denied any knowledge of the crime. About three weeks after the murder, however, he'd returned to the district attorney's office, recanted his earlier accounts and implicated Reagan and Jackson. At the time, LaBord had represented *both* Layus and Reagan.

As the case was outlined to him, Evseroff realized the defense would hinge on his cross-examination of Layus. There was no question of either Reagan or Jackson taking the stand. Both had long criminal records. Reagan's was replete with arrests and convictions for burglary and grand larceny; indeed, he'd once boasted of being "the best burglar in Brooklyn." Jackson had once received a 25-year sentence for a Connecticut kidnapping.

"Beautiful situation! It's not easy when you have no affirmative defense."

Evseroff went to court on Tuesday, December 11, to try the case. He found himself a stranger in a world he hadn't made. The judge was Supreme Court Justice Joseph Corso, a balding man with a hairline mustache, a product of the Brooklyn Democratic organization who ran a tight ship in court. The prosecutor was Gordon Haesloop, a stocky, somewhat scholarly assistant in the homicide bureau. Jackson's lawyer was Jack Wlodawer, an attorney Evseroff knew only slightly. The jury was in the box— *"not particularly the kind of jury I'd choose"* —both sides had opened and Haesloop was about to call his first witness.

It proved to be Evseroff's only triumph of the trial, albeit a short-lived one. Dr. Dominick DiMaio, the assistant medical examiner, took the stand and testified that the doctor who had performed the autopsy on Appnel had left the office. Evseroff successfully objected to DiMaio's reading the results of another's examination. DiMaio was excused, and Haesloop sent detectives searching to summon the doctor who'd performed the autopsy.

The rest of the day went quickly. Patrick Appnel supplied the required identification of his brother as the murder victim. Patrick Shea, a 26-year-old heroin addict, put the participants at the Parkside bar on the fatal day. Shea provided the trial's only touch of humor, black humor, to be sure. He'd lost his right hand and the court officers had difficulty deciding whether he should take the oath with his left or with the stump; they finally opted for the stump.

Among other things, Shea testified that Appnel had been carrying a large amount of money, but Haesloop was not permitted to bring out how much or how he'd gotten it: He had what was left of $1100 in receipts he'd stolen from a 7-Up bottling plant in the Bronx earlier that day.

At the end of the first day's session, after the jury was excused, Haesloop asked Justice Corso to remand Reagan for the remainder of the trial. Jackson was already behind bars, unable to raise bail.

"One of the witnesses, who has yet to testify—his life may be in danger," the prosecutor explained.

Evseroff protested, calling Haesloop's assertion "the oldest dodge in the world."

Justice Corso declined the request, which Haesloop would repeat throughout the trial, but warned Reagan: "If any proof comes before me that even a witness is looked at, [you] will reckon with me."

Wednesday's opening hours were devoted to scientific evidence. Patrolman Daniel Bouldi testified that he'd taken blood samples from the floor of the Parkside bar and Dr. Alexander Wiener, a serologist, said they matched Appnel's blood. The former medical examiner, Dr. Milton Wald, took the stand to put the autopsy findings on the record. He said Appnel had been killed by a "blunt impact" to the cervical cord and spine.

"Could such an injury occur, in your opinion, from striking

of the deceased in the back of the head with a blunt instrument?" Haesloop asked.

"Objection!" Everoff shouted.

"I'll allow it," the judge ruled.

"Yes, sir," Dr. Wald said.

"In your opinion," Haesloop continued, "would a pipe be a blunt instrument? . . ."

"Objection!"

"I'll allow it."

Dr. Wald said that a one- or two-inch pipe would correspond with the wound.

Haesloop then called for a conference in the judge's chambers to ask that the courtroom be cleared of spectators when his next witness testified. He explained that the witness was a policeman who, since his involvement in the Appnel murder, had been assigned to undercover work in narcotics. If he testified in open court, Haesloop said, someone might recognize him and his cover would be blown.

Everoff protested that such a move violated the defendants' constitutional right to a public trial.

Justice Corso didn't agree, but he ruled: "I will not exclude the public. I will not give both of you [Everoff and Wlodawer] an additional baseless ground for an appeal."

But Haesloop pressed the point. He had the undercover agent brought into chambers. When Patrolman Nicholas Palmiotto said that he was going to make a buy that very afternoon, the judge reversed himself: "The court is going to grant the application to clear the courtroom."

So the courtroom was cleared and Palmiotto took the stand to relate how he'd found Appnel's body in the gutter at Flatbush and Parkside Avenues at dawn on May 19. He was followed by James Conaboy, the detective who'd arrested both Reagan and Jackson.

(As an illustration of the small-world syndrome: Out of the 2,602,012 people in Brooklyn, the 50-member panel from which the Reagan-Jackson jury was chosen included Conaboy's brother. Naturally, he was excused for cause.)

The jury was excused again while Justice Corso convened a *Huntley* hearing to determine the voluntariness of an inculpatory statement Jackson had made after his arrest.

Conaboy said that he'd given Jackson a *Miranda* warning and started questioning him about the murder. "He said to me," he related, "that he had come to the bar that night to obtain cigarettes and that the body of a—a body was in the street when he got there, and that he called the ambulance on the telephone. And I asked him why he had given a bad phone number to the police communication system. He said that he didn't want to get the bar and the—himself involved in the case."

"Did he say anything else?" Haesloop asked.

"He refused to answer any more questions."

Justice Corso ruled that Jackson's statement was made voluntarily. The jury was brought back and Conaboy repeated his testimony for it.

After the luncheon recess, Larry Layus took the stand. He was a slight man of 33 with straight black hair and black horn-rimmed glasses. Haesloop's direct examination went quickly.

Layus said that he'd been working in the saloon after closing on May 19. Reagan had been behind the bar, Jackson having a drink in front of it. Reagan, he continued, "asked me if I enjoyed life and, if I enjoyed life, I don't see things."

A few minutes later, Appnel came in and ordered a drink. Jackson slugged him with a piece of pipe. Then, "Butch handed Walter the pipe or tire iron and Walter took it and hit Eddie." Appnel fell to the floor, bleeding profusely. Jackson and Reagan pulled a roll of money from his pocket. Reagan offered some of the bills to Layus, saying, "This is for you."

"I didn't take the money," Layus testified.

But he had helped Reagan and Jackson dump the body in the street outside. He'd also taken a bucket of water to swab the blood off the sidewalk and had mopped the barroom floor of bloodstains. He said the murder weapon had also been wiped clean.

Then Evseroff took over for cross-examination.

"Cross-examination is an art. A poor cross-examination can be disastrous because it gives the witness a shot at you, an opportunity to put it to you his way, or to repeat his direct examination, to hammer it home in the minds of the jurors in case they didn't hear it the first time. A good area of cross-examination is to examine into prior statements made by the witness.

"The purpose of cross-examination is to impeach the credibility and believability of a witness. Nobody is going to do a Perry Mason for you on the stand and say, 'I must admit the truth— it was really me who did it.' This does not happen. At least, it's never happened to me. Nor do I know of anybody it's ever happened to. Rather, it's an art to try to break down the general believability of a witness.

"I'm taking him through the classic lines of prior inconsistent statements, trying to show that he's incapable of belief here because he did not make such a statement as he makes here in court to the first officer on the scene, to the investigating detective, to the district attorney."

He went after Layus for the remainder of the afternoon and all day Thursday, reading great globs of the contradictory accounts he'd previously given.

Marshall Blumenfeld, a civil lawyer who rents an office in the Evseroff & Sonenshine suite, had stopped off in Justice Corso's courtroom to watch the confrontation.

"I think it's going pretty good," Evseroff confided to him during one recess. "I think the jury really eats up this business of prior inconsistent statements."

Blumenfeld replied without saying a word, just the traditional thumbs-down gesture of doom.

Later in the afternoon, Haesloop took over again for redirect. He asked that the jury be excused while he made an offer of proof. If Evseroff could question Layus about prior inconsistent statements, he argued, he had the right in rebuttal to ask about prior *consistent* statements.

He put the question to the witness: "Did you ever tell anyone what you testified to here?"

"I told the whole story to Mr. LaBord," Layus replied.

Justice Corso recessed the trial until Monday, so he could spend the long weekend researching the law as to whether such testimony was admissible.

Monday's session opened with him ruling that it was. Layus repeated it for the jury, and the prosecution rested.

"It's devastating! Here's a jury that knows LaBord because he selected them and he opened to them. We weren't planning to put a defense in, but it's become absolutely necessary for me to bring LaBord in as a witness."

LaBord came up from Delaware and testified on Tuesday. In the witness chair the law professor squirmed and stuttered. To be charitable, his account can best be described as "equivocal." He said that Layus *had* told him about Jackson's role in the murder, but he couldn't recall what he'd said concerning Reagan's participation.

Haesloop had only one question on cross-examination: "Weren't you Reagan's attorney?"

"I know the jurors didn't buy his testimony," Evseroff said afterward.

The remainder of the trial, the attorneys' summations on Wednesday and the judge's charge on Thursday, was anticlimax. LaBord's testimony had sunk the defense. The jury needed only six hours to find both defendants guilty of *both* felony murder and manslaughter, the alternative crime charged in the indictment.

On February 15, 1974, Justice Corso sentenced each of them to 15 years to life in prison.

"I've never done this before in twenty-four years, nor will I ever do it again—walk into a courtroom once a jury has been selected by another lawyer and he has opened to the jury and he himself is involved in this manner in the case," Evseroff said after the trial.

"I feel very bad about it. I really don't think that justice was done to the defendant in this case. I'm not passing on the question of whether he's guilty or not. But I don't think that he had his day in court as he should have, had the case been properly handled.

"It was a mistake, an effort to make some money, to gross three thousand dollars. But it was a big mistake."

The Gambler and the Deadbeat

Over Christmas, Evseroff vacationed in Puerto Rico. He booked his passage through travel agent William Landsman. Two weeks after he returned, he was defending Landsman in Federal District Court. The trial opened on Foley Square on Wednesday, January 16, before Judge Whitman Knapp.

Until two years before, Knapp had lived in the obscurity appropriate to a Wall Street lawyer. Then Mayor Lindsay named him to head a commission to investigate police corruption and he was thrust overnight into prominence. President Nixon rewarded him with appointment to the bench.

Although he was famed in legal circles for making the shortest argument in history before the U.S. Supreme Court, Judge Knapp was anything but laconic when he presided in the courtroom. He was long-winded and pedantic in his explanations to potential jurors, so much so that jury selection, normally a speedy process in the federal courts where the judges do all the questioning, lasted the entire day. A panel of eight women and four men was finally sworn.

The prosecutor, Michael Eberhardt, a special attorney from the Justice Department's strike force, opened the following morning. Tall and blond, he looked like an all-American boy. But he was young and inexperienced, without frill or flourish. His remarks lasted barely 15 minutes. Melvin Fogelson, he said, had owed $17,000 to Landsman, a gambling debt. When he'd failed to pay, Landsman had hired Fred Votto to collect the debt. In the course of the collection, Votto and the third defendant, Salvatore Marino, had made threats to Landsman and his wife.

In reply, Everoff lashed at Fogelson as a "deadbeat": "Your tax dollars and my tax dollars have been enlisted to help the Fogelsons avoid paying their just debts. . . . My client, Mr. Landsman, conspired with nobody, made no unlawful agreements and made no threats against anybody." Yet he didn't disclose much of the defense case.

"In an opening you just want to infuse into the jury some sort of annoying doubt."

After Marino's and Votto's lawyers offered their openings, Eberhardt called his first witness, Gary Kramer, an auto dealer from New Haven, Connecticut. In September 1972, he said, Landsman had called and asked if he could recommend a collection agent in the area. Kramer couldn't, but said he'd ask Joseph Baronne, a nearby concrete contractor. As a result, he'd contacted Votto, who'd handled collections for Baronne and for the local bank, and referred him to Landsman. A few months later, at Landsman's request, he'd advanced Votto $200 for expenses.

"Did he ever ask you to get any kind of strong-arm guy up in Connecticut?" Everoff asked on cross-examination.

"No, sir. . . . If he wanted a tough guy, he never would have called me," the auto dealer replied.

Baronne confirmed Kramer's account. Everoff managed to turn around both witnesses and use them as character witnesses for Landsman.

Fogelson followed. He was 46, a balding man with a hawk nose who looked like Uncle Fester on *The Munsters.* He'd been in the cuff-links business, but it had gone broke, because, he explained, men had stopped wearing cuff links. "At present," he said, "I'm unemployed."

Fogelson was a compulsive gambler. In 20 years, he'd lost "somewhere in the neighborhood of a quarter of a million dollars," including the $17,000 he'd owed to Landsman.

In December 1970, he continued, Landsman had summoned

him to his travel agency on Madison Avenue.

"I've taken enough of your bullshit," he quoted Landsman as saying.

"Bill, my intentions are good," he'd replied. "I'm going to pay you. Besides, I'm not looking to get killed."

"Nobody's going to kill you," Landsman supposedly had replied. "We're just going to break your arms and legs."

He didn't speak to Landsman again. About six months later, the Fogelsons left their home in White Plains, telling no one where they were going, and slipped into an apartment in Stamford, Connecticut.

Eberhardt tried to elicit Fogelson's state of mind when he'd fled. Evseroff jumped to his feet: "I object to the question as vague and indefinite—and leading and suggestive."

"It can't be both," Judge Knapp said.

Fogelson was permitted to explain: "I was . . . in no position to pay off my gambling debts. . . . I had a fear for my wife and family."

After about a year in Connecticut, Fogelson continued, a "Dan Sabbatini" started to dun him for payment. Although he'd never met "Dan"—he'd hidden in the closet when he'd come to the house—he'd spoken with him on the phone. By then, he'd gone to the FBI and the calls were monitored.

Tapes of two conversations between "Dan" and Fogelson, set up across state lines to create a federal jurisdiction, were played in court. In the first, made January 30, 1973, Fogelson pleaded for more time to pay, explaining that he'd just started training for a new job, selling textiles throughout the South; he mentioned recent stopovers in Charlotte, North Carolina, and Charlottesville, Virginia. He promised to pay $2000 or $2500 by March. In the second, made March 19, Fogelson reversed himself, claiming he had no money, but offering a diamond ring instead. "Dan" agreed to pick it up the next day from Mrs. Fogelson. The last five minutes of the conversation were lost because of a malfunction on the tape recorder.

The next day's cross-examination was delayed by an extraneous matter: One of the alternate jurors had been arrested on a marijuana charge. The remaining jurors were not told why he was excused from further duty.

When the trial resumed, Evseroff, wearing a maroon suit, rose and approached the lectern. He adjusted his shirt-sleeves before he posed the first question. "See," he said, "some people still wear cuff links."

He quickly elicited that Fogelson's company had gone into receivership not because of changing styles in men's fashion, but because Fogelson had "borrowed" $100,000 of company funds to pay his gambling debts. He'd also gone into personal bankruptcy for $150,000, had lost $100,000 in the stock market, had run up $48,000 in gambling debts and owed another $11,000 to a shylock.

Evseroff asked Fogelson about the stocks he'd touted to his White Plains neighbors: How much had they lost?

"What they lost I don't know," Fogelson replied. "But did they tell you about all the money they made?"

"I could answer that question, but I'd better not, Mr. Fogelson," Evseroff replied.

His answer would have been "no." Evseroff, rushed to trial, had had no opportunity to talk to the neighbors. The information about Fogelson's finances had been gathered by Landsman and his friends.

As Evseroff pressed his questions, Fogelson proved to be hopelessly confused about dates. He couldn't even remember when he'd moved from White Plains to Stamford (in the course of the investigation, he'd given different answers on four different occasions) even though moving day had been his 45th birthday.

"Do you have records to show—" Judge Knapp started.

"No, I have nothing."

Evseroff pressed the point: "Do you have anything to show whether you moved in 1970 or 1971?"

"May I ask you a question?"

"No."

"August 20, 1971," Fogelson insisted.

Evseroff continued, telling his client to stand. Landsman was a balding, mustached, pot-bellied man of 52, whose height barely reached five feet.

"Did Mr. Landsman try to break your arms and legs . . .?" Fogelson was forced to admit he hadn't.

Finally, Evseroff asked about the missing minutes on the tape: "Did it malfunction because somebody stepped on a foot-pedal?"

"Objection!" Eberhardt snapped.

"Sustained," Judge Knapp ruled. "Let's try *this* case."

The jurors laughed. Evseroff had hit home with his reference to Watergate and "Rose Mary's Baby."

The other defense lawyers took over on Monday. Marino's counsel, Paul Flynn, was brief, eliciting little more than that Fogelson had never seen Marino until he'd come to court. Votto's attorney, Ira Grudberg, was as awkward as Flynn was dapper, but his manner concealed the spring of a cobra.

He started asking Fogelson about his conversations with "Dan." Fogelson admitted that all his talk about the textile job was a lie. He explained that his remarks were "in character."

"You lied to him on any number of occasions, didn't you?" Grudberg pressed.

"Yes, sir."

"And that was in character, wasn't it?"

"Yes, sir."

Charlotte Fogelson followed her husband to the stand. She was a small, birdlike woman with an affected accent. She told of going to Landsman's office a week or two after her husband's visit and offering him a diamond pin as a token of their "good faith." At first, Landsman refused, then he'd accepted it. She'd paid $625 or $675 for the pin, she couldn't remember which, but she recalled that she'd had only $500 with her at the time and had to borrow the rest from a friend, Mrs. Sylvia Greene.

In the fall of 1972, she continued, "Dan Sabbatini," whom she identified as Votto, started dunning them. On his first visit, he'd left a note in the mailbox. He came again on January 15, 1973, accompanied by Marino, and she'd invited them inside for coffee. She'd said her husband was away on business; actually, he was hiding in the bedroom. They'd discussed Fogelson's gambling and his debts.

"When people are desperate, they do funny things," she quoted Votto as saying. "The word is out that should he gamble or shoot craps, he's a dead duck."

She'd replied, "If he gambles again, I'll kill him myself."

She'd pleaded with them for more time to pay, saying they had no money, no jewelry, not even life insurance.

"We know you have no life insurance," Votto had said.

At this point, Marino supposedly spoke for the first time: "If your husband had twenty-five thousand dollars' insurance, there'd be a contract on his life."

Then a series of nine taped telephone conversations between "Dan" and Mrs. Fogelson was played. Only on the last, made March 19, a few minutes after the call to her husband, was there anything that could be construed as a threat.

"Dan" and Mrs. Fogelson were discussing the diamond ring. "Dan" wanted to be sure that Fogelson, once he'd delivered it, wouldn't report it as stolen.

"Wouldn't my husband be a silly fool to do that?" she said.

"No, he wouldn't be a silly fool," "Dan" replied, "he'd be a dead silly fool."

"This is the biggest bunch of shit I've ever seen in my life. Of all the cases I've ever seen, this is one of the strangest. This case is absolutely weird. I don't see a conspiracy here for nothing. I don't see any extortion here."

Evseroff speculated that the government pressed such a flimsy case because Fogelson had told the FBI that Landsman was a garment-center shylock tied in with organized crime. Landsman had offered to cooperate with the strike force, but could not come up with any useful evidence. It was *not* a point he planned to press in court:

"I don't think it's good tactics in this case. It may be good in

*a political case to put the government on trial. But in this case
I think it's better to make them the victims of the Fogelsons. As
I said in my opening, Fogelson's a deadbeat who enlisted the
government's help to avoid paying his debts. It's the truth, but
not the whole truth."*

Evseroff's cross-examination took up most of Tuesday morning. It was slow going because Mrs. Fogelson proved an obtuse
witness. She kept saying, "I didn't understand the question—
would you rephrase that," or "I don't remember." She couldn't
even remember where Landsman's office was.

Evseroff brought Mrs. Greene into court so Mrs. Fogelson
could identify her as the woman who had loaned her the money
for the pin.

As he lunched on an omelet at Stark's Chop House on Lower
Broadway, Landsman came to his table and informed him that
Eberhardt wanted to see Mrs. Greene.

"She doesn't have to talk to anybody if she doesn't want to,"
Evseroff replied.

Mrs. Greene did not visit the prosecutor.

Evseroff planned to lead off the defense with Mrs. Greene's
testimony, but Grudberg's lengthy cross-examination of Charlotte Fogelson made it evident that the defense wouldn't get
under way until the following day.

During the mid-afternoon recess, he chewed out Grudberg:
"You ruined my whole case. This woman's flying to Puerto
Rico tomorrow."

Grudberg suggested that they ask Judge Knapp for permission to call the witness out of turn.

"How can I do that?" Evseroff protested. "The prosecution
hasn't finished its case yet."

"Ask," Grudberg replied. "Ask and it shall be granted. But
don't ask me not to cross-examine. I've got to defend my client.
My guy's the guy who's in the tank."

So they asked Judge Knapp, who denied permission. But, at
Evseroff's and Landsman's urgings, Mrs. Greene arranged to
postpone her flight for another day.

Actually, the prosecution didn't finish until Wednesday morning. Its final witness was FBI agent Angelo Melonas, who testified to Votto's statements after arrest. He said that Votto had admitted using the alias "Dan Sabbatini" so no one would trace him and had admitted making statements "to scare the Fogelsons and make them pay the money."

In a multidefendant trial, statements made by one defendant cannot be used as evidence against another. But Evseroff started to question Melonas about what Votto had said concerning his instructions from Landsman. He was, in effect, making the agent a defense witness. Judge Knapp warned that he was opening the possibility of a prosecution cross-examination on *everything* Votto had told the FBI. Evseroff took exception and a heated legal discussion ensued.

"It's not my intention to argue with the court," Evseroff said at one point.

"If it's not your intention, you should be disbarred," Judge Knapp replied. "That's what you're here for."

Votto, it turned out, had told the FBI that Landsman never instructed him to threaten the Fogelsons. On that note, the government rested.

The jury was excused while the defense attorneys, both in chambers and in open court, made their motions to dismiss. Eberhardt agreed to drop the conspiracy count, leaving only the substantive charges of extortion, one against all three defendants, the other against Votto alone.

There was no chance that the charges against Votto would be dismissed: His voice was on the tapes and he had made admissions to the FBI. As for Landsman, Judge Knapp said: "If I were the finder of fact, I would throw it out." But he left it for the jury to decide. Evseroff considered it a judicial cop-out:

"His whole theory is that he's leaving it in because the debt is unenforceable at law. 'If I'm wrong, you'll have a great issue on appeal. But I don't think it will get that far. You should have tried this without a jury.' Fat chance."

As for Marino, Judge Knapp told Flynn: "You have the strongest case. If the jury convicts, I will consider very strongly a motion to set it aside. That doesn't mean I'll grant it." He offered Marino a severance, which the defendant declined.

Although his rulings went against the defense, Judge Knapp had some harsh words for the prosecutor: "The testimony as it stands is absolutely incredible. . . . You obviously don't know how to deal with a witness. She [Mrs. Fogelson] told obvious untruths on immaterial matters."

After lunch, Evseroff launched his defense. Mrs. Greene said she had *not* loaned Charlotte Fogelson money for the pin or been with her when she'd bought it. Eight character witnesses followed, including Al Aronne, who'd served in the air force with Landsman during World War II.

Evseroff had a problem with the character witnesses, not with what they said, but with the way he posed his questions. Showing more regard for the subtleties of syntax than for the law, Judge Knapp protested whenever Evseroff asked: "Did you have occasion to discuss with them his reputation for truth, honesty, veracity and peaceableness?"

"Of course, he had occasion," the judge snapped. "The question is, 'Did he?' "

Evseroff tried to rephrase the question, but he found it hard to break a habit of 25 years.

Private detective George Palocsik testified that Landsman had asked him to collect the debt from Fogelson. He'd explained that he wasn't licensed in Connecticut and suggested that Landsman get someone who was.

Thursday's session opened with Evseroff asking for a conference in chambers. He had no legal issue to raise; he was stalling until his character witnesses arrived. None showed up in time, so he put his client on the stand.

Landsman said he was a travel agent who arranged gambling junkets to Las Vegas and the Caribbean. "I've always been a gambler," he explained, "for all my life—successfully at times, not so successfully at others."

In the mid-1960s, he continued, he'd made a deal with a bookie named Jack Ulrich; he'd refer customers to Ulrich in return for 25 percent of the profits, but he had to guarantee the losses. Among those he'd referred was Fogelson, who'd lost $22,000 to $24,000 and wound up owing $17,000.

Landsman admitted discussing the debt with Fogelson, but denied threatening him: "Actually, what I did was beg him." He denied that he'd accepted promissory notes from Fogelson, as Fogelson had claimed, or that he'd accepted a pin from Mrs. Fogelson.

He told of going to Palocsik and Kramer to get a collection agent in Connecticut. Asked why he'd hired someone else rather than do it himself, he explained, "I would have to quit my job to go up there and wait for him."

He hadn't authorized Votto to make any threats. "I just said, 'Dun him for it.' "

"Did you ever enter into any agreement with anybody directly or indirectly to threaten Melvin Fogelson or Mrs. Fogelson?" Evseroff asked.

"No, I did not."

Eberhardt's cross-examination was surprisingly tame. But Evseroff was not satisfied. He remained incredulous that the case was on trial at all.

"Can you believe it? You've got Watergate. You've got Nixon and his taxes. You've got every other goddamn thing that's happening in Washington. And we're trying this piece of shit."

Evseroff presented two more character witnesses, then told Judge Knapp at the sidebar that more might show up in the afternoon. The judge denied permission to call them out of turn. "Their testimony would just be cumulative," he explained.

Flynn's defense of Marino went quickly—three character witnesses, then Marino himself. A policeman in West Haven, Connecticut, he was a stocky man with slick black hair and a ruddy face. He wore rose-tinted glasses and red plaid slacks. He told of going on three rides with his friend Votto; once to Landsman's office in New York, twice to the Fogelsons' apartment in Stamford, but he insisted that he'd never discussed the purpose of the visits with Votto. He claimed that Mrs. Fogelson, not he, had made the remark about her husband's life insurance. He said that he hadn't said a word during the entire conversation, not even "hello" or "good-bye." By the time he finished, the jurors were shaking their heads in disbelief.

Grudberg followed on behalf of Votto with a few New Haven policemen as character witnesses and a couple of friends who testified to a luncheon meeting on the day of his arrest.

Evseroff interrupted the presentation to call a sidebar conference: Another of his character witnesses had arrived. Judge Knapp explained that he'd already denied permission to call them out of turn.

"But this one is black," Evseroff explained, "and there are two blacks on the jury."

Judge Knapp relented and Inez Cooper, owner of a soul-food restaurant, testified to Landsman's good character.

Grudberg rested without putting the volatile Votto on the stand.

The attorneys summed up on Friday. Evseroff led off, insisting that the prosecution's case was based on "surmise and suspicion."

"This case in its entirety is a farce," he shouted. "It's a joke, an insult to your intelligence."

For the benefit of the two blacks on the jury, he noted that the two FBI agents, Melonas and William Booth, who'd assisted Eberhardt on the prosecution, came from South Carolina and Mississippi.

By contrast, Flynn was low-key, Grudberg sarcastic, his voice filled with the inflections and idioms of the Grand Concourse: "You should believe him [Fogelson]? You should convict on this?" He called Fogelson "the king of the con-artists" and jumped on one point in his testimony of his claims that he'd actually been to Charlotte, North Carolina, and Charlottesville, Virginia: "His wife's name is Charlotte—and he's a charlatan."

Judge Knapp charged on Monday. The jury retired at 12:35.

Evseroff braced himself for a long wait: "You can't hope for a quick verdict in a case like this. It's inconceivable."

He was right. After lunch, the jury asked to hear all the tapes again. The recorder was set up in the jury room and the replay took most of the afternoon.

Shortly before dinner, the panel reported, "We are quite divided in our opinions," and asked for further explanation of the law of extortion.

Evseroff saw it as a good sign: If the jury hadn't found anyone guilty yet, they never would. Eberhardt agreed, saying that if they convicted, he wouldn't defend the verdict on appeal: "I'd be embarrassed to go up there [the U.S. Court of Appeals] and say that I participated in this mockery."

Evseroff and the Landsman family dined in nearby Chinatown, returning to the courthouse just in time to get word that the jury had reached a verdict.

"It looks bad," Evseroff whispered to Landsman as the jury filed in.

It's an axiom of criminal practice that "hanging juries" avoid looking at those they've condemned; those that acquit smile at the defendants. None of the jurors had looked their way.

The clerk asked the forewoman for the verdict.

"Not guilty," she said.

Landsman's wife and daughter let out shrieks of joy and broke into tears.

Judge Knapp called for order, then asked: "I presume you mean all defendants?"

"Yes."

Evseroff and the Landsmans went off for a drink of celebration. Votto and Marino, Grudberg and Flynn piled into a car for the two-hour drive to New Haven. Someone suggested that they stop off in Stamford and ask Fogelson to pay up.

"No way," Votto said.

The Pirouetting Policeman

On Monday, March 4, Evseroff appeared before Judge Jack Weinstein in Brooklyn's federal court, representing one of five defendants accused of hijacking a truckload of dresses.

Weinstein, a former Columbia law professor, had some novel ideas about courtroom procedure. Unless a case was being presented to a jury, he conducted court clad in mufti at the counsel table, sitting alongside the defendants and attorneys.

He sounded out the parties about the possibilities of a plea, then called a recess to give them time to discuss it. The prosecution's case was cold: Not only had the FBI recovered the stolen goods, it had had two informers inside the gang and had photographed the entire operation. Like the other defense lawyers, Evseroff saw no point in going to trial.

But one of the defendants refused to plead to anything more than a misdemeanor, even though the assistant U.S. attorney, Paul Lazarus, told him, "The boss downstairs won't buy it." He offered a plea to conspiracy, carrying a maximum sentence of five years, rather than the ten they otherwise faced. But the deal was all five defendants or none—and the one still balked.

Evseroff and the other defense lawyers wondered aloud what kind of defense they could present if the case went to trial.

"I've got it!" Evseroff said. "No defense, no witnesses, no cross-examination. Just get up at the end and say to the jury, 'Don't you think this case is a little too pat?' And hope there's one nut out of 12 who won't convict."

Gus Newman, who represented another defendant, chimed in: "How about: 'Would five Italian boys do something like this?' "

The holdout was finally persuaded to plead. While Lazarus returned to his office to draft the new information, Evseroff slipped into a phone booth and called his office. He learned that Justice Cowin had ordered him to trial on another case in Brooklyn Supreme Court at 2 P.M.

Evseroff had no desire to start the trial. He asked Judge

Weinstein's clerk to ask if the pleading could be put off until 2 P.M. If he was engaged in federal court, the Supreme Court case would be put off, and another case might be moved ahead of his on the calendar. The clerk asked, but the judge declined.

So Evseroff continued to pace the sixth-floor corridor until Lazarus returned at 12:30 with the new information. Judge Weinstein reconvened court at the counsel table, got each defendant to sign a waiver of his right to indictment by the grand jury on the new charge, then took his plea.

After lunch, Evseroff appeared before Justice Cowin. He had three cases on the calendar, all of ancient vintage, and the judge wanted to push one of them to trial. Evseroff explained that the defendant in one case, Anthony Lisi, the *mafioso* accused of contempt, had died. Evseroff and the prosecutor, his old courtroom adversary Henry Sobel, his hair considerably trimmed since their last encounter, agreed to go to trial on the case of Robert Kennedy and George Cooper as soon as the court's schedule permitted. The third case was marked "ready and passed"—another postponement.

Kennedy and Cooper were a study in contrasts. Both were suspended Manhattan detectives accused of shaking down a Brooklyn storeowner for $500. Kennedy was a small, peppery man with blond hair and a ruddy face. At 45, he'd suffered three heart attacks and gulped pills for his coronary condition; he also took frequent nips from a hip flask. Cooper was a tall black with close-cropped hair and a thick mustache, as taciturn as Kennedy was talkative.

Their trial started four days later. The first order of business was a *Wade* hearing to determine the accuracy of the eyewitness identifications. The proceeding was conducted with the usual decorum of Justice Cowin's court. While Sergeant John Ryan of the police department's internal-affairs division took the stand to describe how eight lineups of black and white policemen had been held at the Brooklyn district attorney's office on October 22, 1970, the judge kept interrupting with questions: "Which one is Kennedy?" "Which one is Cooper?"

"Let me see if I understand this. . . . I just don't know what it's all about."

At the defense table, Evseroff was having problems with his sinuses.

"Do you want some water maybe?" Justice Cowin asked.

"No, judge."

"Do you, Sobel?"

"No, I'd like some coffee."

"What?"

"Light coffee with sugar."

Gabriel Borgo, a short, balding man of 65, followed Ryan to the stand and identified Kennedy as one of the two policemen who'd come to his bargain store on 11th Avenue on Friday, October 9, 1970. "Him and a colored officer," Borgo said, though he couldn't identify Cooper. On cross-examination, Evseroff elicited that Borgo had been convicted in federal court as a receiver of stolen property, although the New York City police had no record of the arrest.

Although Borgo had not identified Cooper, Evseroff had little hope that the identification would be ruled invalid and thus lead to dismissal of the case.

"That's not really our aim. The purpose of this hearing is to give us a preliminary look at what they've got."

Armed with a little knowledge, the volatile Kennedy had his own ideas about the proceeding. As they walked to lunch at a nearby deli, he protested to Evseroff about Borgo's appearance: "The CPL [Criminal Practice Law] says he can't testify."

"The CPL doesn't say that," Evseroff snapped. "And I don't want you giving me any fucking legal arguments. If I'm going to try the case, I'm going to be the only lawyer in the case. Understood?"

Because Sobel had mislaid some necessary papers, the afternoon session was canceled. Borgo returned to the stand on Monday morning and this time identified Cooper as the other policeman who'd been in his store four years before. Evseroff

noted that he'd picked out the only black among 16 persons in
the courtroom.

Sobel's next witness was William Bauer, a young man who
assisted his father in a marine salvage wholesalers. He recalled
that two detectives had come to their Brooklyn warehouse on
October 12, 1970.

How long had they stayed? Sobel asked.

"Until they were thrown out."

He identified Kennedy as one of them; he did not identify
Cooper.

He was followed by his father, Conrad, a man with the build
of a stevedore, a big beer-belly and a belligerent manner. Like
his son, Bauer identified Kennedy, but not Cooper. On cross-
examination, he explained why: "I wasn't looking at the colored
officer. This little fellow was the guy doing all the talking."

As Evseroff pressed his questions, Bauer exploded in outrage:
"Now don't look like that at me. . . . I don't like his tone of
looking at me," he explained to the judge.

"Have you ever been in a mental institution?" Evseroff asked.

Bauer rose a foot out of his seat. "You're lucky I'm under
oath or I'd ask you the same question."

"No?"

"Is this guy for real?"

As soon as Bauer stepped down, Justice Cowin called Evseroff to the bench and suggested, "You'd better wear an iron
vest."

"You ain't seen nothing yet," Evseroff replied.

The judge refused to suppress the identification of Cooper.
"The question of credibility of the witness is for the jury to
decide and not for me to determine."

Jury selection started that afternoon and lasted through
Tuesday. A panel of ten men and two women, including two
blacks, was finally chosen. It was a middle-class, middle-aged
assortment.

*"That's the kind of jury you want in a cop case, the kind of
jury the D.A. would normally want, if somebody like Borgo was*

the defendant. You don't want young people on the jury in a case like this. In this day and age they're ready to believe all cops are crooks."

Sobel started his case on Wednesday. Borgo led off, identifying Kennedy and Cooper as the two detectives who had come to his store on October 9, 1970. With them was a man, later identified as Jack Pilger of the Little Jones Company, who'd visited the store the previous week.

"He [Kennedy] says the stuff I sold to this young fellow was taken from a warehouse—it was stolen goods. . . . He says I was in big trouble and he has to lock me up and I was very frightened," Borgo related.

He'd told the cops that he'd bought the goods from Bauer's firm and produced the receipts for them. Kennedy and Cooper had loaded the supposedly stolen porcelain figurines into the trunk of Cooper's car, then driven to a phone booth about eight blocks away where Borgo tried unsuccessfully to contact his next-door neighbor, Augustine Vesce. They'd dropped Pilger off at a subway stop, returned to the store just in time to see Vesce return from work and gone upstairs to Borgo's apartment.

"What do you want to do about it?" he'd asked Kennedy.

The detective, he said, had spun around and held up one finger.

"What is it—a hundred you want?"

"A thousand," Kennedy had replied.

"I haven't got that kind of money."

"How about five?" Kennedy had replied, holding up five fingers.

"That's still too much for me."

Borgo had suggested going to his sister's to borrow the money, but Kennedy had insisted: "No, it's got to be done here."

So Borgo went to his next-door neighbor, Vesce, to borrow the money. Vesce had come to his apartment and handed the bills to Kennedy.

During cross-examination, both Evseroff and the judge started to question Borgo at the same time.

"Let me finish and you keep quiet!" Justice Cowin snapped.

"Let the record indicate that the court is shouting at me," Evseroff said to the stenographer.

"That's exactly right," the judge said.

Evseroff moved for a mistrial.

"Denied."

He asked for a recess.

"Denied."

He asked for permission to go to the bathroom.

"O.K., you can go."

"Thank you so much, Your Honor."

"Without the sarcastic remarks."

On his return, Evseroff asked Borgo to demonstrate again the spin Kennedy supposedly had made.

"He made a spin and I don't have to show you again, because I showed you before," Borgo snapped back.

Vesce, a stooped man of 53 who owned a pizzeria in Greenwich Village, related how Borgo had come to his apartment and said, "I'm in trouble—I need five hundred dollars." Vesce had got the money from his receipts, followed Borgo into his flat and gave it to one of two men there. He couldn't identify the men, except to say that one was white and one was black.

In his brief cross-examination, Evseroff elicited some minor inconsistencies between Borgo's account and Vesce's.

"They're not important. The important thing is the improbability of his handing over the money without asking any questions."

William Bauer followed, relating how two detectives had come to the warehouse on October 12 and asked his father if he knew Borgo.

"Yes," his father had replied.

"Do you know that you're in a lot of trouble?" Kennedy had said. "He's in a lot of trouble."

"If anybody's in a lot of trouble it's you two fellows," his father had yelled back. "You'd better return the money you took from him."

The elder Bauer then told them to get out.

"And what did they do then?" Sobel asked.

"They got out."

Conrad Bauer confirmed his son's account, adding only that the two cops "ran out like scared rabbits."

Then Evseroff rose.

"Your Honor, might I ask Mr. Bauer one or two questions?"

And that's all he asked. There was no need for the iron vest.

Sobel's final witness was Sergeant Ryan, who introduced Kennedy's and Cooper's memo books, which showed they'd visited Borgo's store on October 9 and Bauer's warehouse on October 12, though neither man was mentioned by name on any of the documents they'd prepared for the police files.

Evseroff's cross-examination was brief: "Did they do everything that was required. . . ?"

"Yes."

He showed Ryan the calling card Kennedy had given Borgo.

"Did you ever hear of a detective shaking someone down and leaving his business card?"

"Objection!" Sobel shouted.

"Sustained," Justice Cowin ruled.

Evseroff's defense started the following morning. He led off with nine character witnesses for the two detectives, then put Kennedy on the stand. The detective said he was 45, married, the father of two sons. He'd been on the force for 20 years and had served as a helicopter pilot in the military before that.

"Mr. Kennedy, do you remember the day you were indicted in this case?"

"I can't forget it. That's the day I had my first heart attack."

"How many heart attacks have you had?"

"Objection!" Sobel shouted.

"Sustained."

But Evseroff had scored his point.

Kennedy's account jibed with Borgo's up to the point where

they'd left the store. Kennedy said they'd started out for Bauer's warehouse, but Borgo thought it might be closed for the day, so they stopped and made a phone call. There was no answer, so the detectives decided to put off their visit until Monday. They'd dropped off Pilger at the subway stop, then dropped off Borgo a block later. He'd never gone to Borgo's apartment, had never seen Vesce until he'd come into court.

"Did you ask Borgo for money?"

"Positively not."

"Did you ever ask for a thousand dollars and do a pirouette?"

"Pirouettes aren't my strong suit."

"Did you ever receive any sum of money either from Vesce or Borgo?"

"No, sir."

Kennedy's account also corresponded with Bauer's. But he noted that the salvage dealer "went bananas."

"What?" Justice Cowin asked.

"Bananas."

"What does that mean?"

"Crazy."

He quoted Bauer as saying: "You two guys get out of here. Kennedy, you get out of here and take that black bastard with you."

During the break between his direct and cross-examination, Evseroff clapped Kennedy on the shoulder and said, "You're doing great, *bubee*. Don't die on me."

But Kennedy made a near-fatal slip on cross-examination. He noted that Cooper had checked with police BCI (Bureau of Criminal Identification) to see if Borgo had a record. Evseroff feared that Sobel might follow up the point with his own check of BCI and find out that Cooper had asked about *both* Borgo and Vesce, even though they'd supposedly never met Vesce.

"If these two guys get convicted, it's their own damn fault. I don't know if they took the money—I wasn't there—but they've always protested their innocence to me."

"It could have been a lot worse," he consoled Kennedy when the cross-examination concluded.

Kennedy boasted that a Legal Aid lawyer once told him he was "the best liar he'd ever seen." "I'm a little out of practice now," he added.

Cooper confirmed Kennedy's account. Like his partner, he was 45, married, the father of four. He'd had 17 years on the force.

After his direct examination, Evseroff said, "You killed them, George." But he warned that Sobel would zero in on why he hadn't returned the receipts he'd taken from Borgo, and he supplied the answer: "That was the evidence of why you didn't arrest Borgo—not because he paid you five hundred dollars."

Indeed, Sobel put the question to him the following morning.

"If I didn't have those bills," Cooper replied, "everybody would have said, 'Why didn't you lock this guy up?' "

Evseroff presented 15 more character witnesses, a Brooklyn detective on a point of procedure, a private detective who said he'd been unable to trace Pilger. He even called Douglas LeVien, the detective who was assisting Sobel, in an attempt to show that the D.A.'s office had made no attempt to locate Pilger, but Justice Cowin barred that line of questioning.

Sobel called two witnesses in rebuttal, both on points of police procedure, and the attorneys summed up on Monday morning.

Evseroff called the case "a rather transparent attempt by a bunch of crooks and receivers to blemish the reputations of two policemen so that they themselves would not be the subject of continuing investigations.

"Do you think that if they were crooks and shook down a man for five hundred dollars, they would leave their calling card?" he shouted. "What crooked cops would take the property and voucher it?"

In rebuttal, Sobel said: "They are common crooks. They have broken the law and having broken the law, they are subject to the judgment of the law."

Justice Cowin charged Tuesday morning and the jury retired at 11:45 to render its judgment. It returned after lunch to ask

"What the Hell Is Justice?"

that Borgo's and Vesce's testimony be reread. The reading
lasted until 4:45 P.M.

"What do you think, Jack?" Cooper asked as they stepped
into the corridor for a cigarette.

"I think you're going to get convicted—that's what I think.
Why? Because of the times we live in."

At 5:29, the jury sent word that it had reached a verdict. The
clerk came into the corridor to inform Evseroff.

"I don't think it's good," he confided.

"I don't think so," Evseroff agreed.

Because of Kennedy's heart condition, there was a tank of
oxygen in readiness behind the bench and four court officers
stood around the defense table in case he collapsed. But as the
foreman rose to read the verdict, repeating "not guilty" 14
times, once for each defendant on each of seven counts of grand
larceny, bribery and official misconduct, it was the normally
cool Cooper who broke down and started bawling like a baby.

13   Black and Blue

South Jamaica is a suburban slum. Although it is part of the big city, in the outer reaches of the borough of Queens, some of its side streets are dirt roads, most of its houses drain into cesspools and many of its lots lie vacant, covered with weeds and scrub and littered with trash. Its population is almost all black. To the police, it's a jungle; to the civil authorities, a tinderbox.

At about 5 A.M. on Saturday, April 28, 1973, two people walked down New York Boulevard, the thoroughfare that bisects South Jamaica: Add Armstead, a 50-year-old junkyard "burner," and his ten-year-old "stepson," Clifford Glover. In the opposite direction came an unmarked police car carrying two plainclothes officers: the driver, Walter Scott, and the passenger ("recorder," in police parlance), Thomas Shea. Armstead and the Glover boy were black; Scott and Shea were white.

The car made a U-turn and pulled up alongside the two blacks. Shea jumped out. A few seconds later, Clifford Glover lay dying in an adjoining empty lot, felled by a bullet from Shea's gun.

As always when a policeman fires a fatal shot, the department's brass descended on the scene to ferret out the facts. Throughout the day, Shea repeated his account over and over again, both at the scene and back at the 103rd precinct stationhouse. Finally, an assistant district attorney took a formal, stenotyped statement. After giving Shea a *Miranda* warning, Martin Bracken asked:

Q. Now, in your own words, can you tell me what happened at approximately five A.M. on the morning of April 28, 1973, in the vicinity of New York Boulevard and 112th Road?

A. Yes. I was proceeding to the stationhouse on New York Boulevard with a prior—to continue a prior investigation. . . . We were proceeding north on New York Boulevard when my partner drew my attention to two male Negroes who were walking south on New York Boulevard. They fit the description of a past armed robbery of a taxicab. . . .

And they were just crossing [the] street. My partner made a U-turn. He was driving the vehicle. He made a U-turn. We were abreast of the two individuals. I stepped from the vehicle with my shield and my ID card, which is all in one folder, and I says, "Stop! Police officers." . . .

Q. Then what happened at that time?

A. At that point, the fellow in the yellow waist jacket with a white hat [Glover] said, "Fuck you! You ain't taking me." And he started to run, followed by the other male with the brown leather jacket.

Q. Where did they run?

A. They ran down New York Boulevard for a short distance and then cut into a wooded area.

Q. What did your fellow officer do?

A. He took his vehicle and drove around to 112th Road and came in along the fence from 112th Road.

Q. What was his name?

A. Walter Scott. . . . At this time, I chased the two suspects. They ran to the fence and started to run down the fence. I started to run down behind them. At that point, I seen the male Negro in the yellow jacket go where his front pocket would be and as his hand came back there was a black type revolver in it. . . .

Q. How far were you behind them at this time?

A. I was approximately ten to fifteen feet behind them.

Q. What did the individual do at this time?

A. He started to turn with the gun in his hand and at this point I fired three shots.

Q. What happened then?

A. The male Negro in the yellow waist jacket staggered forward and the other Negro—he handed the gun to him and said, "I'm shot." At this time, the male Negro in the brown leather jacket [Armstead] continued running and as the yellow jacket staggered he passed him the gun.

Q. Where was your partner at this time?

A. He was behind me.

Q. Directly behind you?

A. Well, I don't know exactly, because I stopped at this point to see if I could give any aid and find out what was wrong with the shot individual. And I yelled to my partner to continue to chase the other individual. And my partner continued the chase and I lost sight of him. I then heard two reports that I believed to be gunshots.

Scott supported Shea's account, adding that he'd chased the second suspect into a clump of trees beyond the fence and traded shots with him, but the man had escaped.

Armstead gave a different version. He'd fled the scene and flagged down a police car about two blocks away. He'd been brought back to the lot and placed under arrest. At the station-house he claimed that Shea had jumped from the car without identifying himself as a policeman. He'd yelled, "Stop, you black son-of-a-bitch!", then started firing. Armstead insisted that neither he nor his "stepson" had had a gun and that no gun had been passed between them. He denied exchanging shots with Scott.

A search of the area proved fruitless. The police could not even find the spent slugs—at least three from Shea's gun and one from Scott's. But the following day a toy pistol was found in a lot across the street and two days later a starter's pistol, for firing blanks, was unearthed in a nearby sewer.

News of the fatal shooting spread quickly through South Jamaica. By mid-afternoon, angry blacks, led by the local assemblyman, Guy Brewer, had gathered outside the stationhouse demanding action. The department's deputy commissioner for community affairs, Roosevelt Dunning, came in to try to pacify them.

The authorities were in a quandary. Two weeks before, Queens District Attorney Thomas J. Mackell had been indicted for conspiracy and misconduct and had resigned just in time to escape removal proceedings. Handed the hot potato of the Shea case, Bracken, the weekend "duty" man, contacted acting D.A. Frederick Ludwig, who immediately tossed it back to him. At about 7 P.M., Shea was arrested for murder.

To some, it seemed a patent attempt to defuse the explosive community. If so, it failed. That night saw the first of three days of scattered violence in South Jamaica as hordes of black youths swarmed through the streets smashing windows, tossing firebombs and looting stores. On another front, black militants picketed Shea's home in suburban Brentwood, Long Island, and poison-pen letters were sent to him and his family. Shea, free on $25,000 bond, was placed under police protection.

Ludwig, flustered, fluttered like a shuttlecock. On Sunday, after scores of angry off-duty policemen picketed the courthouse, he reduced the charge against Shea to negligent homicide. The following day, he reversed himself again and reinstated the murder charge. On June 12, a grand jury duly indicted Shea for murder, saying he'd shown "a depraved indifference to human life."

For those who kept such records, the case set two firsts: Glover was the youngest person ever killed by a New York City cop and, according to newspaper reports, Shea was the first policeman to be charged with murder for a killing in the line of duty.*

The battle lines were drawn for a classic confrontation in the deadly warfare between the black community and the blue knights of New York's Finest.

The police brass may have supported the D.A.'s action, but the rank-and-file certainly did not. Robert McKiernan, the president of the Patrolmen's Benevolent Association, called Shea's arrest an "outrage" and the PBA put up $10,000 for his defense. Evseroff was retained as trial counsel.

After kicking around the courts for nearly a year, the case came up for trial on Wednesday, May 8, before Justice Bernard Dubin in Queens County Supreme Court. At the appointed hour, 10 A.M., Evseroff took a place in the front row of Part IV on the third floor of the Queens County Criminal Courts Building and waited while the court plodded through the calendar.

In the row behind sat Shea, at 37 a surly, stocky man with a ruddy, pockmarked face. The long locks and mustache he'd worn at the time of the shooting had been trimmed off. He wore, as he would throughout the trial, his only suit, of dark brown. Beside Shea sat James Cahill, a prematurely gray PBA lawyer who would serve as Evseroff's co-counsel, McKiernan and Shea's ever-present bodyguard of two plainclothes policemen.

Justice Dubin is a roly-poly man with a shock of silver hair, a big nose and black horn-rimmed glasses. He'd climbed the ladder of Queens' Democratic politics—assistant D.A., assemblyman, Criminal Court judge—to his Supreme Court sinecure. Although he blustered long and loud, he had little command

---

*It turned out that Shea was *not* the first. After his trial, James B.M. McNally, a retired Appellate Division justice, reminded *The New York Times* (June 30, 1974) of the 1924 trial of Patrolman Robert McAllister, who was tried for murder and acquitted and who went on to become a deputy inspector.

of his courtroom. Just as schoolchildren instinctively know which teachers they may terrorize, so lawyers had learned that Dubin's docket didn't demand punctuality.

"Isn't there a lawyer here on any case?" the judge shouted as the clerk droned through the calendar call. "Oh, boy! This is ridiculous. You mean to say we have eight or ten different lawyers and not one is here, except you [he pointed at one] and your client's not here."

Evseroff saw it as a good opportunity for a smoke break. He spent the next hour, as he would the opening hour or two of almost every trial day, pacing the corridor.

When the case was finally called, he took his place beside Shea and Cahill at the defense table facing the prosecutors—the trial attorney, Albert Gaudelli, a short, chubby man with a full-moon forehead and a toothbrush mustache, and his bureau chief, Thomas Demakos, squarely built and ruggedly handsome. Evseroff soon discovered that both his adversaries had the annoying habit of interrupting him in mid-sentence.

Gaudelli immediately objected to Cahill's presence at the defense table: "There may be a problem, because he may be a witness."

As PBA counsel, Cahill had represented both Shea and Scott at their interrogations.

After a lengthy colloquy, Justice Dubin ruled: "He's a lawyer. He's got a right to represent someone. . . . I don't see that I have a right to exclude counsel."

Evseroff had called for *Huntley* and *Wade* hearings to determine the legal admissibility of Shea's statements and the eyewitness identifications of him. He had little hope of winning on either point.

"The purpose of it is to see who their witnesses are and to give us a chance to get a little defense in."

During the two days of the *Huntley* hearing, Gaudelli called eight witnesses (seven policemen and Assistant D.A. Bracken) who had talked with Shea on the fatal day, either at the scene or at the stationhouse. Shea's comments fell into three categories: first, offhand remarks he'd made to the officers at the scene;

more formal interviews by the police brass; and finally, transcribed statements, complete with *Miranda* warnings, taken by Bracken and by Inspector Robert Johnson.

Only Johnson, one of the department's few ranking blacks, said that Shea had given an account that differed from the others. When he'd questioned Shea at the lot about 10 A.M., Johnson said, the patrolman had not mentioned Glover's gun or its passage to Armstead. Johnson said he'd made no notes of the conversation but when he'd taken a formal statement a few hours later, Shea had mentioned the gun.

"That inspector saying he changed his story and he didn't have any notes! I'll eat his eyeballs out in front of a jury."

Evseroff confined his cross-examinations to asking if Shea had appeared ill, drunk or drugged, just in case, as had been rumored, the prosecution tried to show that he'd been drinking. All the witnesses said Shea had seemed normal, if a little excited.

Gaudelli was surprisingly ill-prepared for such a major case. With some witnesses he did not have the documents he was required to turn over to the defense and he didn't even know that some existed. At points, he was surprised by what his own witnesses said.

Justice Dubin's growing impatience with the prosecutor was evident. It culminated when Captain Leonard Flanagan was on the stand.

Evseroff concluded his cross-examination: "I have no more questions of this witness."

"Do you, Mr. District Attorney?" Justice Dubin asked.

"No, sir."

"Well, I do." He turned to the witness. "At the time you asked these questions, was he under investigation?"

"I don't think so."

"Was he in custody?"

"No."

"Thank you." He turned back to Gaudelli: "Obvious questions."

When court convened for the hearing's second day, Demakos

called Evseroff aside and told him that the new D.A., Nicholas Ferraro, had directed that *he* try the case with Gaudelli assisting. Demakos added that he planned to ask for a week's adjournment to give himself time to prepare.

"What am I going to tell him—'No'? He'll get it anyway. But what I want is a direction from the judge that I'm actually on trial in this case, so I don't get glommed into starting a trial somewhere else."

But when court broke for lunch, Demakos, apparently realizing that a delay would push the trial's end into the long hot summer, approached Evseroff again. "Jack, I'm not going to ask for a delay," he said.

"Why not?"

Demakos shrugged. "I'm just going to have to work my balls off over the weekend."

"You're not going to start picking a jury tomorrow?"

"Oh, no."

Evseroff produced no witnesses at the *Huntley* hearing. When Gaudelli concluded, Evseroff made his motions. He did not object to the transcribed statements. But he did object to the other statements Shea had given to the police brass because he'd been given no warnings, even though he'd obviously been the target of the investigation. "When a man is interrogated over and over again by teams of policemen, they're not talking to him to learn the time of day." He also objected to the offhand comments at the scene, because the officers couldn't differentiate who'd said what, Shea or Scott.

But Justice Dubin ruled that *all* the statements were admissible. He then ordered the prosecution to call its witnesses for the *Wade* hearing.

"There is nothing to be the subject of a *Wade* hearing," Gaudelli replied.

"They ain't got no eyeball. They ain't got no witnesses. They ain't got no one except Armstead. It seems to me that to convict a cop of murder you've got to have a lot more than just Armstead and a theory. It just won't work."

Demakos asked for an adjournment until Monday.

"Why wait till Monday?" Justice Dubin asked. "Why not tomorrow?"

Demakos explained that a fresh jury panel would be available on Monday. Justice Dubin reluctantly agreed to the delay.

Where Gaudelli had been stumbling, Evseroff had been smooth. Yet he was also playing it by ear. Before Monday's session, as he sipped coffee with his client and Cahill in Ann's Cafe across the street from the courthouse, he had Shea sketch the layout of the lot on a paper napkin. In 13 months, he'd never visited the scene.

"You think I'm crazy! M'ken dort geharget verden." [*A man could get killed there.*]

Then they crossed the street to start picking a jury.

"Judge Liebowitz told me many, many years ago that in his opinion the selection of a jury was seventy-five percent of the trial of a criminal case. I agree.

"There are no hard and fast rules with respect to the selection of a jury. It varies with each case."

In several recent celebrated criminal cases, the defense retained sociologists to conduct surveys to determine what kinds of jurors would be most likely to acquit: Jay Schulman and a team of Columbia University sociologists in the cases of the "Harrisburg Seven," "Camden 28" and "Gainesville Eight"; a team of black psychologists in the trial of Angela Davis; and "think tank" operator Marty Herbst in the trial of former cabinet members John Mitchell and Maurice Stans. But Evseroff preferred to work by more traditional rules of thumb.

"It's a concept that's foreign to me. In picking a jury, you should rely on your own experience, your knowledge of the community, your voir dire *and what rapport, if any, you can establish—gut reactions."*

He needed no scientific survey to tell him what kind of jury he wanted. In the case of a white policeman charged with the murder of a black boy he wanted a jury of 12 hardhats. He was hopeful that he would get it: After all, Queens is Archie Bunker country.

"Can you imagine a jury in Queens convicting a cop for shooting a Negro kid? Have you talked to the Jews in Forest Hills who live near the project? Or the Poles in Woodside who walk around with American flags in their lapels?"

Justice Dubin's courtroom ran with its usual efficiency. The trial was scheduled to start at 10 A.M. Not until noon was the calendar call completed, and it took another half-hour before the panel of 66 prospective jurors was led into the corridor outside the courtroom.

Like most New York City jury panels, it was predominantly male (women may opt off jury duty simply by claiming their sex) and composed largely of civil servants and utility employees, who receive full salary while on jury call and thus cannot claim exemption on grounds of economic hardship. It was also disproportionately white and middle-aged. Only seven of the 66 were black; only one of the 66 was a woman.

Evseroff sized up the group and murmured aloud, "It looks good."

The prospective jurors were led into the courtroom's spectator seats.

"The people move the trial of *The People* versus *Thomas Shea. . . .*" Demakos said.

"The defendant is ready," Evseroff answered.

The clerk pulled the names of 12 veniremen from a drum and the jury box was filled. The dozen included two blacks and one Puerto Rican.

Justice Dubin rose to deliver his introductory remarks. Arms flailing, his big belly bouncing beneath his black robe, he resembled "What's-the-story-Jerry?" of the TV commercials. Among other things, he asked the jurors to cast aside any racial or religious prejudice: "When you sit in this courtroom, we're all the same color, we're all the same religion, we're all the same nationality. There is no prejudice in this courtroom."

Wishful thinking. The racial issue erupted a few minutes

later when Demakos took over for his *voir dire*, "to speak truly," the examination of prospective jurors. He asked if any member of the panel knew any party to the case or was familiar with the scene of the crime.

One juror, a white machinist, raised his hand. "I live right there," he said. "They had a riot there and everything else. The neighborhood—you couldn't live there for two days."

He was excused for cause, as were seven others who indicated bias or inability to serve at a three- or four-week trial because of personal, medical or financial reasons. Those excused included the two blacks.

More names were pulled from the drum and a panel of 12 was finally seated for closer questioning:

1) a lighting engineer, 30ish, German, single.

2) a postal clerk, 40ish, Puerto Rican, married with three children.

3) the president of the Cemetery Workers Union, 50ish, Italian, married with four children.

Under Demakos's questioning, the union official, Savino Cimaglia, said he faced a 20-day sentence for contempt of court for defying a no-strike injunction handed down in another part of Queens Supreme Court. Yet he vowed to follow the law as defined by Justice Dubin.

"Despite the fact that you didn't obey the judge's order?" Justice Dubin asked incredulously.

"Objection," Evseroff snapped.

"Overruled," Justice Dubin said, allowing his own question.

"Yes," Cimaglia replied.

Cimaglia added that he also faced strike charges in New Jersey. He had been arrested while on a hunger strike. "They locked me up for praying in church."

"Were you praying for food?" Justice Dubin asked.

Demakos pressed Cimaglia on incidents that had occurred during the strike.

Evseroff jumped up again: "Objection, Your Honor. Now we're trying a cemetery case."

The attorneys quickly became embroiled in the first of many verbal clashes which Justice Dubin proved unable to control.

When order was restored, Demakos resumed his *voir dire:*

4) a gas station manager, 40ish, Irish, married with two children.

5) a Transit Authority supervisor, 50ish, Italian, married with four children. He worked with transit policemen and had two nephews on the force.

6) a Con Edison mechanic, 30ish, Irish, married with two children.

7) a subway motorman, 40ish, Irish, married with four children.

8) a flamboyantly dressed Florida real-estate salesman, 50ish, Jewish, single, with a head of hair that looked like a cheap toupee.

9) another Transit Authority supervisor, 50ish, Italian, married with one child.

10) a crew-cut post office manager, 40ish, German, married with three children.

11) a bookbinder, 60ish, German, married with two children.

12) a retired textile company manager, 60ish, Jewish, married with three children.

In questioning the textile man Demakos mentioned for the first time that the victim was "a ten-year-old black boy." Evseroff objected that the prosecutor was "injecting an element of racism in this trial."

"Just say it's a nine-year-old [*sic*] boy," Justice Dubin ordered.

All the information was elicited by Demakos. When Evseroff's turn came, there was little new that he could glean. Yet he questioned the panel at length, in part to ingratiate himself, in part to press his case.

"When I ask questions on the voir dire, *I'm just pumping them full of 'reasonable doubt.' "*

He zeroed in on number 7, questioning him closely, not in an effort to disqualify him—the subway motorman was acceptable to the defense—but as a diversion. Moments later, he posed the same questions to the Puerto Rican postal clerk. He did not want to appear bigoted by first questioning the panel's only minority member.

Finally, he asked if any member of the panel knew of any other reason why he couldn't serve. Juror number 1, the lighting engineer, raised his hand and stated his reason at the sidebar: His religious scruples wouldn't let him return a guilty verdict. Justice Dubin excused him for cause. Since the questioning had lasted so long, his place was not immediately filled.

Then number 9, the second Transit Authority supervisor, raised his hand. He whispered that number 8, the real-estate salesman, had the worst case of halitosis he'd ever seen and he couldn't stand to sit next to him for three weeks. Justice Dubin ruled that that was not a valid ground to be excused, but Evseroff almost felt tempted to say, "Don't worry, buddy, that's not going to be your problem." The salesman struck him as "a head case."

Under New York law, in a murder case the prosecution and defense have 20 peremptory challenges each, that is, they may excuse 20 prospective jurors without stating a reason. A rack containing the cards of the 11 prospective jurors in the box was passed to the prosecution. Demakos excused numbers 3, 4, 5, 6, 7 and 11 (Cimaglia, the gas station manager, the first Transit Authority supervisor, the Con Ed mechanic and the bookbinder). Then the rack was passed to the defense. Evseroff excused numbers 2 and 8 (the Puerto Rican postal clerk and the real-estate salesman with halitosis).

The three who were left were sworn in as jurors numbers 1, 2 and 3: the foreman, Leo Savarino, the second Transit Authority supervisor; Charles Kutch, the crew-cut postal manager; and William Seplowe, the retired textile man.

The process had taken all afternoon. The attorneys had gone through 20 of the panel of 66 and chosen only three. Their challenges were a mirror-image of those the prosecution and defense normally make: the defense challenging liberals, "bleeding-hearts" and members of racial minorities; the prosecution challenging hardhat, law-and-order types. The prosecution had used five of its 20 peremptory challenges; the defense, two.

Evseroff was pleased with the three jurors chosen; he didn't concern himself with the might-have-beens, those rejected by the prosecution. Before heading back to his office and the late-afternoon round of appointments, he paused to point out to a black newsman that it had been Demakos, not he, who had first raised the racial issue.

Jury selection resumed Tuesday morning, but at the outset it was juror exemption. Kutch told Justice Dubin that a sudden illness in the family made it impossible for him to serve, and he was excused. Then Savarino explained that he feared conflicting pressures on his job from the blacks he supervised and from the transit policemen he worked with if he continued. He too was excused. Seplowe was left as foreman and the lone sworn juror.

Justice Dubin threw up his hands and exclaimed, "It looks like we're going backwards."

Fifteen more prospects, including the only woman on the panel, were excused before the box was filled again:

2) a retired postal clerk, 65, black, married with six children.

3) an army clerk, 42, Irish, single.

4) a computer programmer, 30ish, Scandinavian, single.

5) a truck driver, 50ish, Italian, married with two children.

6) a retired insurance salesman, 60ish, Jewish, married with four children, the only venireman who read *The New York Times.*

7) a hippie-haired sheetmetal worker, 20ish, Italian, single, member of a gun club.

8) a bearded Western Electric installer, 20ish, Italian, single.

9) a frozen-food salesman, 50ish, German, married with nine children.

10) a bearded accountant, 50ish, Jewish, married with three children.

11) a sanitation worker, 40ish, Italian, married with four children.

12) a truck driver, 50ish, Italian, married with two children.

During the questioning, Justice Dubin raised the possibility that he might sequester the jury.

The prosecution used four peremptory challenges to eliminate numbers 3, 5, 7 and 9. Evseroff quickly knocked off numbers 2, 4, 6 and 10, hesitated for several minutes, then pulled the card of number 8.

The two remaining men were shepherded into the front row to be sworn. Then number 11 volunteered that no one had asked him, unlike the others, if he had any friends who were policemen. Evseroff deliberately had *not.* The juror added that he had a very close friend on the force, and Demakos promptly used another peremptory challenge and excused him. Then number 12 said he couldn't be sequestered, so the judge excused him.

Despite the lack of progress, Evseroff was pleased with the strategic situation.

"He's got to pick eleven jurors with nine peremptory challenges," he noted to Cahill and Shea as they caucused in the men's room during the morning recess. He speculated that Demakos had left jurors 11 and 12 only because he'd feared to use up more challenges. The defense had 13 left.

More cards were pulled, but only eight men were in the box when the initial panel of 66 was exhausted. A new panel was summoned after lunch, an hour late.

"It looks O.K.," Evseroff said.

Of the 54 on the new panel, only two were black, only two women. Women, Evseroff theorized, were more likely to sympathize with the ten-year-old victim.

Five more potential jurors were excused for cause before the box was filled. Among them was a plump blonde woman named Miriam Seplowe.

"Might we ask if this lady is related to the foreman of our

jury?" Evseroff asked as she stepped forward. He'd seen them together at lunch.

"My wife," Seplowe said.

She was excused before she reached the jury box.

The lawyers questioned the new panel:

2) a sales manager for Macy's, 50ish, Jewish, married with one child.

3) a paper-company employee, 60ish, Italian, married with one child. He'd been convicted of bookmaking and for dealing in fireworks.

4) a State Department of Labor investigator, 60ish, towering in physique, Irish, married with five children, two of them policemen.

5) a typewriter repairman, 50ish, German, married with one child.

6) a letter carrier with the build of a football tackle, 50ish, WASP, married with two children.

7) a telephone installer, 30ish, Irish, married with four children.

8) a retired restaurant owner, 60ish, Jewish. (His family was never elicited.)

9) a subway motorman, 60ish, black, married with three children.

10) a sanitation worker, 30ish, black, married with two children.

11) a big bearded man of 27, a dispatcher who had once worked for Catholic Charities, Irish, divorced.

12) a data processor, 30ish, German, married with two children.

The prosecution used its twelfth and thirteenth challenges to excuse numbers 7 and 12. Evseroff knocked off numbers 9, 10 and 11 (the two blacks and the onetime charity worker), then pulled the card of number 5, the typewriter repairman.

"I was iffy about him and I could afford the challenge."

Five jurors were sworn: Sidney Horn, the Macy's manager; Dominic Consalvo, the onetime bookmaker; William Meehan, the towering labor investigator; Gordon Peck, the muscular mailman; and George Stell, the retired restaurant owner.

So the selection process went into its third day. Two more prospects were excused before the box was filled again:

7) a welder, 50ish, Irish, single.

8) a postal employee, 50ish, German, married with five children. His father-in-law was a retired policeman and his brother was also a cop.

9) a long-haired motorcycle mechanic, 28, Jewish, single.

10) an engineer, 50ish, German, married with four children.

11) a retired telephone company employee, 60ish, German, single.

12) an engineer for the navy, 50ish, Jewish, married with two children.

Evseroff went after the motorcycle mechanic in an unsuccessful effort to elicit some submerged bias.

"I don't know anybody involved with motorcycles who hasn't had a run-in with the cops."

Then he turned to the Jewish engineer. At this stage of the selection process the name of the game was to excuse a potentially hostile juror without consuming a challenge. This time Evseroff was successful. The prospect said he couldn't be sequestered because "my wife can't handle the finances."

Then Consalvo raised his hand and asked to speak with the judge. His wife, he said, had reminded him the night before that a cousin had been shot a few weeks before by a policeman during a stickup.

"Last night at home I start thinking about these things. I didn't sleep all night."

He was excused. Evseroff speculated that he'd been talking not to his wife, but to some of "the boys."

Then Seplowe raised his hand. His emphysema had flared up, he said, and he too was excused. This time, Evseroff speculated, the juror *had* been talking to his wife.

The number of sworn jurors was reduced to four. Horn became the panel's third foreman in three days.

Demakos asked that the box be filled again, but Justice Dubin directed him to exercise his challenges on the five prospects in the box. Demakos excused numbers 7 and 8, the Irish welder and the German postman. Evseroff eliminated numbers 9 and 10, the motorcycle mechanic and the German engineer.

"He [number 10] gave me bad vibes. He was too anxious to serve."

Frank Gedgard, the retired telephone man, became the fifth sworn juror.

"How he left that guy on I'll never know."

Evseroff remained pleased with the strategic situation: "He's got to pick seven jurors with only five challenges left." The defense had seven challenges to go.

Five more prospects were excused before the box was filled again. Demakos asked to make an application, but Justice Dubin ordered him to start questioning the panel; he said he'd entertain the application after lunch. Evseroff suspected what it would be. Before he went to lunch, he called his office and had Jeff Rabin check the law on granting additional challenges. Before he returned to court, he made another call and came before the bench armed with the appropriate citations.

With the sworn and potential jurors excluded from the courtroom, Demakos asked Justice Dubin to grant both sides additional challenges because jurors had been excused after they'd been sworn.

"We do not consent . . ." Evseroff said. He called Demakos's plea "an argument made by a district attorney who has not used his peremptory challenges as prudently as he might have." He cited the cases to support his view.

Justice Dubin agreed, saying he knew of "no law that allows further challenges."

The jurors were brought into court and Demakos resumed his questioning of the new panel:

6) a hippie-haired telephone company employee, 25, Italian, single.

7) a bank guard, 60ish, Irish. Although he carried a gun, he'd never fired it except in practice.

8) a bearded man who insisted he was not a "social worker," as stated on his card, but a "supervising human resources specialist," 30ish, Jewish, single.

9) an accountant at Merrill Lynch, 50ish, Irish, single.

10) a retired liquor-store owner, 60ish, Jewish, married with one child.

11) a billing clerk, 30ish, German, married.

12) an electrician for American Airlines, 40ish, black, married with four children.

Under Demakos's questioning, the Irish accountant said he couldn't predict how he might act in the jury room. Demakos challenged him for cause. Evseroff, eager to have Demakos consume another peremptory challenge, objected and questioned the prospect, "testing the challenge" as it's called. The venireman reversed himself, but Justice Dubin granted the challenge for cause, despite the way a "clever lawyer" had twisted his words.

Demakos used his sixteenth peremptory challenge to eliminate number 7, the bank guard. Evseroff challenged numbers 6, 8 and 12 (the hippie-haired telephone man, the "human resources specialist" and the black electrician). Of all the blacks who'd appeared in the box, he'd struck Evseroff as the best prospect.

"The only reason I didn't take him is he has to go back to St. Alban's."

William Heller, the retired liquor-store owner, and Daniel Ehring, the billing clerk, were sworn as jurors numbers 6 and 7. Each side had four peremptory challenges left.

"You're even," Justice Dubin said. "The situation solved itself."

Nine more prospects were excused before the box was filled:

8) a retired United Parcel Service employee, 60ish, Irish, married with three children.

9) a retired bank clerk, 60ish, Irish, married with five children.

10) a retired clerk, 60ish, Italian, married.

11) a clerical employee in a textile firm, 50ish, Italian, married with one child.

12) a foreman for Brooklyn Union Gas, 50ish, Irish, married. His brother-in-law was a retired policeman and he looked more like a cop than many of those who'd testified.

The prosecution's seventeenth and eighteenth challenges eliminated numbers 8 and 9, the two retired Irishmen. Juror number 10 struck Evseroff as "a little unstable," so he used his seventeenth challenge on him.

Angelo Sicurella, the textile clerk, and Martin O'Brien, the gas company foreman, were sworn in as jurors numbers 8 and 9.

Six more prospective jurors were called, but only one was left in the box when Evseroff rose for his part of the *voir dire.* Privately, the defense attorney grumbled that Justice Dubin was excusing for cause so the prosecution wouldn't exhaust its challenges. He questioned the lone venireman, a 29-year-old professional magician with an arrogant air, at length.

"No challenges," Demakos announced when Evseroff finished.

"Peremptory?" the judge asked.

"No peremptory."

The court officer handed the rack to Evseroff. With a look of contempt he flung away the lone card.

"I got up to examine him and I knew I was going to challenge him. But it gave me another chance to get my thing in."

Evseroff's eighteenth challenge had exhausted the second panel. On Thursday morning, a new panel of 30 was brought into the courtroom. In age, it was somewhat younger than the previous panels and it included six women and four blacks.

Three prospects were called to the box:

10) a female social worker, 30ish, Italian, single. Evseroff elicited that she was a ballet buff.

11) a female supervisor in the Manhattan probation department, petite, black, 40ish, married to a postal worker.

12) a telephone company employee, 30ish, Irish, married with two children. Evseroff elicited that he was a member of a gun club.

"The jury is satisfactory to the people," Demakos said.

The rack was presented to Evseroff and he faced a dilemma. Neither of the women was satisfactory to him, but if he challenged both, he'd be left with two places to fill and only one challenge. He decided to risk the known peril rather than the unknown. He used his nineteenth challenge to excuse the Italian social worker.

Mrs. Edrica Campbell and Dennis Connolly were sworn in as jurors numbers 10 and 11.

"I think she was the best black juror I saw. She's Establishment."

One seat remained. The first prospect was a bosomy blonde divorcée in a miniskirt. When she said she'd been dating a policeman, Demakos used his nineteenth challenge to eliminate her. Evseroff called a sidebar conference and chided the prosecutor: Why not leave a little pulchritude on the panel?

Two more prospects were excused for cause, then a 60ish IRS examiner, Irish, single, a former naval intelligence agent, took the seat. Demakos asked if he'd read about the case. He had. Demakos asked if he'd formed an opinion about it.

"No opinion—except an opinion that you couldn't form an opinion on what was in the papers."

Demakos used his last challenge to excuse him.

A retired Jewish furrier was called, a widower who spoke with a thick accent. Evseroff asked how old he was.

"Seventy-two," the man replied and he was automatically excused. The cut-off age for jurors in New York is 70.

Evseroff was pleased. He'd eliminated the prospect without consuming his last precious challenge.

Next was a retired garage attendant, 67, German, married

with four children. Demakos had no choice but to accept him.

"If Your Honor please," Evseroff said, "the juror is satisfactory to the defense."

"I'd have to be crazy to waste a challenge on him."

George Rickehoff was sworn in as juror number 12.

The afternoon session was devoted to selection of four alternates. Each prospect was questioned individually; each side had two peremptory challenges per seat.

Of the four alternates, number 1 was the most important since he'd fill in if any juror couldn't serve. The first prospect was a black social worker who was excused by Evseroff. Next, a black who worked for the Maritime Administration was also excused by Evseroff. Demakos knocked off an Irish railroad clerk. Finally, Thomas Gucciardo, a 30ish, bushy-bearded engineer in the city's hospital system, was accepted by both sides.

Both sides quickly agreed on alternate number 2, Mrs. Catherine Dudzinski, the plump wife of a transit worker.

The prosecution challenged a retired sanitation worker for the third seat. Then both sides agreed on Amerigo Filosa, a retired postman.

Filling the last seat took longer. Evseroff excused a black salesman. Then the seat was filled by a subway motorman who was divorced.

"Who do you live with?" Evseroff asked.

"Myself—me and my dog."

Evseroff cupped a hand over his mouth and whispered to Justice Dubin, "Me, too." He told the prospect, "I understand the situation—for reasons I don't care to go into."

Demakos immediately challenged the prospect.

The prosecutor also excused a navy electrician, while Evseroff challenged a black postal driver. Finally, both sides agreed on Mrs. Grace Seller, a 60ish postal clerk.

The process had taken four days. One spectator suggested that it would have been simpler to send a court officer into the subway, have him round up the first 12 people he found and bring them back to court—with a Spanish interpreter! Evseroff was content with the panel, expressing doubt only about Mrs.

Campbell. But he felt that when the chips were down, she'd go along with the others. On the other hand, Assemblyman Brewer took one look at the panel and muttered, "There's not a chance of convicting with that jury. Even the hippie [Gucciardo] looks like a conservative hippie."

Gaudelli opened on Friday, May 17, relating Armstead's version of the incident. He told how Shea had been questioned and how he'd claimed that the boy had had a gun. He said an "extensive search" had uncovered no weapon and called the shooting "reckless and without any justification." He was finished in ten minutes.

Evseroff was briefer, but louder. He gave Shea's version and told how black protestors had gathered outside the stationhouse:

"Things began to happen at that stationhouse. . . . Patrolman Shea was 'it' and he was arrested for murder."

He said the authorities then tried to justify the arrest. Pointing a finger at the prosecution table, he accused Gaudelli of threatening Scott with criminal charges unless he changed his story and implicated Shea.

The practical effect of his opening was to put the prosecution on the defense and to "steal" the headlines with the charge that Gaudelli had threatened Scott. Reporters grabbed Cahill and PBA President McKiernan in the corridor and pressed them for details. A black reporter cornered Evseroff. "Is this a political trial?" he asked.

"I'm not saying."

The trial received considerable coverage. A dozen reporters and artists from three television stations were stationed inside the courtroom, while camera crews photographed Evseroff and Shea as they arrived at the courthouse each morning. By its nature, the coverage was pro-prosecution: The capsulized accounts could carry the meat of the testimony, but not the nuances of cross-examination. Yet Evseroff was not upset at the bad press.

"The worse it appears, the better I like it."

A victory would make him appear a miracle worker. And, of course, a bad press was better than none at all.

During the first day, Demakos presented technical evidence from a policeman who'd mapped the lot and from three others who'd photographed it. Evseroff didn't dispute their exhibits, but he subjected them to nit-picking cross-examination "to needle Demakos on the little things."

When court resumed on Monday afternoon, Demakos called his star witness, Add Armstead. He was a short, wiry man of 51 who wore a checked sports jacket, no tie and carried a cap in his hand. He spoke in monosyllables with the loud, forced tone of one who isn't used to speaking, especially in public.

Armstead said he lived at 109–50 New York Boulevard with "Louise" Glover and (at the time of Clifford's death) her four children—two his, two by another man. He also had nine children by his first wife. Armstead admitted that he'd served a six-month sentence for statutory rape and another 23 days (in lieu of a $125 fine) for having had stolen license plates on his car.

He said he worked at an auto-wrecking yard at 115–07 New York Boulevard, about six blocks from his home. On the morning of April 28, 1973, he'd left home at about 4:50 A.M. to walk to work with Clifford. In his pockets he'd carried a monkey wrench, a pair of pliers and $114 in cash.

"In your own words, tell the jury what happened . . ." Demakos said.

"I heard a car pulled up to the curb," he started. "I turned."

A white man had jumped out with his fist clenched.

"He said, 'You black son-of-a-bitch!' I whirled to my right. I heard a gunshot. I ran into the lot. I heard another gunshot."

Armstead said he'd kept running through the lot. He'd tripped and "Clifford fell on my leg." He'd gotten up, run into the bushes and climbed a fence to emerge on the street. He'd flagged down a police car and told the officers, "There's somebody shooting at me over there." Back at the lot, "I saw my son laying on the ground."

"Did you have a gun . . .?" Demakos asked.

"Nope."

"Did your son have a gun?"

"Nope."

"Did your son hand you a gun after he fell?"

"Nope."

But he admitted that he'd kept a gun at the junkyard, which he'd turned over to the police.

After a half-hour, Evseroff took over for cross-examination: "You told us on direct that you work at a certain place. What's the name of that place, Mr. Armstead?"

The witness sat silent for nearly a minute, then pulled a card from his pocket and read, "Power Automotive"—the place where he'd worked for 11 years!

It was a point Evseroff had gleaned from his cursory reading of Armstead's grand-jury testimony, which the prosecution, under the state Court of Appeals' *Rosario* ruling, was required to turn over to the defense.

Evseroff hopscotched, confronting Armstead with variant accounts he'd given to the police or grand jury. Armstead said he couldn't remember what he'd said. He denied that Shea (whom he was never asked to identify) had flashed a shield or identified himself as a policeman. He insisted that he'd heard only two shots, though he'd told Inspector Johnson that he'd heard "about five."

"All I know, I was running," he explained.

Why had he run?

"Because he called me a 'black son-of-a-bitch' and I had money in my pocket."

After 35 minutes, Evseroff asked for a brief recess. He wanted to hit his next point with the jury fresh and relaxed.

He returned to the dash across the lot: "Did you know your son was shot at that time?"

"Nope."

"Do you consider him your son?"

"I call him my son."

"And do you have a feeling of affection for him?"

"Yep."

"And do you worry about his welfare, Mr. Armstead?"

"I worried about him."

"At no time did you ever stop . . . to see what happened with respect to Clifford Glover, isn't that a fact, Mr. Armstead?"

"Yep. Right."

"You never went back to see if he was shot?"

"Nope."

"You never looked to see what condition he was in when he tripped over your leg?"

"Nope."

"You never looked back to see who was coming at you, did you?"

"Nope."

"You never looked back when you heard a second shot fired in the lot, did you?"

"Nope."

"You loved this boy, didn't you, Mr. Armstead?"

"Yep."

Under further questioning, Armstead insisted that he'd been going to work at 5 A.M., even though he'd never otherwise started before 7 or 7:30—a point Evseroff had gleaned by having private detective Herman Race interview Armstead's boss.

In conclusion, the defense attorney elicited that Armstead had been arrested for illegal possession of the gun and also for having a blackjack in his home. Both charges were still pending (indeed, they'd been on the court calendar that very day), but Armstead insisted that he'd made no deal with the D.A.

"I think I did pretty good with him. You never know how you're doing while you're doing it."

Over the next three days, Demakos called the policemen who'd arrived at the scene and the senior officers and Assistant D.A. Bracken who'd interviewed Shea. Evseroff cross-examined them closely (though he was surprisingly tame with Inspector Johnson), making each repeat again and again Shea's account of the incident.

"I'm putting the defense in through their witnesses."

On Tuesday, two policemen, Thomas Scott (no relation to Shea's partner) and Albert Farrell, told of statements they'd taken from Armstead. They had not been turned over to the defense after Armstead's direct, as required under *Rosario.* Evseroff moved for a mistrial. Justice Dubin denied the motion, but said Evseroff could recall Armstead for further cross-examination. The defense attorney thought the ruling was "reversible error."

The three days were marked by frequent clashes between Evseroff and Demakos and so many calls for conferences at the sidebar that Justice Dubin was finally moved to mutter, "I feel like a jumping jack—back and forth."

"It's all bullshit—a lot of fighting over nothing."

Sergeant Thomas Donohue inadvertently provided one of the trial's lighter moments. He said Shea and Scott "spoke collectively" to him immediately after the shooting, but he couldn't distinguish who'd said what. But he remembered that it had been Shea who'd quoted Glover because of the "expletive" he'd used.

"And what was that 'expletive,' Sergeant?" Evseroff asked.

" 'Fuck you!' "

"Thank you," Evseroff said, sitting down as the courtroom erupted in laughter.

Demakos also played the tape of the precinct's radio calls for the morning of April 28. On it was the alarm for the taxicab stickup suspects: "Two black males, early twenties, possibly armed." One had worn a white hat and a black overcoat; the other, a brown leather jacket. Glover had worn a white hat but a yellow jacket; Armstead, a brown leather jacket.

The tape also included Scott's "10–13" alarm ("assist policeman") and the first reports of the shooting.

". . . Who did the shooting?" the dispatcher had asked.

"That's both sides, K," a unit in the field had replied. "The good guys won."

Several jurors smiled.

They might not have smiled had they heard the entire tape.

Justice Dubin had ordered that all calls unrelated to the incident be "redacted." Also excised was a remark made by one policeman as he'd stood over the wounded boy, apparently unaware that his walkie-talkie was on: "Die, you little fuck!" Even Gaudelli conceded that it was too inflammatory for the jury's consideration.

On Friday, Gaudelli offered the fruits of the police search. Detective Henry Sephton said he'd found the starter's pistol in a sewer two days after the shooting. Finally, Demakos called Joseph McKeefery, a florid-faced retired policeman whose voice was barely audible. He said he'd walked his dog nearly three miles to the shooting scene on Sunday, some 36 hours after the incident, "looking for a gun."

"You were just looking on your own?" Demakos asked.

"Yes, sir."

He'd found the plastic toy and turned it over to the authorities.

Over Evseroff's objections that he was trying to impeach his own witness, Demakos brought out that for six years before his retirement McKeefery had been on limited duty because of a "drinking problem." To Evseroff, he was more to be pitied than pilloried; he asked no questions on cross-examination, and the trial recessed for the long Memorial Day weekend.

In six days, 30 witnesses had testified for the prosecution. Only one, Armstead, had presented evidence inculpating Shea. Evseroff was baffled. At first, he gave some credence to the rumors of a surprise witness. That had ended when Gaudelli said there were no witnesses for a *Wade* hearing. Then he leaned to the view that the prosecution would try to prove a "theory"—that Shea was guilty because it couldn't have happened as he'd said. By the end of the week he was convinced "they have no case at all."

On Saturday night, a black man found a rusted gun in the lot and turned it over to officers in a passing police car. Cahill, who learned of it through the PBA grapevine, called Evseroff with the news on Sunday morning. When court reconvened on

Tuesday, Demakos announced the find at the sidebar and gave Evseroff the police ballistics report. The gun was a Belgian-made automatic, without magazine or ammunition, incapable of being fired in its rusted state. There was no indication of how long it had been in the lot.

Meanwhile, Evseroff had done some sleuthing on his own. He had met with Scott at the Jaeger House restaurant on Manhattan's East Side. Scott had been suspended when Shea was indicted, only to be reinstated as the result of a court action brought by the PBA. Since then, he'd refused to talk to the authorities. But he talked freely with the defense counsel and corroborated Shea. Surely, he was not the prosecution's secret witness. But the prosecution could not afford *not* to call him; it had to call him and attempt to impeach him.

Evseroff's partner, Bill Sonenshine, had developed a theory: If the prosecution called Scott and he supported Shea's version, then the prosecution was presenting "affirmative evidence of justifiable homicide" and the case should be dismissed on motion. He started preparing the papers, although Evseroff doubted that Justice Dubin would summarily dismiss so controversial a case.

Scott, 26, slightly built and pouty, took the stand when court resumed Tuesday afternoon. He spoke in a whiney voice. Demakos, who had addressed previous police witnesses by their titles, pointedly called him "Mr. Scott." He elicited that Scott was assigned to clerical duties in Brooklyn, then asked where he'd worked before August 1, 1973.

Evseroff objected that Demakos was trying "to impeach the credibility of his own witness," but Justice Dubin allowed the line of questioning.

"I was suspended . . . as Mr. Gaudelli said I would be," Scott shot back.

Scott went on to describe the fatal day. He told of driving along New York Boulevard and spotting the two blacks: "I nudged Patrolman Shea. 'Tommy, there're the two guys from the taxicab stickup.' . . . I told Police Officer Shea to watch out for the guy on the left [Armstead] because I believed he had a gun."

Demakos had difficulty eliciting the answers he wanted and asked Justice Dubin to declare Scott a hostile witness. Justice Dubin dismissed the motion as "previous," meaning "premature."

The questioning resumed. Scott said Shea had jumped from the car yelling, "Stop! Police!"

"Did he have a gun in his hand?" Demakos asked.

"I don't believe so."

"Did he have anything in his hand?"

"A shield."

Continuing the trend to malapropism, Scott said that Glover had shouted "words that could be interpreted as an epitath."

"What did he say?" Demakos snapped.

" 'Fuck you! You're not going to take us.' "

They'd started chasing the pair. "Tom yelled back at me, 'Scotty, get the car and head them off.' "

By now, Demakos was cross-examining his own witness, and Justice Dubin granted his motion to declare Scott hostile, "on the grounds that he was this defendant's partner at the time of this incident and he has shown some hesitancy in his answers." Evseroff protested in vain that a hostile witness is not one who has an adverse interest, but one who has changed his story.

Under Demakos's questioning, Scott said he'd driven around the corner while radioing for assistance. He'd jumped out of the car, dashed back into the lot and joined Shea in the chase.

"The one in the white hat [Glover] made a turning motion," he said, "and that's when I heard the shots. . . . I saw him come forward with his arm outstretched and the father . . . took a gun in his left hand . . . I believe it was a revolver . . . I started pursuing the father."

Demakos asked how far away Scott had been at the time. Scott said about the distance Demakos stood from him.

"Twenty-five feet?" Demakos asked.

Evseroff jumped up objecting, "About twelve feet."

"Fifteen?" Demakos suggested.

"No way," Evseroff said.

"Let the jury decide," Justice Dubin ruled.

Scott continued, saying he'd chased Armstead into the clump of trees. "He turned and fired at me. . . . I returned fire."

Armstead had fled. Scott had run back to the car and pulled it around another corner, but had lost his suspect. He'd returned to the lot where Shea stood over the fatally wounded boy.

"Did the boy say anything to you?"

"Yes, sir."

"Did you say anything in return?"

"Not that I recall . . ."

Demakos called for a sidebar conference, asking Justice Dubin's permission to get the remarks in evidence. Evseroff protested that a conversation between Scott and Glover wasn't evidence against Shea. Actually, he was baiting a trap for Demakos, and Justice Dubin's ruling triggered it.

Demakos asked Scott what the boy had said.

"Glover said, 'Don't shoot! Don't shoot!' " Scott replied.

"Did you say anything in return?"

"No, sir."

"Are you sure about that?"

"Yes, sir."

"Did you tell him to die?" Demakos asked, as Evseroff leapt to his feet objecting. "Did you tell him, 'Die, you little fuck.' "

"I didn't say it," Scott screamed back.

Evseroff roared his objections at the top of his lungs, accusing Demakos of "prosecutorial misconduct": "He knows who said it and he knows this witness did not."

Justice Dubin, barely able to keep his robe on, was even less able to maintain order. "You don't have to yell and scream," he yelled at Evseroff.

"I object to the court yelling at me," Evseroff said, as the spectators laughed and the officious court officers yelled for order.

Evseroff's outrage at Demakos had been calculated, but he remained incredulous at Justice Dubin's rulings.

"He's dead wrong. He's not even close. John Murtagh, Joe Sarafite, Sam Liebowitz, none of the so-called hanging judges would have permitted this."

Although many spectators found Scott's account "incredible," Evseroff was unruffled.

"I don't think he hurt me. These people on the jury believe what they want to believe."

It had become the defense strategy to cast Gaudelli as the trial's villain. The next morning as they caucused over coffee at Ann's Cafe, Evseroff told Scott, "You've got to throw it to Gaudelli. You've got to do it on direct. You've got to throw it in his fucking teeth."

When court opened, Demakos called for a sidebar and asked leave to play the previously deleted portion of the tape. Justice Dubin allowed it as a test of Scott's credibility.

Evseroff insisted on registering his objection in open court. He called the comment "collateral, irrelevant, immaterial and highly prejudicial." He said the comment had been made by Sergeant Donohue and that Donohue had so informed both Gaudelli and Demakos, but "the district attorney says he doesn't believe what Sergeant Donohue says."

Demakos replied that Donohue had come on the scene later, that Glover had said, "I'm dying," and that Donohue had replied, "That's right, you little fuck, you're dying." He insisted that the two statements were "quite different."

The tape recorder was set up, the jury was called in and the tape was played. Amid the police calls came the comment, "Die, you little fuck!"

Demakos asked Scott if that was his voice.

"No, sir, it wasn't and you know it wasn't. It was Sergeant Donohue and he told you so."

On his turn, Evseroff elicited that Scott had a one-month-old baby and that he'd been stabbed on duty in January 1973. He asked Scott about his interrogation by Gaudelli.

"He told me that if I didn't tell him what they wanted to hear, they would fire me. They would indict me for perjury and hinderance of prosecution."

Scott said he'd arrested Armstead for attempted murder, but the arrest had been countermanded by Inspector Johnson. He said the station had been filled with black civilians and he'd heard one man say, "If something isn't done about this, Jamaica is going to burn."

Most of Evseroff's questions dealt with the chase, establishing that "everything was split-second" and that Scott had not been able to measure distances, note landmarks or observe that Glover was only ten years old.

"Is Patrolman Shea your friend?" Evseroff asked.

"Yes, sir."

"Is he still your friend?"

"Yes, sir."

"Have you told the truth here?"

"Yes, sir."

"I have no further questions of this witness."

But Demakos did. He returned to the chase, noting Scott's failure to make observations, asking over and over, "You're a trained police officer, are you not?"

Finally Scott replied, "I'm still a human being."

Demakos asked if Scott had challenged Inspector Johnson's order countermanding Armstead's arrest.

"I couldn't believe what he was saying," Scott said.

"Did *he* believe what you were saying?"

"Objection," Evseroff snapped.

"Sustained," Justice Dubin ruled.

"Did *anybody* believe what you were saying?"

"We had a very good morning. We got all our defense in. We could rest right now."

In the afternoon, Demakos started calling a string of neighborhood residents who'd seen or heard parts of the incident and whose accounts differed from Shea's and, in some cases, Armstead's. Evseroff called them "woodwork witnesses—the kind that appear out of the woodwork just before the trial." His cross-examinations were marked by frequent verbal clashes with the peppery prosecutor.

He questioned Mrs. Elaine Fryer at length as to whether she'd heard two shots, as she said in court, or "a lot of shots," as she'd told the grand jury. He read her grand-jury testimony, but she couldn't recall what she'd said. Evseroff asked for a stipulation that he'd read the testimony accurately.

"I must admit that I must give Mr. Evseroff 'A' for reading," Demakos said.

A few minutes later, as Evseroff continued to read the Q. and A., Demakos popped up, insisting that Evseroff read other questions.

"You can't conduct his cross-examination," Justice Dubin told him.

Evseroff charged that Demakos was making a "conscious effort" to disrupt his cross-examination: "I'm very upset at having my cross-examination disrupted in this manner."

"You've been around too long to be upset," the judge said.

"I don't start these things. But he starts needling me and I rise to the bait. But I always manage to get a zinger in in front of the jury."

On Thursday afternoon, Mrs. Katie Robinson, an elderly black domestic, took the stand. She spoke in a piping, mile-a-minute, barely audible voice. She said she'd heard somebody shout, "Halt!", then looked out the window to see a man with a gun. He'd fired one shot. Then she'd heard a voice say, "Don't shoot! Don't shoot!" "And he shot four times."

Evseroff spent a long time reading through her previous statements. She'd given several conflicting versions, even one in which she'd said that the policeman was completely justified. Then he rose to question her.

"Miss Robinson," he started. "Is it 'Miss' or 'Mrs.'?"

"Mrs."

"Mrs. Robinson, how old are you?"

"Thirty-four years old."

Evseroff paused for several seconds, then returned to the counsel table and conferred with Cahill.

"If Your Honor please, I have no further questions."

Demakos made no effort to rehabilitate her. Instead, he called Jane Booles, a young, miniskirted bookkeeper with the bosomy figure of a go-go dancer. She said she'd been returning from a dance with her sister and brother-in-law. When they'd come to the lot, she'd seen two men running. A white man had jumped from a car and started chasing the two men. The car had speeded around the corner, nearly cutting them off.

"I got out of the car and ran to the lot and saw the boy's body, but no one else."

Then a heavy-set woman had leaned out a window and screamed, "Stop that man! I saw him kill the kid."

When her direct ended, Evseroff waited for Demakos to turn over her prior statements. Demakos said there were none. "I see counsel looking at me funny," he added.

"I was just getting up to question the witness," Evseroff protested.

Demakos said he meant Cahill. Evseroff said Demakos was "paranoid."

Justice Dubin said, "Don't look at him funny."

But Evseroff had something more valuable than *Rosario* material. One of Shea's bodyguards had handed him a note: "There's a Booles locked up for killing Policeman Hurley."

He pounced on the point: "Isn't it a fact that your brother is arrested for killing Patrolman Hurley?"

"Yes," she admitted.

Sonny Osbourne Booles had been arrested on March 8 for killing Patrolman Timothy Hurley during a tavern holdup. Evseroff elicited that she hadn't come forward with her information in the Shea case until after that.

Demakos made a brief effort to rehabilitate her. He brought out that she'd taken the test to become a policewoman. He asked how she felt about her brother's arrest.

"If he's guilty, he deserves any punishment that he receives," she replied. "I didn't want to testify—"

Demakos cut her off. The damage had been done. Her sister and brother-in-law, who had been waiting to testify, were sent home without being called.

Evseroff wondered why Demakos would present, and thus vouch for, witnesses like Mrs. Robinson and Miss Booles. He speculated that the prosecutor was operating on the "kitchen-sink theory"—to throw in everything, lest he be accused of covering up.

Then Demakos called a series of ballistics experts to testify about the guns. Evseroff didn't dispute their findings and asked few questions on cross-examination, except to elicit from one detective that there had been activity at the lot on May 9, 1973, and that it had been directed by Gaudelli. Through the police grapevine, he'd learned that the prosecution had "reenacted" the shooting for videotape.

On Friday morning, Mrs. Eloise Glover, a big woman in a beige suit, her voice barely audible, took the stand. Her direct examination was brief, Demakos eliciting only that she'd identified Clifford's body and that he had been ten years old.

Normally defense attorneys don't cross-examine the next-of-kin at murder trials because it rouses too much sympathy for the victim. But the PBA's army of 27,000 investigators had been at work on Mrs. Glover. Evseroff asked her if Armstead had ever threatened her with a gun. She said, "No." Hadn't she made such a complaint to Patrolman Winberry? Again, she said, "No."

Finally, the deputy medical examiner, Dr. Yong-myun Ro, testified that one bullet had struck Glover, entering at mid-back, traveling up and slightly to the left to exit beneath the collarbone. Demakos used himself as the dummy to demonstrate the path, prompting Evseroff to ask: "Your Honor, may I move over so I can see where the bullet entered Mr. Demakos's back?" Glover, the doctor continued, had died of internal bleeding.

With that, Demakos informed Justice Dubin that the prosecution was finished except to recall Armstead for further cross-examination and one policeman with an exhibit the defense had requested.

"They're not going to put in the run-through [reenactment]. They're going to save it for rebuttal."

For a moment he considered crossing up the prosecution by resting without calling a witness. Instead, he told reporters that he planned to call some 70 witnesses for the defense.

Armstead returned on Monday morning, denying any threat to Mrs. Glover. Then Demakos announced, "The people rest." In 11 trial days he'd presented 47 witnesses. Evseroff moved to dismiss, arguing that Scott's testimony had "established *prima facie* justification." As he'd expected, Justice Dubin denied the motion and ordered the defense to start that afternoon.

"Who's your first witness?" a reporter asked Evseroff in the corridor.

"Thomas Shea," he replied. "But don't you tell nobody. I want to catch them flatfooted."

No pun intended. Ordinarily, Evseroff likes to build up to a defendant's testimony, presenting him last. But he calculated that Demakos had relaxed over the weekend and would be unprepared to cross-examine Shea.

When court resumed after lunch, Evseroff rose and announced, "If Your Honor please, the defense calls Thomas Shea."

It was the most electric moment of the trial. The courtroom, jammed to overflowing with blacks bused in, as their leaflets put it, "to insure justice," hushed. The jurors sat up.

Clearing his throat nervously, Shea spoke in a loud, clear voice, answering questions promptly. Evseroff elicited that he was 37, married, the father of two daughters, an air force veteran. In 13 years on the force he'd participated in 700 to 1000 arrests. He'd used his gun on three prior occasions.

Then Evseroff said, "I would like you, if you would, Patrolman Shea, slowly and clearly, to relate to this court . . . what happened."

And Shea told the same story he'd told since that April morning. He said that "everything happened too quickly" for him to have made observations of time and distance, or of Glover's age and height. At one point, when Evseroff asked how long a time interval was, he replied, "It seemed like a lifetime to me."

"Did you ever intend to do anything other than do your job?"

"No, sir. . . ."

"Did you believe that Clifford Glover had a gun?"

"Yes, sir."

"Did you believe that he was going to use that gun against you?"

"Yes, sir."

Evseroff's questioning lasted less than 15 minutes. He had kept it short so Demakos wouldn't have an overnight adjournment to prepare his questions. Surprisingly, the prosecutor didn't even ask for a brief recess. He rose to cross-examine immediately, snapping at Shea with such ferocity that the witness blurted out, "Mr. Demakos, please don't scream at me. I'm not screaming at you."

At times the prosecutor stood silent for long stretches, as if wondering what to ask next. When he failed to shake Shea, he expressed his incredulity by tone of voice. He asked Shea to demonstrate how he'd stood when he'd fired.

Shea did so, saying, "At that point, I brought my gun up and fired."

"Just like that," Demakos commented.

Finally, Demakos turned to the other incidents when Shea had used his gun. Shea explained: One had been against a man with a meat cleaver; another against a knife-wielding dope addict; the third against a burglary suspect.

"Did you find a gun on that individual?" Demakos asked.

Evseroff objected and Justice Dubin sustained him: "That case has nothing to do with this case. We're not trying that case here."

Demakos turned to an incident in which Shea had allegedly pistol-whipped a 14-year-old boy.

"I didn't do anything to that boy," Shea insisted.

"Is that case still pending?" Demakos asked.

"Objection," Everoff screamed. "There's been no showing that there is any case."

"Sustained," Justice Dubin said.

Again, the jury didn't get the details. Two of Shea's fellow officers had been convicted in a departmental trial not of pistol-whipping but of failing to file a report on the incident and had been subjected to "command discipline"; the case against Shea remained pending.

After about an hour, Demakos gave up.

"I think we caught Mr. Demakos with his pants down. He was completely, totally unprepared to cross-examine, which was just what I figured."

The following morning at Ann's Cafe, Everoff met with Marshall Banks, the black man who'd found the rusted gun in the lot a week before. Straddling a chair at a back table, Everoff sipped his coffee and asked what had happened. Banks said he hadn't found the gun, as he'd originally claimed. He'd taken it from his brother's home, but when he'd seen a police car approaching, he'd panicked, and fearing to be caught with the gun, he'd claimed he'd found it and turned it over to the cops.

"Who got you to change your story?" Everoff asked.

Banks got up and walked out. He was not called by the defense.

Everoff's second witness was Anthony Buffalano, the PBA attorney who'd accompanied Scott to the D.A.'s office a year before. He was a short, stocky man, only four years out of law school. He testified over Gaudelli's repeated objections, so many that Demakos finally had to restrain his assistant. Buffalano said that Gaudelli had threatened Scott: If Scott told the story the D.A. wanted to hear, he'd be allowed to resign; if not, he'd be fired. Gaudelli had also hinted at a perjury indictment unless he cooperated.

Justice Dubin interrupted the questioning: "Did you hear his testimony here?"

"No."

"Do you know if he changed his testimony?"

"Objection," Evseroff snapped.

Justice Dubin thought a moment. "Overruled," he said, as the spectators laughed.

"No," Buffalano said.

On cross-examination, Demakos asked, "You're implying that Mr. Gaudelli urged Scott to commit perjury, is that correct?"

"Yes."

"Weren't you appalled at that?"

"Of course," the lawyer replied. "In all my years I'd never heard anything like that."

Sergeant Donohue was recalled by the defense and asked if he'd had a conversation with Clifford Glover at the lot. He said he had.

"What was said, sergeant?"

"Glover said, 'I'm dying.' And I said, 'That's right, you little fuck, you're dying."

He added that he'd related the conversation to both Demakos and Gaudelli before the trial.

Evseroff then called Patrolman Thomas Winberry, the officer who'd taken Mrs. Glover's complaints of threats by Armstead. Gaudelli objected, demanding an offer of proof, that is, proof that Winberry's testimony was relevant. Justice Dubin deferred a ruling, so Evseroff called six other policemen to the stand, most of them testifying that the neighborhood witnesses had initially given accounts to the police that varied from their courtroom testimony. Then he recalled Winberry. After a lengthy sidebar conference, Justice Dubin ruled that the policeman's testimony would be a "collateral" attack on a witness and sustained Gaudelli's objection.

Evseroff insisted on stating his exception in open court—"for the record," he said; for the press, in actuality. He said that Winberry would have testified that in May 1970, Eloise Glover had complained that Armstead had assaulted her with "a big silver gun" and that she'd later made two other complaints of assault by Armstead. He loudly protested the judge's ruling. *"Of course, he's absolutely right as a matter of law. My big worry wasn't Winberry. It was Buffalano. I was afraid he wasn't going to let it in. I wouldn't, if I was him."*

Wednesday morning opened with Evseroff calling Sergeant Charles DiRenzo. The defense attorney wanted to show that Inspector Johnson had ordered the gun charge against Armstead reduced from one requiring arrest to one that meant merely the issuance of a summons. However, Gaudelli successfully objected to the line of questioning.

Evseroff threw up his hands: "If Mr. Gaudelli doesn't want me to bring this out, I have no further questions."

For the next two days he presented character witnesses: 15 civilians, including a Roman Catholic priest and a black telephone operator at the 103rd precinct stationhouse; 32 policemen, including nine blacks and three Puerto Ricans, which, if nothing else, proves that the bonds of blue are stronger than those of black.

Sometimes Demakos or Gaudelli rose to cross-examine a witness, asking him about the previous shoot-out or the pistol-whipping. Sometimes the questions backfired. Lieutenant Charles Mancuso, formerly Shea's superior on youth gang duty in Brooklyn, was asked if such incidents altered his opinion.

"If Tom was the type that lost his head, I never would have had him in my outfit," he replied.

Before the jury filed into court on Thursday, Evseroff asked Justice Dubin to order a hearing on the circumstances under which Banks had changed his story about finding the gun. He intimated that Gaudelli had coerced the witness.

Justice Dubin denied the motion as "wholly irrelevant and immaterial to the issue": "The court can see no necessity for a hearing in this matter. . . . The court does not believe that the district attorney would bring pressure on a man to change his story."

As Evseroff sat down, he whispered to Cahill, deliberately

loud enough for the prosecutors to overhear, "Call Nadjari"—
Maurice Nadjari, the special prosecutor for New York charged
with investigating corruption in the administration of justice.
He repeated the call later for the newspaper reporters and
television cameras, not that he really wanted an investigation,
but to raise another collateral issue and to discombobulate the
prosecution.

As he questioned Thursday's character witnesses, he continued his counteroffensive against Gaudelli. Under department
regulations, all police witnesses, for either prosecution or defense, must sign in at the district attorney's office. Evseroff had
learned that his police character witnesses had also been ordered to see Gaudelli and that the D.A. had questioned them
about their testimony, which was perfectly proper, but it ac-
quired an ominous air when presented to the jury.

A few minutes after 1 P.M., when his 47th character witness
stepped off the stand, Evseroff announced: "The defendant,
Patrolman Thomas Shea, rests at this time."

But he was back in court the following morning asking Justice Dubin to reopen the defense. The night before, he said, he'd
read a year-old *New York Times* interview with Armstead
which was "substantially inconsistent" with his courtroom testimony. In the interview, Armstead had said he'd left the lot by
a different route than the one he'd claimed in court to have
followed, one that had brought him to the street right where the
starter's pistol had been found. Evseroff said he'd sent an investigator to the *Times* office to subpoena the reporter who'd
talked to Armstead.

Demakos argued against calling the reporter, though one
reporter suggested that if the interview was anything like the
Times's coverage of the trial he had nothing to worry about
(among other things, the *Times* had misstated the judge's
name).

Loath to delay the trial, Justice Dubin suggested that Demakos proceed with his rebuttal and Evseroff, if he wished, could
reopen the defense on Monday. The prosecutor called two witnesses in rebuttal. First, Armstead's boss, Anthony Minutello,

who confirmed that Armstead "was supposed to get in early" on the day of the shooting. Demakos then asked him about the gun.

"I knew a gun was there," he replied. "He said he found it in a car and put it on a shelf."

On cross-examination, Minutello said that by "early" he hadn't meant 5 or 6 A.M.

Then Alan Parente, a former assistant D.A. who'd gone on to become law secretary to a state Court of Claims judge, testified that he'd been present when Gaudelli had questioned Scott and denied that Gaudelli had threatened him. He said Gaudelli had stated that he thought Scott was "lying" and that if he told the truth he'd be allowed to resign from the force. Scott, Parente said, had replied, "That's my story and I'm not going to change it."

Under Evseroff's cross-examination, Parente insisted that Gaudelli hadn't told Scott what would happen to him if he didn't tell the "truth."

With that, Demakos rested. He hadn't presented the "run-through." For his part, Evseroff had not offered the results of Shea's lie-detector test; they were "inconclusive."

"I don't think Parente hurt us at all. I don't think the jury liked Parente—a smart-ass kid politician."

But Evseroff directed Cahill to bring Buffalano back to testify at Monday's surrebuttal. He also planned to call private detective Herman Race to rebut parts of Minutello's testimony.

"The more collateral issues you raise, the better it is for the defendant."

Over lunch, Evseroff ticked off what he considered the prosecution's major errors: 1) making a summary arrest rather than waiting to present the case to a grand jury; 2) charging Shea with murder, rather than manslaughter or negligent homicide; 3) not indicting Scott as an accomplice; and 4) threatening Scott. But he also cautioned against overconfidence: "The biggest hurdle we have to overcome is that this was a ten-year-old boy."

Monday's session saw the *Times* reporter, Ronald Smothers,

in court along with a *Times* executive and an attorney from Cahill, Gordon & Reindl, the Wall Street law firm that had represented the *Times* in the Pentagon Papers case. Evseroff informed Justice Dubin that the *Times* was resisting his effort to subpoena Smothers: "As I was told, he will go to jail before he testifies."

Eugene Scheiman, the *Times* attorney, argued that Smothers's testimony was "immaterial" and that forcing it would not only violate his First Amendment rights, but "harm him as a civil rights reporter."

"As long as he's here, I don't see any damage to it," Justice Dubin said. "I can't see where all this is that important."

"I think it's important to Mr. Smothers," Scheiman said.

Demakos joined the argument, and for the first time Justice Dubin realized when the article had appeared: "A year ago! I thought it was yesterday."

He called a five-minute recess to read the article, then returned and ruled that it was "not proper evidence to put in surrebuttal." Evseroff retorted that he wasn't offering it as surrebuttal, but as part of the defense case-in-main. Justice Dubin stuck to his ruling.

Plainly piqued, Evseroff decided not to call Buffalano or Race and rested. Justice Dubin directed the attorneys to sum up after lunch.

"This judge is doing everything he conceivably can to zing us."

What irked Evseroff even more than Justice Dubin's refusal to let Smothers testify was his decision to include the lesser counts of manslaughter in his charge to the jury. Rather than the all-or-nothing of finding Shea guilty of murder or freeing him, the jury could "cop out" and convict on the lesser charge.

By afternoon, the long, hot summer had set in. The temperature was 95 degrees. Con Edison, unable to meet the soaring demand for power as thousands of air conditioners were switched on, had "browned out" the city. With voltage reduced, the courthouse air conditioning went dead and Justice

Dubin's windowless courtroom soon resembled a Finnish sauna. Evseroff asked permission to remove his jacket.

Justice Dubin acceded: "Being comfortable is never an offense—or offensive."

It was a scene reminiscent of Darrow and Bryan at the Scopes trial in the sticky summer heat of Dayton, Tennessee, as the shirt-sleeved defense lawyer filled the air with old-time histrionics.

He opened by confronting his biggest hurdle head-on: "Let's face it—there was a ten-year-old killed in this case. . . . This is tragic." But he insisted that Shea had "acted justifiably."

Shouting at the top of his lungs, sometimes cupping his hands to his mouth for emphasis, he denounced Armstead as "a convicted rapist, a gangster" and a coward. "He split and ran. He had no more concern for Clifford Glover than the man in the moon." He implied that man and boy had set out to commit crimes at that early morning hour and fled the police because they were guilty . . . of something.

He noted Gaudelli's threat to Scott: "You didn't see Mr. Gaudelli get on the stand and deny this." And the prosecution's claim that Scott had said "Die, you little fuck!": "Whoever said it, it wasn't Shea." He noted the prosecution's claim that they knew Scott wasn't telling the truth because of the "other evidence."

"Where is that 'other evidence'?" he shouted.

Then, his forehead dripping sweat, his shirt sticky with perspiration, he turned to Justice Dubin: "Judge, I really need a recess at this point."

But there was little solace in the sun-baked corridor. He returned for his peroration.

He said the "woodwork witnesses . . . insult your intelligence." He didn't argue that Armstead had tried to shoot it out with the starter's pistol: "I don't know what gun he used, but he had five to ten minutes to get rid of that gun."

Finally, he pointed to his client. "This is the cop on the street," he said. "This is the type of policeman who stands

between you and me and the crime in the streets. . . . Tom Shea
—his sin and his crime is that he was doing his job.

"I speak to you for every man in blue," he concluded, asking
the jury to return a verdict "for law and order and justice."

Demakos, his jacket still on, rose to respond. Where Evseroff
had been dynamic, he was discursive.

"A trial," he said, "is a search for truth, not a search for
reasonable doubt."

Using the map of the scene, he recapitulated the eyewitness
accounts to demonstrate the prosecution contention that Scott
had driven all the way around the lot and had been "nowhere
near when Shea shot that boy." And, therefore, the story of the
passage of the gun was a fabrication.

"I can't help but feel indignation at the colossal gall and
arrogance of Shea in concocting his incredible, preposterous
story," he said.

Given the oppressive heat he was mercifully brief.

The air conditioners were back on the following morning for
Justice Dubin's charge. The jurors retired at 11:25 A.M. They
returned at 11:50 with a series of requests for some exhibits; for
a rereading of the testimony of Shea, Scott, Armstead and one
of the eyewitnesses; and the law on whether a citizen is required
to stop when a policeman calls "Halt!"

Instead of the law on that point, Justice Dubin reread his
charge on justification: A policeman is justified in killing if he
has reasonable grounds to believe that he is about to be at-
tacked. It stressed the point that was the main defense contention.

*"I take back everything I've said about Judge Dubin. He was
marvelous."*

The rereading of Shea's testimony took most of the afternoon. Rather than have the testimony of the other witnesses
reread in open court, Justice Dubin sent the transcripts into the
jury room. The panel went to dinner at 6:30.

*"You want to know what I think? That black woman is all
alone on that jury."*

But as the night wore on, Evseroff's mood blackened. At

9:30, the jury sent out a note asking for a rereading of the charge on manslaughter. As they entered the courtroom together, Evseroff told Demakos, "I think you've got a winner here."

Showing emotion for the first time in the trial, Shea hung his head and wrung his hands as Justice Dubin reiterated the law covering manslaughter.

The jury retired again. At 10:55 the panel was lodged overnight at the International Hotel at John F. Kennedy Airport.

"I need a drink bad," Evseroff said as he left the courthouse.

A reporter told him, "You can get a bad drink across the street."

The following morning, about 20 mostly white members of something called the Queens Coalition for Peace and Justice picketed the courthouse. Their placards read:

10-YR-OLD SHOT IN BACK BECAUSE HE WAS
BLACK
A BADGE IS NOT A LICENSE TO MURDER
CHILDREN
LET JUSTICE BE DONE—JAIL THE RACIST KILLER
QUEENS COALITION FOR PEACE AND JUSTICE
DEMANDS SHAY [*sic*] PAY

The jurors did not see the signs. They had been brought back to the courthouse early and had resumed their deliberations at 9:20 A.M. At 11:13, they sent out a note: "We have reached a verdict. [Signed] Sidney Horn, foreman."

Evseroff was not hopeful. All morning he'd been hearing rumors that the jurors were compromising on manslaughter.

It was 11:20 A.M., Wednesday, June 12, 24 hours after Shea's fate went to the jury, 31 days since his trial started, 365 days since his indictment was returned.

Shea stood and faced the jury. The clerk asked for the verdict.

"Not guilty," Horn said.

Shea buckled. He fell into his chair, buried his face in his hands and wept.

Evseroff beamed.

Justice Dubin thanked the jury and discharged the defendant. Shea's bodyguards, pressed into something more than "gopher" service for the first time, hustled the defense entourage out of the courtroom and into an adjoining conference room where Shea composed himself. Then they led the group down a side stairway and outside onto the courthouse steps where camera crews and newsmen clustered around, thrusting microphones in their faces and peppering them with questions.

"Thank God for the jury system," Evseroff said.

Shea was asked how he felt. "Believe me, it's been a year out of my life."

What would he do now? "All I want to do is go back to work as a police officer."

From the fringes of the crowd an angry black shouted, "You better not go back to South Jamaica!"

The bodyguards hustled the entourage two blocks down Queens Boulevard to Luigi's restaurant where the proprietor presented Shea a congratulatory snifter of brandy.

A few minutes later, several jurors came into the restaurant's bar for a post-trial drink. Shea jumped up to thank them, kissing Mrs. Campbell, the black woman, on the cheek.

Evseroff and Cahill cornered one juror, led him outside and spoke to him on the rain-spattered sidewalk.

"There was no way we were going to convict," he said.

The first ballot had been 6–3–3, six to acquit, three to convict, three undecided. This soon shifted to 9–3. By the time they'd gone to dinner, it was 11–1. Mrs. Campbell had been the lone holdout.

"We were ready to kill her last night," the juror said.

He added that they had never really considered a manslaughter verdict and had asked for a rereading of the charge merely to humor Mrs. Campbell.

"When we saw how bad he [Shea] looked, we were ready to call it quits right then," he said.

Mrs. Campbell had not slept all night. In the morning, she'd told the others, "O.K., I've seen enough. I'll go with the majority."

She'd been convinced by juror Dennis Connolly, the young telephone company employee. What finally convinced her was a point seemingly so inconsequential that Evseroff had not even mentioned it in his summation: One of the policemen who'd picked up Armstead had testified that he'd told them, "They shot my son back there," while Armstead had testified that he hadn't seen what had happened to the boy. This discrepancy led her to doubt Armstead's account.

Evseroff's initial prediction was confirmed: In the end, she "went along."

"The selection of the jury—Sam Liebowitz said it's seventy-five percent of the case. He's wrong. It was one-hundred percent of this case."

Euphoric, Evseroff returned to the restaurant, hoisted a Beefeater Gibson on the rocks and reveled in his triumph. "It's better than getting laid."

A black reporter praised Evseroff for his performance. He'd done a good job on behalf of his client. But didn't he have a deeper obligation . . . to society . . . to see that justice was done?

The defense attorney replied, "What the hell is justice?"

Postscript

The day after Shea was acquitted, a second New York City policeman was charged with murder. Brooklyn District Attorney Eugene Gold had held up the announcement to avoid influencing the Shea jury.

Patrolman William Walker, who is white, claimed he'd shot and killed a 23-year-old black in self-defense, thinking the man had pulled a gun. A toy pistol had been found beside the body. But two other policemen testified that they'd seen Walker with the toy gun earlier in the day.

As a result of his victory in the Shea case, Evseroff was consulted about defending Walker.

"The guy fired one shot in his life. Right between the eyes. He was bleeding something terrible. His brains were splattered all over the place. Another policeman came running up, turned the body over and there was the [toy] gun.

"I asked him [Walker] one question: 'Was there any blood on your clothes?'

"He said, 'No.'

"The case has possibilities. . . ."

New York City
June 14, 1974

Notes

Most of this book is based on personal observation and interviews. I had the cooperation of Jack Evseroff, his partners Gus Newman and Bill Sonenshine, their associates and staff. But I want to stress that the opinions expressed are mine, not theirs.

Among those whose assistance I want to acknowledge are: Peter Andreoli and the Manhattan D.A.'s office; A. C. Aronne; Marshall Blumenfeld; James Cahill and the legal staff of the Patrolmen's Benevolent Association; Mort Davis and the Nassau D.A.'s office; Paul Gorman; Gordon Haesloop and the Brooklyn D.A.'s office; Jeremiah McKenna; and Supreme Court Justice Burton Roberts. Again, my thanks to Congressman Ed Koch and his staff.

Whenever possible I have quoted from trial transcripts; I have not hesitated to correct obvious errors or to repunctuate the texts to my style. Unfortunately, transcripts are not routinely filed in the New York State courts, and those that are are often incomplete. (The reason is economic. Trial transcripts cost more than $1 a page, even for district attorneys' offices. For a defendant, stenographers' bills may outrun the legal fees. In this era of the tape recorder and the Xerox copier, the stranglehold of court stenographers would seem a fit subject for judicial reform.) In such instances, it was necessary to reconstruct the courtroom colloquy from newspaper accounts and the participants' memories.

The citation of a case in the Notes does not necessarily mean that there is a transcript on file with the clerk of the court or in the briefs and records on appeal. Newspaper references are cited only when quoted.

1. A Week in the Life

This chapter is based on personal observation.

2. The Making of a Mouthpiece

For Liebowitz's career, see Quentin Reynolds, *Courtroom* (1950). *People* v. *Miller,* 6 N.Y.2d 152 (1959); 9 N.Y.2d 838 (1961). *New York Post,* June 9, 1961.

3. A Crazy Business

This chapter is based on personal observation.

4. Around the Rim and Out

For another view of the baseketball-fix scandal, see David Wolf, *Foul!* (1972). *People* v. *Molinas,* 21 A.D.2d 384 (1964); *cert. denied,* 380 U.S. 907 (1965). *Molinas* v. *Mancusi,* 370 F.2d 601 (1966); *cert. denied,* 386 U.S. 984 (1967). *New York Post,* November 6, 1972.

5. "They Are Framing Me"

People v. *Grande,* 19 A.D.2d 655 (1963).

For the Portelli investigation, see Raymond V. Martin, *Revolt in the Mafia* (1963). *People* v. *Portelli,* 15 N.Y.2d 835 (1965); *cert. denied,* 382 U.S. 1009 (1966). *New York Daily News,* May 23, 1962.

6. A Cop Cops a Plea

The statistics are from New York State, Administrative Board of the Judicial Conference, *Report* (1973).

7. Men of Respect

For the origins of the Gallo-Profaci War, see Martin; for recent developments, see Nicholas Gage, *The Mafia Is Not an Equal Op-*

portunity Employer (1971) and Gage, ed., *Mafia, U.S.A.* (1972). Martin Garbus, *Ready for the Defense* (1971).

For Itkin's career, see Walter Goodman, *A Percentage of the Take* (1971). *U.S.* v. *Keilly*, 445 F.2d 1285 (1972); *cert. denied*, 406 U.S. 962 (1972).

U.S. v. *Cioffi*, 472 F.2d 1404 (1973); *cert. denied*, U.S. (1973).

8. Appealing Propositions

Mapp v. *Ohio*, 367 U.S. (1961); 368 U.S. 871 (1961).

People v. *DeLucia*, 21 A.D.2d 805 (1964); 14 N.Y.2d 294 (1965); *cert. denied*, 382 U.S. 821 (1965). *U.S. ex rel. DeLucia* v. *McMann*, 373 F.2d 759 (1966). *People* v. *DeLucia*, 19 N.Y.2d 837 (1967); 20 N.Y.2d 375 (1967).

Miranda v. *Arizona*, 384 U.S. 436 (1966) at 446.

9. A Killing in Camelot

Newsday, March 20, 1972.

The police corruption case is noted in Peter Maas, *Serpico* (1972), and New York City, Commission to Investigate Allegations of Police Corruption and the City's Anti-Corruption Procedures, *Report* (1972), published commercially as *The Knapp Commission Report on Police Corruption* (1973).

10. Ring Around the Collar

The New York Times, November 5, 1966, and October 4, 1967.

U.S. v. *Giordano*, 498 F.2d 327 (1973).

11. The Cloud

For Zelmanowitz's career, see my book, *Tiger in the Court* (1973). U.S. Senate, Permanent Subcommittee on Investigations, Hearings, *Organized Crime—Securities: Thefts and Frauds*, 2d series (1973). *The New York Times*, July 17, 18 and 27, 1973.

12. A Year in the Arena

People v. *Lagana*, 43 A.D.2d 834 (1974).

13. Black and Blue

The New York Times, April 30, 1973.

About the Author

PAUL HOFFMAN was born and raised in Chicago. He received his A.B. and A.M. degrees from the University of Chicago and started his reportorial career with the City News Bureau of Chicago. He first met the subject of this book 12 years ago when he was a reporter for the *New York Post* and Evseroff was defending basketball fixer Jack Molinas. In addition to numerous articles, he is the author of two books about lawyers, *Lions in the Street* and *Tiger in the Court.*